The Screenplay

D1027241

Also by Steven Price

OSCAR WILDE: *SALOME* (*with William Tydeman*)

THE PLAYS, SCREENPLAYS AND FILMS OF DAVID MAMET

The Screenplay

Authorship, Theory and Criticism

Steven Price
Lecturer in English, Bangor University, UK

First published 2010 by
PALGRAVE MACMILLAN

Palgrave Macmillan in the UK is an imprint of Macmillan Publishers Limited, registered in England, company number 785998, of Houndmills, Basingstoke, Hampshire RG21 6XS.

Palgrave Macmillan in the US is a division of St Martin's Press LLC, 175 Fifth Avenue, New York, NY 10010.

Palgrave Macmillan is the global academic imprint of the above companies and has companies and representatives throughout the world.

Palgrave® and Macmillan® are registered trademarks in the United States, the United Kingdom, Europe and other countries

ISBN 978-0-230-22361-5   hardback
ISBN 978-0-230-22362-2   paperback

This book is printed on paper suitable for recycling and made from fully managed and sustained forest sources. Logging, pulping and manufacturing processes are expected to conform to the environmental regulations of the country of origin.

A catalogue record for this book is available from the British Library.

A catalog record for this book is available from the Library of Congress.

10   9   8   7   6   5   4   3   2   1
19   18   17   16   15   14   13   12   11   10

Printed and bound in Great Britain by
CPI Antony Rowe, Chippenham and Eastbourne

For Domini, Joey, and Abigail

Contents

Preface

One of the first screenplays I ever read was *The Autobiography of Malcolm X*. I was writing a postgraduate dissertation on David Mamet, who with great generosity had permitted me, through his agent, to read much of his voluminous unpublished work. The screenplay was an adaptation of the text written by Alex Haley in collaboration with the black political activist, which Haley completed after Malcolm's assassination in 1965. The film was never made, and the script never published; for the first time, I was experiencing the thrill of studying material by a major writer that very few people had even heard about, let alone read.

At that time, I hadn't read Haley's book either. With the monomania of the doctoral student, what interested me instead were the connections to Mamet's plays, most notably *Edmond*, completed like the screenplay in 1983. The protagonist of each story proceeds through the lower depths of New York towards some form of spiritual enlightenment, although in each case that conclusion is overwhelmed by irony: Malcolm is murdered, Edmond is jailed and forcibly sodomised. The narrative structure of each work appears to be strongly indebted to a mythic paradigm drawn from Joseph Campbell's *The Hero with a Thousand Faces* (1949), which – as I discovered later – rivals Aristotle's *Poetics* for the title of screenwriting's holiest book.

By 1983, Mamet had already been nominated for an Academy Award for *The Verdict* (Sidney Lumet, 1982), his second produced script after *The Postman Always Rings Twice* (Bob Rafelson, 1981) – two further unpublished gems from the treasure trove. As I turned now to these screenplays, obvious stylistic connections emerged. As with the plays, scenic description was minimal, and on the page, at least, the dialogue – pithy, sometimes aphoristic, consistently lean, and unsentimental – was predominant. Individual scenes, of course, were shorter than in most of the stage plays (though not all: both *Edmond* and *Sexual Perversity in Chicago* [1973] appear to owe something to cinematic construction). More significantly, although Mamet routinely referred to Aristotle when interviewed about his plays, it was in the structure of the screenplays that the debt was more keenly felt. The linear narrative was more sharply etched, and the cathartic structure of recognition and reversal was facilitated by the short scenes and insert shots of the screenplay form, with later events echoing and transforming the meaning of earlier episodes.

This became still more apparent when I read Haley's book, and saw that the Campbellian mythic pattern was largely Mamet's invention. In other words, there was no difficulty in examining this screenplay in much the same way as any other text. That it was unfilmed was irrelevant; it could be compared to a known source for evidence of compression, addition, and structural alteration, and if I was interested in Mamet the writer, I was going to be more interested in what he was doing in someone else's work than with what a future director might do to his. Clearly the method of adaptation was prescribed to some extent by the transformation from prose narrative to screenplay, but the process also revealed continuities with his work for the stage. In short, it was very easy to write about *The Autobiography of Malcolm X* in the context of Mamet's own *style*.

Nothing about this struck me as strange at the time. I had previously read the published script of his 1987 film *House of Games*, after seeing the movie, which acquainted me with some of the distinctive features of screenplay form; but I doubt that any prior experience was really necessary. Once I had worked out for myself that 'INT' meant 'interior' and 'EXT' meant exterior, I was in. It was only later, as I became more familiar with film studies as a discipline, that I began to encounter the argument that *because* the screenplay is an industrial form, *therefore* it is peculiarly difficult or unrewarding to read. My experience of reading unfilmed screenplays indicated that this was a non sequitur, and in that conviction lay the seeds of the present book.

What I did not fully appreciate at the time was that Mamet was very far from being a typical Hollywood writer. *The Postman Always Rings Twice* was something of an apprentice work, during which Rafelson schooled him in the art of screenwriting, to the satisfaction of all concerned. *The Verdict*, while ostensibly an adaptation of a potboiler novel, was much more Mamet's own creation, and although Lumet intervened to alter the ending, he otherwise respected the writer's work, and indeed only agreed to direct the movie on condition that Mamet's script was reinstated. *The Autobiography of Malcolm X* had been planned as another Lumet film, and because Mamet was working with directors who were willing and eager to see what a brilliant dramatist might do in a different medium, these early scripts preserve the crackling dialogue and hardbitten world view of the plays while revealing the writer's fascination with the new possibilities of time and point of view presented by the screenplay form. Much the same can be said of Pinter's screenplays for Joseph Losey.

Soon, however, Mamet would encounter the reality confronting most writers in Hollywood, when he lost artistic control over the adaptation of *Sexual Perversity in Chicago* into *About Last Night ...* (Edward Zwick, 1986). Wounded by the experience, he dug his heels in when asked for last-minute rewrites on *The Untouchables* (Brian DePalma, 1987). By this time he was directing his first movie, *House of Games*, and arguing that the work of the director was essentially an extension of that of the writer, as his own subsequent career as a writer-director affirms. In these ways Mamet has largely managed to preserve the kind of authority over his screenplays that he and other dramatists routinely enjoy over their work for the theatre.

Yet this is very much the exception in a Hollywood in which the writer is almost invariably a worker for hire, contractually obliged to relinquish control over the text on submission to the studio, which customarily subjects a 'final draft' to ongoing revisions from many different writers. In this context, the very notion of authorship itself is questionable, and this loss of authority over what is in any case an inherently unstable text contributes to a widely held perception among writers and literary critics that the screenplay is by definition non-literary. Such arguments, however, invoke an essentially Romantic perception of literature as the product of an individual, autonomous sensibility, which is at odds with the empirical facts surrounding most 'literary' authorship – not least that of Romantic poetry itself. Recent scholarship in these fields is increasingly inclined to see single authorship as, at best, the exception to a general rule of collaboration expressed in the 'socialised text'. If this is the case, then the practices of collaboration and revision characteristic of screenwriting and openly acknowledged in the Hollywood credit system are a general condition of literary production, and it is the 'literary' text, and not the screenplay, that is embarrassed by these practices. These questions are discussed in Chapter 1.

The corollary of multiple authorship, as practised in Hollywood, is textual instability. This was the second charge that could routinely be laid against the screenplay, and another that was obscured in the Mamet scripts that had first sparked my interest. As Steven Maras argues in his recent book *Screenwriting*, the 'blueprint' theory of screenplay production holds that a film is little more than a cinematic realisation of the script marked 'final'. This is how Mamet apparently conceives of his own scripts: as completed texts that are not to be revised by others, with the director's work being in effect a completion of the writing process. This accounts for the peculiarly affectless quality of the films he directs himself, with the actors audibly reciting lines rather than inhabiting the role in the manner of a Method actor. The unique strangeness of the results, nevertheless, is an exception that seems to prove a general rule: the screenplay is not so much a blueprint as an enabling document, necessary for the production but transformed by directors, actors, vagaries of the weather, and a multitude of other factors that occasion the rewrites that are the bane of the screenwriter's craft. As with multiple authorship, however, textual instability in and of itself does not explain the marginalisation of the screenplay in literary studies. Indeed, as argued in Chapter 2, in many ways the screenplay exemplifies the reorientation from 'work' to 'text' that was theorised by Roland Barthes in the 1960s, and which has informed much of literary scholarship – 'traditional' or otherwise – ever since. From this point of view, it is again difficult to see why the screenplay should be seen as something exceptional within the field of literary studies, unless one concedes that the radical claims of critical theory have made little headway in an institutional study of literature that still constructs its canon around authors and stable texts.

Chapter 3 examines the various ways in which the screenplay has been made to disappear, within the fields of both literary and film studies. The evidence of the senses confirms that screenplays exist as texts, but as they pass through production they are always in the process of transformation, to the point at which it is often difficult to speak of *the* screenplay of a film at all. This instability is compounded, particularly by film makers and theoreticians, in metaphors and rhetorical strategies that seek to eliminate the screenplay altogether, not least because of its troublesome ghostliness in relation to the film: it is both absent and present, dead and alive, erased yet detectable. The chapter concludes with a discussion of adaptations as particular manifestations of this peculiar dynamic.

The next three chapters explore the consequences for criticism of some of the theoretical questions addressed in the first part of the book. Chapter 4 discusses some of the stages through which a given script may pass in production, while Chapter 5 gives a detailed study of a particularly striking example: the collaboration between Evan Hunter and Alfred Hitchcock in scripting *The Birds* (1963). The aim here is not to provide a teleological narrative of how an idea was progressively refined until it became an authorial masterpiece, of the kind familiar in 'the making of...' studies. Instead, a detailed study of the script materials shows that certain problems kept recurring and refused to go away, no matter how hard Hitchcock sought to eliminate them. These include the main questions raised by, but rarely articulated and never resolved within, the film: why are the birds attacking, and in what ways, if any, are the attacks connected to the developing relationships between the characters? The script conferences and memos, and Hunter's three drafts, indicate that the developing tension between writer and director resulted from their differing responses to these questions. Very broadly, Hunter attempted to resolve some of them within the script, while Hitchcock later developed more visual methods of addressing the same concerns. This is qualified by the director's commissioning of rewrites that explicitly verbalised aspects of Melanie's personal history that had been repressed (or simply didn't exist) in Hunter's drafts, and in so doing articulated some of Hitchcock's recurrent 'thematic' concerns, especially surrounding the relationships between parents and their adult offspring.

The existence of these late rewrites, and of further changes the director made during production and post-production, illustrates that films are liable to generate a large number of drafts and other materials, no one of which is likely to correspond with any great precision to the final cut. Chapter 6 addresses the questions that arise for editing and publication (which is seemingly a precondition of the screenplay being taken seriously as a textual form): which of these multiple versions should be selected for the copy text? Does every rewrite produce a new version? Again, examining these questions from the viewpoint of both literary and film studies suggest that each discipline is beginning to deploy methodologies more frequently encountered in the other: film-centred studies of screenplays routinely address questions of the social text that are relatively new within literary studies, while screenplay publication has to date, with some notable exceptions, rarely paid attention to matters of textual provenance that are detailed as a matter of course in critical editions of literary works.

The final two chapters continue this dual approach by attempting to establish the ways in which both literary and film theory may illuminate the critical reading of screenplays, while also seeking to establish the distinctive textual properties of the screenplay form. (For those unacquainted with these properties, the Appendix presents sample pages of a professionally written screenplay, with brief commentary.) As argued in Chapter 3, one reason for the lack of critical attention to screenplays as texts is undoubtedly the tendency to regard them as mere pre-texts for movies, which kill or erase them on completion. Accordingly, these chapters insist on the extensive differences between screenplay texts, especially regarding the inclusion or excision of commentary within the prose narrative, a practice routinely prohibited in screenwriting manuals but widely followed by screenwriters themselves. This suggests that many writers reject the blueprint metaphor, and instead see the text as a literary (or perhaps simply textual) creation that invites directors, actors, and other members of the production crew to find correlatives for the verbal text within their own fields. Accordingly, Chapters 7 and 8 draw connections between the screenplay form and other kinds of text, while insisting that a distinction always exists between screenplays and films.

It is this distinction that occasioned the writing of the epilogue. On one level, Billy Wilder's film of *Sunset Boulevard* (1950), written with Charles Brackett and Dave Marshman, Jr., is a classical tragedy about the crumbling of an old order and its replacement by something newer and more ruthless, a timeless dramatic theme that runs through innumerable works in different media, from the Greeks through *The Cherry Orchard* to *The Magnificent Ambersons* to *Tinker, Tailor, Soldier, Spy* and *The Long Good Friday*, all of which are splendid. The problem with *Sunset Boulevard* is that the transition has already happened, twenty years before the events of the film. Norma cannot win, because she has already lost. Consequently she is little more than a deluded victim of that cruellest of genres, the comedy of embarrassment, the only counter-dynamic lying in her ability to inflict humiliation after humiliation upon Gillis and Max. And everything is made worse because both men know they are only enduring this torment so that she can continue a decades-long, hammy, absolutely delusional performance from which there is no escape except in death.

When I read the screenplay, however, I suddenly saw something completely different. Instead of a nasty tale of the dying suffocating the living and the living stamping on the dead, the screenplay was a celebration of words: the beautifully honed put-downs of studio executives, the resourceful inventiveness of Gillis as narrator, whole stories told in a sentence. Reading the screenplay liberates the tale: instead of being restrained in Norma's mansion, Gillis freely wanders, the title indicating not so much literal or cultural confinement as a recognition of the diversity and opportunity represented by the vastness of this extraordinary stretch of road. Unlike the protagonist of a true film noir, of which Wilder was a master, Gillis really does have choices. He goes to parties, he establishes his relationship with Betty Schaefer, his stories take on new life, and all the while the screenwriters have a ball with the possibilities of dialogue, voice-over, and description.

It is often noted that screenplays differ from stage plays in being written with only a single performance in mind. As anyone who has read a screenplay they consider better than the film will have observed, however, a movie doesn't move, insofar as it fixes in perpetuity an interpretation of a script that is otherwise amenable to multiple possible realisations. Perhaps because it is so vivid, the images of Wilder's *Sunset Boulevard* have the effect of confining, even replacing, the verbal panache of the written text. That text is one of the finest examples of screenwriting, a testament to the irreducible differences between a verbal medium and a visual and auditory one, and a pinnacle in the careers of Wilder and his chief collaborator, Charles Brackett.

As the present book debates the value of screenplays as verbal texts, it seemed inappropriate to consider in detail those that were only available to me in translation; accordingly, most of the discussion of individual texts is confined to screenplays written in English, although the question of translation is briefly considered in Chapter 6.

In a professionally written screenplay, characters' names and dialogue are customarily indented using the margins illustrated in the excerpted screenplay reproduced in the Appendix. For reasons of space, I have sometimes departed from these conventions.

Acknowledgements

I am indebted to the British Academy, for a research grant that enabled me to visit several libraries in the United States, and to the Arts and Humanities Research Board for a research leave award that enabled me to write up the results. The book would not exist were it not for Christabel Scaife, my commissioning editor at Palgrave Macmillan, whose enthusiasm, support, and patience have been invaluable at every turn. I am also indebted to the anonymous reviewers of the original proposal, whose suggestions helped to define the limits of what might reasonably be accomplished within a single book.

During my time in Los Angeles I was faintly stunned by the generosity and thoughtfulness of the library staff at every institution I visited. I would like to express my particular thanks to Karen Pedersen, Director of the Shavelson-Webb Library at the Writers Guild of America – West, and Barbara Hall, at the Margaret Herrick Library, Academy of Motion Picture Arts and Sciences, for their tireless assistance and expert advice; and also to Ned Comstock, an equally knowledgeable and hospitable guide to the resources held at the University of Southern California. Steven B. Kravitz, on behalf of the Trustees of the Alfred Hitchcock Trust, unhesitatingly granted permission to quote from the archival material on *The Birds* that the Trust has donated to the Margaret Herrick Library. Shannon Fifer, at Warner Bros., was also most helpful in responding to permissions requests. Sarah Kaplan, and Sam and Paige Farmer, were excessively generous hosts, as were Tony and Jen Walton in New York.

In London, staff at the library of the British Film Institute were unfailingly helpful in providing materials and tracking down obscure pieces of information, and the work also benefited from the resources and assistance of staff at the British Library and Senate House Library, University of London. David Hughes very generously granted me free use of unpublished scripts. I am grateful to my colleagues at Bangor University, especially Stephen Colclough, for comments on particular areas in which their expertise greatly exceeded my own.

David Mamet and the staff at the Rosenstone/Wender agency, especially John Gersten, started me off on this trail long ago by granting me access to a wonderful array of Mamet's unpublished scripts. This isn't a book about Mamet, but it would never have been written had his work not alerted me to the potential of the form. Over the years the friendly discussions and exchange of ideas with many who have written on his work have continually helped me to clarify my thinking about screenwriting; of these, I should particularly like to thank Leslie Kane, David Sauer, Ira Nadel, and Johan Callens. Bill Baker, Bob Lee, and Justin Edwards all offered great encouragement when it was most needed, as did Harold Pinter; I regret that the opportunity to thank him in print has arrived too late. Inevitably, the greatest debts are personal, so thank you Domini, Joey, and Abigail.

1
Authorship

On 22 January 2009, an article in *The Guardian* announced the year's Academy Award nominations. Below the story in the online edition, 'uniquescreenwriter' observed with exasperation that writers had been subjected to predictable ignominy on the official Oscars website. At least the Writers of Best Adapted and Best Original Screenplays 'were actually named – but they were right down at the bottom of the list after Sound Mixing, Animation Short and Achievement in Make-up'.[1] A quick visit to the Oscars page confirmed that this was true – there they were, right at the bottom. 'Writing' was at the bottom because the list had been compiled in alphabetical order.[2]

Ideology at the birth of screenwriting

Uniquescreenwriter is not alone, since paranoia among members of that profession seems not so much understandable as mandatory. Writing has always been the poor relation in the family of cooperative arts convened after the birth of cinema. Film was at least in part a product of late-Victorian fascination with scientific and technological progress: for the first time, natural movement in real time could be mechanically recorded, reproduced, and exhibited. As with most inventions with a mass commercial application, its potential was expressed through perpetual innovation and refinement. The transition from the earliest *actualités* to the beginnings of narrative cinema, for example, was the result as much of technical advances in cameras and film stock as of audiences' weariness of scenes of everyday life. Yet it is this transition that is generally assumed to have occasioned the emergence of screenwriting as a necessary discipline, with the creation of relatively lengthy narrative films around 1902–3 by figures such as Georges Méliès in France and Edwin S. Porter in the United States.[3]

In practice, scripts (soon to be termed 'photoplays' or 'scenarios') for early pictures usually consisted of little more than a numbered list of shots, written down to facilitate the pre-arrangement of story events into a coherent order prior to filming. This required no particular facility with words, and very few such materials have survived. Films could even be derived from textual sources, such as plays or newspaper reports, without necessarily going through any intermediary stage of textual adaptation. Writing had no value in a medium that at this stage (often termed 'primitive' by film historians) could not begin to approximate the intellectual and artistic revolutions taking place in modernist literature. The French had coined the term *films d'art* in the early 1900s, but this designated not the quality of the films themselves but merely of their source materials. Such a film was an adaptation of a recognised literary classic, with Shakespeare as a popular source, despite the impossibility of reproducing either the language or more than a fragment of the plot. It was not until later, in the first decade of the twentieth century, with the emergence of embryonic studio systems requiring the circulation of a standardised script to different members of the production team, that written texts entered the film-making process as a matter of course.

Many of the most successful professional scenario writers were journalists like Roy P. McCardell, who began working for Biograph in 1898 and was the first of 'the flood of newspapermen turning screenwriters'.[4] Tom Stempel suggests that McCardell's experience in editing and writing captions for cartoon and photo stories for newspapers may have influenced his decision to write for the movies. The relatively lawless state of copyright in America at this time exacerbated the hostile relations between cinema and literature, and it was not until 1911 that a US Supreme Court ruling ended the cannibalisation of published source material that had previously had no protection. Changes to the copyright law meant that 'features and shorts were at last perceived to be the products of authors, rather than stories that just happened to be made up by the actors on the screen'.[5]

The film-makers' immediate response translated into social terms a class distinction that already pertained to the texts themselves. Reluctant to increase their costs either by using copyrighted material or by importing established professional writers, they instead actively promoted 'scenario fever' in the early teens through the pages of popular film magazines. Such classical divisions between 'high' and 'low' forms of writing were reinforced by American literary geography: the East was the home of the serious writer, the West of lowbrow popular culture – 'Westerns', in all their various stage, screen, and literary manifestations. A familiar Hollywood joke contends that 'it is the writer's job to get screwed. Writers are the women of the movie business'. Bitterly unfunny, it would also be spectacularly sexist were it not for the conspicuous irony that its author is said to have been a woman, although it is sufficiently emblematic to have been credited by two different female film historians to two different female screenwriters.[6] Moreover, while the joke threatens to emasculate the men who outnumber women by an uncomfortably large majority in contemporary Western screenwriting, it also invokes a folk memory of the silent years when women including Jeanie Macpherson, Gene Gauntier, Elinor Glyn, Frances Marion, Beulah Marie Dix, Alice Guy Blaché, and Anita Loos were some of the best-known writers in Hollywood. Estimates vary: Lizzie Francke suggests that around half the scripts stored in the Library of Congress between 1911 and 1929 were by women,[7] while Marsha McCreadie cites the Writers Guild of America (WGA) in suggesting that 'from the turn of the century to the mid-twenties, women outnumbered men in the screenwriting trade ten to one'.[8] It is almost unimaginable. The situation changed rapidly in the 1930s and 1940s, to the point that by the time the United States entered into the Second World War, 85 per cent of industry writers were men.[9] Although the imbalance was redressed to some extent during the war years, and women also attained prominent positions elsewhere in the industry, the female screenwriter remains very much the exception. In 1988, at the height of the producer-driven 'high concept' movie, a Film Writers Guide revealed over one thousand five hundred men and only thirty-three women.[10]

McCreadie and Francke advance several explanations for the early prominence of women: the first companies were often organised as family businesses; actresses might have gravitated towards writing to prolong their careers; women appear to have developed networks between themselves; and with a preponderance of women in cinema audiences, female writers may have been better placed to cater to their tastes. Equally important is that, regardless of the sex of those making the films, the style and genres of early cinema strongly favoured extremes of emotional affect that have always been gendered as feminine.[11] The dominant mode of the narrative motion picture was melodrama: a survey of early scripts preserved in the Selig, Dawley, and Lubin collections at the Academy of Motion Picture Arts and Sciences in Los Angeles, and the Museum of Modern Art in New York, reveals moral worlds that are predictably confined to family values, easy distinctions between good and evil, and the most simple of character motivations. Comedies aside, almost every one is either a melodrama or has pronounced melodramatic elements, and the same could be said of most of the films of D. W. Griffith.

Although melodrama would later become a complex and significant Hollywood genre, especially in the 'women's pictures' of the 1940s, the surviving scripts and films made prior to the First World War are crude. They suffer terribly from comparison to both the contemporaneous modernist novels of Conrad or Lawrence, for example, which were exploring complex or impenetrable psychology, stylistic difficulty, and moral ambiguity, and the perceived advances in playwriting that George Bernard Shaw associated with Henrik Ibsen, whose *A Doll's House* (1879) challenged the conventions of the sanctity of marriage and the trope of the woman-as-victim.

Seen in this light, the early decades of cinema represent a visible leap backwards. Narrative techniques were rudimentary and had to sacrifice complexity for comprehensibility, while technological limitations required scenes to be filmed in long shot rather than close-up, with an accompanying need for exaggerated emotional gestures on the part of the actors. A triangular association of cinema, femininity, and childishness soon emerged: Loos began her writing career at the age of twelve; Blaché was allowed by Gaumont to use the camera because he said it was 'a child's toy'.[12] Once a studio hierarchy that ensured the writer's subordination to producers and actors had been established, the association of the scenario writer with feminine powerlessness was complete.

'Serious' writers, then, had every reason to be suspicious of the new medium, even disregarding the limitations of the scenario form. Working for Hollywood soon became synonymous with artistic failure, financial opportunism, or both. Edward Azlant has identified two waves of early scenario writers: those who stayed east and also wrote in other genres (McCardell, Sargent, Eustace Hale Ball), and those who 'moved to or started out in the west', such as Macpherson and C. Gardner Sullivan.[13] Ball purportedly wrote sixty thousand words weekly, travelled west, became the type of the journeyman or hack who sacrifices artistic integrity for money, and personified the perception of Hollywood as the destroyer of literary talent. This view took still firmer hold after Sam Goldwyn created the Eminent Authors enterprise in 1919 (Edison had already tried something similar), swiftly followed by comparable initiatives at Vitagraph in 1919 and Metro in 1920.

Yet a more complex set of perceptions seems to have developed among the writers themselves. In *Hollywood and the Profession of Authorship*, Richard Fine examines forty 'Eastern' writers who arrived in Hollywood between 1927 and 1938, mostly after the Depression had ravaged Broadway and curtailed a major source of income in the process. He argues that '[n]either side of the Hollywood-as-destroyer controversy adequately explains the curious paradox ... that many of the Eastern writers most successful in Hollywood [including Ben Hecht, S. J. Perelman, Gene Fowler, and Dorothy Parker] were its harshest critics; others [such as William Faulkner, James M. Cain, Nathanael West, and Thornton Wilder], faring less well in the studio system, complained in far more muted tones .... Not all writers came to sad ends in Hollywood, then, but virtually every writer was disquieted or unnerved by the experience'.[14]

That experience typically confined them to pre-production duties including enforced collaboration, regular hours on-site, script conferences, negotiations with the Hays Office responsible for censorship, and encounters with producers who preferred to digest synopses and outlines rather than novels and screenplays. Initially, at least, the authors were generally employed either for the cachet of their names, or because of a facility with particular aspects of the writing process, most notably dialogue. More experienced Hollywood professionals would generally be responsible for constructing the scenario itself, and the 'authors' could easily come to see themselves as little more than alienated labourers on a Fordist assembly line, albeit peculiarly well-remunerated ones. Partly as a result, writers developed a number of organisations to protect their interests, of which the most effective was the still highly influential Screen Writers' Guild, created in 1920.

Nonetheless Fine concludes that 'a writer's talent was not under attack in Hollywood so much as the profession of authorship as he had known it'. Eastern writers were judging one culture – the Hollywood studio system – in terms of its diametrical opposite, that of literary New York, which had established professional values such as 'creative autonomy, personal independence, legal control and ownership of their work, and fair compensation'.[15] In other words, these writers were members of what Stanley Fish would call an 'interpretive community',[16] whose view of literary authorship has its roots in an essentially Romantic ideology that predisposed them to evaluate Hollywood screenwriting in a particular way. That such writing remains to this day marginalised to the point of near invisibility within departments of literature in Western universities indicates the persistence and pervasiveness of this ideology within academic circles, regardless of the ubiquitous graduate courses in the post-1968 'critical theory' that seemed to have consigned such notions of authorship to the dustbin of history.

The 'auteur theory' and Romantic ideology

One explanation is that at the same time as film theory was in the vanguard of attempts to decentre the individual human subject, a dominant strand in film criticism was committed to the quite opposite project of reconceiving what had previously been considered a collaborative medium as a vehicle for expressing the world view of individual directors. With such a radical devaluation of the role of the writer, which in Anglophone countries had never acquired significant cultural status in any event, it is hardly surprising that film writing became the last place in which to search for evidence of literary merit.

In the 1950s, a group of film critics associated with the journal *Cahiers du Cinéma* advanced a historically and culturally specific *politique des auteurs*. As we shall see later in this chapter, this was an intervention within the French film industry, in which screenwriters were held by critics like Francois Truffaut to possess too much power, to the detriment of French cinema. In 'Notes on the Auteur Theory in 1962' (1962) and *The American Cinema* (1968), the American critic Andrew Sarris instigated a much-criticised approach that drew on the *Cahiers* writers' work in order to advance a very different project: the creation of an evaluative mechanism for promoting the work of mostly American directors. Sarris regarded the directors who were sufficiently distinguished to gain entry into the 'pantheon' as the authors of their films, in much the same way as literary writers were regarded as authors of their texts.[17]

He exerts a powerful sway over his former student Richard Corliss, who in the early 1970s published two books, an edited collection of essays on *The Hollywood Screenwriters* (1972) and the single-authored *Talking Pictures: Screenwriters in the American Cinema* (1974), which attempted to appropriate the term 'auteur' for the screenwriter. While accepting that film is a collaborative medium, in *The Hollywood Screenwriters* Corliss considers the writer, rather than the director, ordinarily responsible in three areas: themes ('as expressed through plot, characterization and dialogue'), tone, and 'fugues', whereby the screenwriter becomes 'an auteur who, through detailed script indications of camera placement, cutting, and acting styles, virtually "directs" his own films. It's no more absurd than to argue that the director writes his own scripts'.[18]

The methodology of his next book, *Talking Pictures*, consciously parallels that of Sarris in sketching a counter-canon of writers to set against his mentor's pantheon of directors. The introductory 'Notes on a Screenwriter's Theory' takes a 'dialectical' approach to the question of authorship by positing Sarris's directorial auteurism as the thesis, the screenwriter as antithesis, and the collaboration between the two as a desirable synthesis. In his preface, Sarris largely agrees:

> I would grant the screenwriter most of the dividends accruing from dialogue, and Corliss would grant the director the interpretive insights of a musical conductor. Where we grapple most desperately and blindly is in that no man's land of narrative and dramatic structure. And here I think the balance of power between the director and the screenwriter is too variable for any generalization.... I tend to agree with Joseph L. Mankiewicz that every screenplay is a directed movie, and every directed movie a screenplay. That is to say that writing and directing are fundamentally the same function.[19]

In practice, it is precisely this conflation that tends to characterise the *auteur* of European art cinema, or the later 'American independent' film, and its relevance to Hollywood studio practice still seems questionable. In this context, it is hard to disagree with Thomas R. Schatz's assertion that '[a]uteurism itself would not be worth bothering with if it hadn't been so influential, effectively stalling film history and criticism in a prolonged stage of adolescent romanticism'.[20] Sarris himself partly acknowledges the full complexity of the studio system in remarking that '[t]he director-auteur is not even a real person as such, but a field of magnetic force around which all agents and elements of the filmmaking process tend to cluster'.[21] Taken a stage further, this insight would undermine the 'auteur theory' and gesture towards the anti-authorial view, persuasively argued by Schatz, that 'style' in Hollywood cinema is not the personal expression of an individual creator but rather the product of what André Bazin termed, in an illuminating oxymoron borrowed by Schatz for the title of his book, 'the genius of the system'.

Although Corliss's attempt to re-establish the screenwriter produces a reading of Hollywood that runs the same dangers of imbalance as Sarris's, his explanation for the marginalisation of the writer in American film remains pertinent. Presented with a screenplay, a director 'can do one of three things: ruin it, shoot it, or improve it'. Crucially, however, while 'the screenwriter *makes* words and situations occur ... the director *allows* actions to occur. Thus, the process of creating a screenplay is more formal, less mystical than the image, which is created by the director, photographer, designer, and actors'.[22] Consequently the direction seems more unconscious and more artistic than the writing. Combined with the ready availability of films but the relative inaccessibility of screenplay texts, the credit system of attribution, the differences between various kinds of adaptation, and the fact that 'the hallmark of many fine screenwriters is versatility, not consistency',[23] this has contributed to the construction of the director rather than the screenwriter as auteur.

More broadly, Corliss examines how the notion of authorship in general functions within a dominant Romantic ideology of cultural production. He identifies a set of three binary oppositions surrounding attempts to distinguish the 'auteur' director from others: art versus entertainment, solitary art versus corporate art, and the creative artist versus the interpretive artist who collaborates with others and adapts material.[24] In each case, the first term is associated with the 'very romantic and American' notion that 'art is the product of one man working alone to carve a personal vision out of the marble of his sensibility'. The second more accurately identifies the conditions under which Hollywood films are usually made. Such distinctions are also frequently deployed to discriminate the American 'independent' or European 'art' cinema from Hollywood studio product: the former are 'films', the latter mere 'movies'. Corliss argues that these distinctions contribute to the perception of the director as *auteur*, while denying the same status to the screenwriter.

Just as Fine sees the frustrations of the author-turned-screenwriter emerging from an ideological perception of the author's profession, Corliss's distinctions describe not absolute divisions between different kinds of writers, but instead different, and ideologically inflected, perceptions or constructions of writing practice. It is arguably these perceptions that bring the category of 'literature' itself into being, with other kinds of writing, such as the screenplay, being defined in opposition to it: as 'non-literature'. Corliss's solitary, creative artist, with its associations of moral seriousness, originality, and spontaneous inspiration, clearly derives from a Romantic ideology that is partly a product of the writings of Coleridge, Wordsworth, Hazlitt, Keats, Lamb, and other writers in late eighteenth- and early nineteenth-century England, but also of the refraction of their ideas through successive eras of literary criticism, persisting to contribute substantially to what remains the dominant paradigm in literary studies today.

Although there is no single or unmixed 'Romanticism', it is ordinarily associated with the idea that the text is an act of personal expression, the translation of inspiration into textual form: the 'emotion recollected in tranquillity' of which Wordsworth writes in the Preface to the *Lyrical Ballads*. Such a construction reaches its apotheosis in the Romantic hero, the genius, of whom Shakespeare is the literary exemplar. In general, Romanticism was opposed to 'systematic thought', for 'just as Blake tells us that exuberance and not formality is beauty, so Wordsworth tells us that we murder to dissect, and Keats that philosophy will clip an angel's wings'.[25] This 'movement from the realm of action and politics to that of thought and inner feeling is fundamental to a major strand of Romanticism', and is articulated also in Romantic criticism of Shakespeare that placed particular emphasis on 'character'; indeed, it was Coleridge who coined the term 'psycho-analytical'.[26] Romantic criticism rejected the constrictions of externally imposed 'rules', especially those deriving from the supposed Aristotelian unities shaping the 'classical' work. Consequently, where classicism valued existing genres, Romanticism delighted in generic hybridity, while at the same time arguing for a different kind of unity, generated organically by the harmonious development of innate qualities. In short, Romantic ideology offers 'an emotionally gratifying respite from the rigors of a mechanized world'.[27]

In this intellectual context, the screenplay text is clearly a product of the kind of advanced industrial practice to which Romanticism is in direct ideological opposition. Much more than with other forms of creative writing, notions of authorship in relation to screenwriting tend to be displaced by legal and contractual relationships and, often, by notions of collective, evolving, and even anonymous authorship. 'Inspiration' is subject to modification not only by the writer but, more importantly, by the studio system to which s/he is subject, while the text itself is caught up in a related system: the internal constraints imposed by industrial designs such as the master-scene format or the numbered shooting script and the demands of genre-specific forms (even if the genre is that of the 'art movie'). And even the staunchest defenders of the screenplay's claims to literary status tend to concede that it privileges exterior action over the interior thought and feeling of the 'character'.

Many of these distinctions result from the bathetic reality that the Hollywood screenwriter is an employee, whereas the truly Romantic writer would be not so much self-employed as beyond the constraints of commerce entirely. Yet recent scholarship on Romanticism has exposed how rarely the practices of Romantic writers actually sustain the ideology that bears its name. Instead, these writers engaged constantly in two activities that are theoretically separable but in practice have become intertwined in much recent scholarship: multiple authorship and textual revision. In an extensive critique of 'the myth of solitary genius', Jack Stillinger details many examples of the multiple authorship of texts conventionally regarded as the work of a single author, including several poems in the *Lyrical Ballads*, all of which are attributed to either Wordsworth or Coleridge but not both, even though significant collaboration appears to have taken place. This critical reorientation is not confined to Romanticism: one of Stillinger's prime examples is the profoundly significant influence of Ezra Pound in editing T. S. Eliot's *The Waste Land* into its published form, while Brian Vickers, among others, has shown that Shakespeare, the very type of the Romantic genius, was an active and frequent collaborator.[28]

Despite such incontrovertible and in some cases long-established evidence, however, '[t]he Romantic notion of individual authorship is now so widespread as to be nearly universal'.[29] This is partly for the ideological reasons noted above, but it is also a pragmatic decision: 'nobody is satisfied with anonymous authorship', partly because 'the myth of single authorship is a great convenience for ... everyone connected with the publication of books, starting with the authors themselves', and including publishers.[30] Accordingly theorists, even 'author-banishers like Barthes and Foucault, all embrace or reject the traditional concept of the single author', even though 'the posited ideal of single-author intention seems a shaky foundation for general theory'.[31]

That a sizeable team of writers and editors contribute to the making of the popular novels published under the name of Jeffrey Archer has undoubtedly contributed to Archer's reputation as a writer of low-grade airport fiction, independently of the merits or demerits of the books themselves.[32] Yet 'popular' and 'serious' fiction are not always as distinct in this respect as may appear at first. Peter Carey, for example, acknowledges the importance of four weeks of collaboration with his editor, not to mention the constructive contributions of his wife and friends, in completing his Booker Prize-winning novel *True History of the Kelly Gang*,[33] and Raymond Carver's stories were often heavily revised by his editor, Raymond Lash, as well as benefiting from the input of Carver's wife, Tess Gallagher.[34]

Empirical evidence of this kind calls into question the basis for constructing the single author as a criterion of literary value. While Stillinger maintains that research into authorship increasingly calls the 'myth of solitary genius' into question, however, he still argues that knowledge of the authorship of a text enriches one's understanding of it. The informed reader is liable to recognise the experimental or unfinished quality of lines that may otherwise appear simply weak, see associations with other texts by the same author, and place the work within relevant contexts such as authorial development or generic tradition. 'Conversely, a reading of the poem without such knowledge is comparatively impoverished', and so, Stillinger says, 'the author-banishing critics are deceiving themselves if they really believe that one can dispense with authors while still retaining an idea of the literary. Indeed, this is probably why the most self-consistent of them also attack the notion of literariness and give their attention to subliterary works – comic strips, James Bond novels, exchanges with waiters in restaurants'.[35]

To this list, we may confidently add the studio screenplays that Stillinger, like so many others, demonstrates to be antithetical to notions of authorship because of the prevalence of rewrites, multiple writing teams, script conferences, and so on. By contrast, the kinds of collaboration that Stillinger discusses in relation to Romantic literature rarely banish entirely the notion of conscious authorial control over a text. For example, he regards the later Wordsworth as a self-collaborator, the older poet revising the younger in producing different versions of *The Prelude*, and traces the collaborations between identifiable individuals – friends, editors, and the like – on works by Keats and others to show that notions of personal creativity and intention can, to some extent, still be recuperated. What at first looks to be an argument that would reorient critical studies towards a direction that might cause the screenplay to be regarded more favourably, then, instead becomes one more means of enforcing its marginalisation.

Much the same can be said of recent work on authorial revision. Part of the Romantic fascination with textual fragments, and with incompletion generally, derives from an ideological preference for spontaneity and a mistrust of the definitive forms apparently imposed by revision. Yet every text goes through a process of development, if only because the writer generates the material in real time; and as Zachary Leader's *Revision and Romantic Authorship* shows, there is every reason to be sceptical of the repeated Romantic affirmations of spontaneous inspiration in the creation of the text.[36] Recent work on Shakespeare has arrived at similar conclusions. In 1987, Stanley Wells and Gary Taylor's *Complete Oxford Shakespeare* printed two versions of *King Lear* in an early demonstration of the now generally accepted argument that disagreement between quarto and folio versions of a play often signifies two distinct Shakespearean versions rather than corrupted or edited versions of a common original; and even the 'bad' quartos are now recognised in many cases to preserve, in however corrupted a form, acting versions of a text that resulted from the common practice of generating alternate versions of a play to meet the particular needs of a given production.

Wordsworth did not argue that composition was spontaneous, but that writing involved rendering spontaneous inspiration into poetic form by means of a process that takes place after the event, 'in tranquillity'. This preserves a certain idealism: the 'powerful feelings' are non-textual, while somehow the writing process involves the 'recollection' of the feelings. Yet if those feelings are to be rendered into text, the separation between the feelings and the text becomes untenable. Either the feelings themselves had a textual form already, or the process of composition textualises them, and thereby makes of them something other than what they were. Nevertheless in Wordsworth's poems about childhood, or the Ancient Mariner's compulsion endlessly to repeat the same tale, revision becomes revisitation, an obsessive return to a primal event in an attempt finally to understand its original meaning. It may not be possible to establish that meaning, or to recover an original intention, but meaning and intention remain at the heart of the literary experience. By contrast, the problem in the case of the multiply authored screenplay text is not that intention cannot be fixed, but that it may never have existed at all.

What distinguishes the screenwriter from the novelist or poet in this respect is partly the extent of the collaboration and revision. Equally significant, however, is that, even when the sole writer of an 'original' script, the screenwriter will engage with producers and directors, leaving a visible paper trail of meetings and textual changes that allows for a relatively precise and detailed reconstruction of collaborative development and composition. These processes, which cause the screenplay to be widely dismissed as a corporately authored and infinitely malleable commercial product, in fact merely eliminate the masking procedures that produce the effect of spontaneous individual inspiration in more 'literary' texts. The novel, for instance, which is almost invariably single-authored, ordinarily introduces no comparable industrial process that would routinely demand the submission of working copy for corporate consultation and revision. The private discussions with the publisher and literary agent, the uncredited assistance from fellow writers, the various drafts that disappear forever at the touch of a computer keyboard, and the processes of editing, previewing, marketing, and so on, are obscured, because the literary author is the owner of the work; the screenwriter is not. Consequently, the studios and writing unions introduced rules and the processes of credit acquisition to settle disputes concerning attribution.

Credit

Especially in Hollywood, the writer lacks the legal status of an author, and unlike the playwright, the screenwriter has little or no copyright or other legal authority in matters relating to the text. Under the US copyright law, films are ordinarily described as 'works made for hire', and '[a]ccording to the work-made-for-hire doctrine it is the employer [in this case the producer] who is regarded as the author of the work, and the rights of the actual creator of the work are given no recognition'.[37] Whereas literary authorship implies ownership of the text, the screenwriter has much the same status as the scientist or other employee whose creative potential relies on facilities owned by the employer. Contractual arrangements may mean that the writer has relatively little control or incentive regarding publication, while studio ownership of production materials can make it harder to secure 'fair use' permissions than is the case with most other kinds of text, contributing to the screenplay's near-invisibility in critical analysis.

Negotiations between screenwriter and employer often focus on credit, the legal and financial ramifications of which are the most obvious way in which screenwriting differs from other kinds of textual authorship. As the most visible acknowledgement of authorship in Hollywood screenwriting, credit is crucial to writers, as its acquisition has significant implications for status and future earnings, for example concerning the payment of 'credit bonuses' and 'residuals' (royalties on sales). The principles of credit are spelled out in the *Minimum Basic Agreement* (MBA), which outlines the rights, responsibilities, and remuneration of writers within the industry. The 2001 edition, effective from May 2001 to May 2004, contains four hundred and fifty-six pages in a large format. As a publication of the WGA itself, however, even this is not definitive, but instead represents advice and information for writers in their negotiations with the studios. As was confirmed by the 2008 writers' strike, sparked by concerns about remuneration from the sales of DVDs and other residuals, these relations are far from straightforward – hence the four hundred and fifty-six pages. For example, on the very first page the 2001 MBA identifies a basic disagreement between the Guild and the companies concerning 'possessive credit' (such formulations as 'a film by X'). The MBA objects to this term if X is not the sole screenwriter, on the grounds that it fails to recognise each individual's contribution, devalues credits, and 'inaccurately imputes sole or pre-eminent authorship' to the director. The companies, however, believed that such credits should be determined by discussions between companies, the WGA, and the Directors' Guild.[38]

The principles subsumed within the MBA's mass of technical detail are helpfully summarised in the WGA's altogether more user-friendly, twenty-nine-page *Screen Credits Manual*. In this document, terms such as 'writer' and 'literary material' acquire very particular meanings. A 'writer' is 'a person employed by a Company to write literary material or a person from whom a Company purchased literary material who at the time of purchase was a "professional writer"'. 'Literary material' itself 'is written material and shall include stories, adaptations, treatments, original treatments, scenarios, continuities, teleplays, screenplays, dialogue, scripts, sketches, plots, outlines, narrative synopses, routines, and narrations, and, for use in the production of television films, formats'.[39] Such definitions may appear bathetic, but they valuably eliminate the impressionism and vagueness of terms like 'literature' and 'authorship' that frequently obscure the real relations between other 'authors' and their own commercial and industrial contexts.

The *Manual* defines several kinds of writing in relation to credit: 'source material is material assigned to the writer which was previously published or exploited and upon which the writer's work is to be based'; 'story' is a contribution 'distinct from screenplay and consisting of basic narrative, idea, theme or outline indicating character development and action'; and a 'screenplay' itself 'consists of individual scenes and full dialogue, together with such prior treatment, basic adaptation, continuity, scenario and dialogue as shall be used in, and represent substantial contributions to the final script'. The most prized attribution is the 'written by' credit, which 'is used when the writer(s) is entitled to both the '"Story by" credit and the "Screenplay by" credit. This credit shall not be granted where there is source material of a story nature'. Additional credit categories are for 'screen story', 'narration written by', 'based on characters created by', and 'adaptation by' (pp. 18–20).

Strict conventions reveal something of the nature of a particular collaboration between two or more writers. An ampersand between two writers' names indicates that they worked jointly on a project; the use of the word 'and' between two writers' names, on the other hand, indicates that they worked separately on the script, with one ordinarily rewriting the other. In disputed cases, each writer must submit all script materials to a board of arbiters, which considers all relevant materials, including if desired submissions of 'breakdowns and illustrative comparisons between the final shooting script and earlier work or any other information which would help the Arbitration Committee to evaluate the writer's contribution to the final shooting script' (pp. 11–12). Writers not seeking credit also submit material to the Arbitration Committee to assist in settling disputes.

When a resemblance to a prior version of the material is detected, regardless of the facts of the case,

> the arbiters must act on the basis that there is presumptive evidence that a writer did, in fact, have access [to prior literary material], in spite of a writer's claim of 'writing independently of prior scripts,' if a significant similarity exists between a prior piece of literary material and a writer's later literary material. The arbiters must proceed on the basis that the similarities in themselves constitute presumptive evidence that there must have been some sort of access even if the literary material of the prior writer was only orally transmitted, as, for example, from a production executive to a later writer.... [T]his presumption is irrebuttable[.]
>
> (pp. 5–6)

The *Manual* then outlines the rules for determining credit. In most circumstances only two writers or teams of writers may be granted credit for a screenplay. 'Any writer whose work represents more than 33% of a screenplay shall be entitled to screenplay credit, except where the screenplay is an original screenplay. In the case of an original screenplay, any subsequent writer or writing team must contribute 50% to the final screenplay' (p. 21). The arithmetic, however, does not imply that the interpretation of credit is free of evaluative criteria. On the contrary, the allocation of credit depends not on a statistical comparison of the final shooting script to the draft materials, but on an interpretation of the relative merit of structural changes. 'The percentage contribution made by writers to [a] screenplay obviously cannot be determined by counting lines or even the number of pages to which a writer has contributed', and therefore arbiters are required to consider a writer's contribution to 'dramatic construction', 'original and different scenes', 'characterization and character relationships', and 'dialogue'.

This situation is not without its possible absurdities, as Tad Friend points out. For example, 'If Writer A of an original script wrote ten per cent of the finished film, and none of the five or six subsequent writers wrote more than fifty per cent, Writer A would get sole credit.' Moreover, 'under the current system there is a huge incentive for writers to make changes for the sake of change, rather than for the good of the film'.[40] Although the statistical basis for credit allocation occasionally risks descending into farce, the *Manual* appropriates for the arbitration committee expertise in what in literary-critical contexts is sometimes termed 'competence':

> It is because of the need to understand contributions to the screenplay as a whole that professional expertise is required on the part of the arbiters. For example, there have been instances in which every line of dialogue has been changed and still the arbiters have found no significant change in the screenplay as a whole. On the other hand, there have been instances where far fewer changes in dialogue have made a significant contribution to the screenplay as a whole. In addition, a change in one portion of the script may be so significant that the entire screenplay is affected by it.
>
> (pp. 22–3)

Although the *Manual* does not give examples, it is easy to think of screenplays that have been radically altered by the addition of a framing device (the 'Rosebud' motif in *Citizen Kane* [Orson Welles, 1941] for instance) which may dramatically alter the meaning of the whole story.

The arbitration committee's presumption of competence in such matters has measurable effects on a writer's income, career, and reputation. Although the acquisition of credit is commendably transparent in certain respects, then, it does not and cannot displace evaluation. Moreover, arbitration is based on the final shooting script, or, if this is unavailable, an uncredited cutting continuity of the release version of the film. This implies that the shooting script is itself a stable textual form; yet the script marked 'final' is itself open to all kinds of alterations once the film is in production.

Nor does it always come close to revealing the actual contribution made by a writer to a particular script, a difficulty compounded by contractual arrangements that may conceal precisely this information. Two examples concerning scripts apparently co-written by David Mamet sufficiently reveal some of the difficulties. Mamet was originally hired to adapt *Hannibal*, the Thomas Harris novel eventually filmed by Ridley Scott for a film released in 2001. In the event, his script was not used. Another writer, Steven Zaillian, then wrote an entirely new version, seemingly without reference to Mamet's, and it is Zaillian's that was subsequently used as the basis for the film, which retains no detectable trace of its predecessor.[41] Nevertheless, presumably for contractual reasons, the screenplay was eventually credited to 'David Mamet and Steven Zaillian', which confusingly implies that Zaillian's version was a rewrite of Mamet's.

A second, and more complicated, example concerns *Wag the Dog* (Barry Levinson, 1998). Very few of the major characters in the film even appear in the ostensible source novel, Larry Beinhart's *American Hero* (1993). That a screenplay can differ so radically from its source indicates the tenuousness of the industry distinction between 'original' and 'adapted' screenplays. Charlie Kaufman's script for *Adaptation* (Spike Jonze, 2002), problematically derived from Susan Orlean's novel *The Orchid Thief* (1999), provides what will probably become a standard case for discussion of this issue (see Chapter 3), but it is also symptomatic of a theoretical embarrassment surrounding the very concept of 'originality', a contentious term in literary studies but retained in a formal distinction largely reserved for screenwriters. Of more immediate interest is the co-crediting of Mamet and Hilary Henkin as writers of *Wag the Dog*'s screenplay. Henkin wrote the initial adaptation, but most Mamet scholars have tended to ascribe the final draft solely to Mamet. Tom Stempel, however, suggests that, irrespective of whether Mamet directly consulted Henkin's version, traces of it remain in his own, possibly as a result of script conferences with Levinson.[42] The final credit allocation may have invoked the 'presumptive evidence' of access to prior material.

There is, then, a general dispute between 'writers', who often argue that only the first writer should get credit, and 'rewriters', who point out that few films get made from one writer's first script, and may want all writers credited.[43] Alternatively, *Hannibal* and *Wag the Dog* are but two examples of films in which the first writer should arguably disappear from the credits altogether. There is also, perhaps, a generic distinction to be made between what might variously be termed 'movies', 'blockbusters', 'Hollywood', or 'studio' productions on the one hand, and 'films', 'art house', 'auteur', or 'independent' works on the other. Increasingly, these distinctions refer less to production (all of the significant 'independent' American labels are actually owned by the 'majors' and the conglomerates of which they are a part), than to the actual or apparent role of an individual 'author' in the creation of a particular film. It is the first kind of movie to which Friend is referring when he notes that 'most Hollywood pictures ... have no particular author. They emerge out of market research and dovetail with the storytelling expectations of the wider commercial culture, the way popular ballads or Punch-and-Judy shows used to'.[44]

This is a nice analogy, but it confuses two notions of popular culture.[45] The first, indicated by 'market research' and 'commercial' considerations, is what is ordinarily meant by 'mass culture'. This is a top-down structure in which commercial interests dictate the production and dissemination of a particular product designed to appeal to a carefully researched target audience. The typical Hollywood blockbuster undoubtedly falls into this category. The second, which would include 'popular ballads' and 'Punch-and-Judy shows', is 'folk culture', a bottom-up structure in which 'traditional' stories and songs are assumed to be the creation of 'the people'. The industrial and technological demands of film mean that it is difficult to conceive of a 'folk' cinema analogous to the essentially oral and evolutionary forms of folk culture. Both mass culture and folk culture largely do away with the individual author, whereas *auteur* movies are generally assumed, by definition, to be products of 'high' culture.

Assigning credit by reference to a paper trail of drafts is a mass-cultural mechanism. What it cannot take into account are traces of other kinds of material: stylistic references that indicate the predominance of a particular writer's style (high culture), or broader intertextual references that indicate a draft's affiliations with wider cultural constructs such as genre conventions (folk culture). Seen in the light of literary theory, credit arbitration looks rather old-fashioned, preoccupied with clearly definable sources rather than with more nebulous intertexts; but as John Ellis points out, seen in the light of credit arbitration, 'literary disputes over authorship seem simplistic in the extreme'.[46]

What is a writer?

Michel Foucault's answers to his own question – 'what is an author?' – further help to establish what it is that distinguishes the screenwriter, consistently and rightly termed the *writer* by the WGA, from the *author*. A short answer to the question of why the *auteur* theory has attached itself to directors, but not at all to screenwriters, is that the latter are not authors but writers. As Foucault suggests, '[t]he coming into being of the notion of "author" constitutes the privileged moment of *individualization* in the history of ideas, knowledge, literature, philosophy, and the sciences',[47] as in the use of a writer's proper name as a means of classifying texts.

Foucault discusses four characteristics of the 'discourse containing the author function' (p. 108). First, it is associated with legal ownership. Foucault is particularly interested in the ways in which the author can thereby become identified with acts that are transgressive or dangerous, but of greater significance to the present discussion is the simple fact that, as we have already seen, the corporate ownership of the screenplay text erases the author function and substitutes for it a multiplicity of writers.

Second, 'it has not always been the same types of texts which have required attribution to an author' (p. 109). For example, scientific discourses (as opposed to individual papers published in scientific journals) tend to be received anonymously; 'literary' texts in former times might have been anonymous, but now they tend to require attribution to an author. It is precisely the struggle for attribution that characterises the acquisition of screen credit. Conversely, the screenplay is unusual among contemporary textual forms in being frequently anonymous or pseudonymous, with major writers often concealed behind an alias, or officially unrecognised for their work as 'script doctors'.

Third, Foucault observes that the construction of an 'author' is a complex process involving psychology, literary value, coherence, stylistic unity, and historical precision. All of these attributes are problematised in the case of the screenwriter. To return to the example of *Wag the Dog*, the screenplay appears very different depending on whether one regards it as an authorial expression or an industrial document. Because the credit system prioritises particular materials in matters of intertextual reference, the existence of Beinhart's novel and Henkin's draft cause Mamet to be designated the co-author of an adapted screenplay. A literary scholar, however, may well be tempted to consider it an original work of Mamet's, either on general stylistic grounds or because its indebtedness to such prior texts is a good deal less extensive than is to be found in many 'original' works. Whichever view one takes impacts significantly on one's reading both of *Wag the Dog* and of Mamet's career as a whole.

Fourth, the 'author' is not simply a real individual, but several selves. For example, '[t]he self that speaks in the[t]he preface to a treatise on mathematics' is not identical to 'the self that speaks in the course of a demonstration' (p. 112). This multiplicity of selves is especially pronounced in the case of the Hollywood screenwriter. In addition to being the co-writer (if that is what he is) of the *Wag the Dog* adaptation (if that is what it is), Mamet is also a writer of original screenplays for other directors (*The Edge* [Lee Tamahori, 1997]), a writer-director, a pseudonymous re-writer (under the name of Richard Weisz), an anonymous script 'doctor', and the writer of prestigious plays either adapted by himself (*Glengarry Glen Ross* [James Foley, 1992]), or others (as in the personally disastrous transformation of *Sexual Perversity in Chicago* into *About Last Night ...* [Edward Zwick, 1986]), as well as being a prolific writer *about* Hollywood.[48] Even as a screenwriter alone, then, Mamet has multiple personae that contribute to the assortment of selves that constitute him as 'author'.

Foucault is suspicious of the author function, because he regards the 'individual', or the 'subject', as an ideological construct, an effect rather than an originator of discourse. The author does not precede and exceed the work; rather, the author function is used to limit the range of meanings a work can possess. 'The author is therefore the ideological figure by which one marks the manner in which we fear the proliferation of meaning' (p. 119). The means by which credit is allocated is one very particular illustration of this general condition, and the potential absurdities of the kind demonstrated by Tad Friend neatly indicate the point at which the limitations of the author function become apparent. Indeed, it is noticeable that screenwriting shares many of the characteristics of a more decentred kind of writing that Foucault and some other French theorists term *écriture*. This writing has freed itself from notions of self-expression and values 'the effacement of the writing subject's individual characteristics'. Writing kills the author, as it were, so that Foucault can ask, with Samuel Beckett: 'What does it matter who is speaking?' (p. 101).

A writers' cinema?

It matters, perhaps, because the question of who is speaking in cinema has rarely been answered in favour of the writer, and the most influential critique of the screenplay in its relationship to cinema insists that it is precisely its transmission of 'literariness' to film that is the problem. In 'A Certain Tendency of the French Cinema', published in *Cahiers du Cinéma* in 1954, François Truffaut traced this regrettable 'tendency' concerning what he saw as the leading role played by screenwriters in the transition from the poetic realism of Jean Renoir and others in the 1930s to the 'psychological realism' of French cinema's 'Tradition of Quality' in the 1950s. He dismissed the latter as a *cinéma de papa* dominated by *littérateurs*. For Truffaut, the films of the post-war French cinema contained too much smoothness, overemphasis on well-turned dialogue, and adherence to narrative conventions, and suffered from an absence of spontaneity and invention. He did not argue against either screenwriting or adaptations in general, but against what he saw as essentially self-serving adaptations that were neither faithful nor cinematic, but instead constantly introduced, in literary ways, the screenwriters' own thematic obsessions. The team of Jean Aurenche and Pierre Bost, for example, he saw as 'the authors of *frankly* anti-clerical films .... When they hand in their scenario, the film is done; the *metteur-en-scène*, in their eyes, is the gentleman who adds the pictures to it'.[49]

In the *nouvelle vague* ushered in by Truffaut and his *Cahiers* colleagues, responsibility for the film would lie with the director, with a corresponding reduction in the status of the screenplay. In this radical reorientation of priorities, the screenplay became, literally, a pre-text: something to be worked from, but ultimately erased, in making the film. Ironically, however, one of the changes the New Wave brought about was that in 1959 the Centre Nationale de la Cinématographie decided to permit funding of a first film on the basis of a script alone. As Corliss notes, Truffaut championed directors who wrote their own scripts, while the Frenchman's emphasis on the visual in his evaluation of American movies may have arisen partly because the Cinémathèque Française eschewed subtitles, thereby compromising the future *Cahiers* critics' ability to appreciate the dialogue.[50]

The *nouvelle vague* created not, necessarily, better films; just different films. Truffaut's essay was less a statement of dogma than a necessary and iconoclastic clearing of the throat that opened cinema up to new ideas, not all of which were antithetical to the writer. Among members of the 'Left Bank' group of French directors, for example, Alain Resnais actively collaborated with major writers such as Marguerite Duras and Alain Robbe-Grillet. Nor is it necessary to look to such radical novelists to discern the possibility of what might be termed a 'writers' cinema' that is not simply literary, but instead responds to different ways of thinking about film. Resnais would soon be followed by Joseph Losey, who actively cultivated Harold Pinter in the justified belief that a profound and unusual dramatic writer might bring something different to the cinema. The resulting film, *The Servant* (Losey, 1963), in conjunction with Pinter's contemporaneous adaptation of his stage play *The Caretaker* (Clive Donner, 1963), commenced a screenwriting career that produced many fine films and several published collections of important screenplays, most of which read superbly as a variant form of dramatic literature. Pinter's name also tended to signify a particular kind of film that the cinemagoer was at least as likely to relate to the author's work in other media as to the other films of whichever director worked on them. This is something other than celebrity. It is the effect of one element of a composite art form, in this case the verbal text of a film, prompting connections to other written texts as well as to other films.

Pinter is a significant test case because there is a political as well as aesthetic debate taking place here. He was extremely unusual in having the right of veto over changes to his script, a right that is axiomatic in the theatre but almost unheard of in cinema. This is one dimension of a struggle between writer and director in which the former is becoming increasingly vocal. Guillermo Arriaga, for example, vociferously objects to the term 'screenwriter' on the grounds that it perniciously deni-grates the work; instead, screenwriters should be acknowledged simply as 'writers'. This lies at the heart of his sometimes bitter dispute with the director, Alejandro González Iñárritu, with whom Arriaga collaborated on the acclaimed trilogy *Amores Perros* (2000), *21 Grams* (2003), and *The Three Burials of Melquiades Estrada* (2005).

One might also argue that certain subgenres seem to refer the specta-tor back to the screenplay as the source of the action, such as adapta-tions of stage plays. More interesting in this context is the recent spate of films that take a highly 'cinematic' approach to time. Temenuga Trifonova shows that several movies made in the late 1990s and early 2000s, including *The Spanish Prisoner* (David Mamet, 1997), *The Matrix* (Andy and Larry Wachowski, 1999), *Fight Club* (David Fincher, 1999), *The Sixth Sense* (M. Night Shyamalan, 1999), *Memento* (Christopher Nolan, 2000), and *Run, Lola, Run* (Tom Tykwer, 2000), erase the distinc-tion between 'real' and 'unreal' events. In most cases it becomes impos-sible to reconstruct the story (the chronological sequence of events as they 'really' happened) from the discourse (the sequence and manner of their presentation within the film), calling into question whether we can still speak of a 'real' series of events, or whether instead we have to think in terms of a new cinematic, imaginary, or virtual time.

Yet it is important to note that what appears to be an exclusively cine-matic conception of time tends to draw attention to the film as a textual construct, thereby making the script obscurely yet tangibly present. Most of the films Trifonova mentions are extremely intricately plotted: they are confidence tricks, of a sort. However, the ostensible explanation from within the story world of how and why events unfolded as they did merely introduces a further level of anxiety. 'There is so much pres-sure to explain how every single detail was part of the plan, to make it fit into a strict causal relationship with every other detail in the story, that the more strongly the film insists that events were planned, the harder it is to reduce them to such a plan.'[51] It becomes implausible that events could 'really' have happened in the way that they do. It is this kind of problem that causes Trifonova, in her preparatory comments, to ask an exceptionally suggestive question: 'Could the narration of an event precede the event itself?'[52] Although this does not lead her towards a discussion of the screenplay, the existence of that document provides one very obvious answer. It is an anxiety that also lies at the heart of film dialogue: the words spoken in the present are recitations of words scripted in the past, and uncomfortably straddle the temporal distinction between present and past time while throwing into confusion the ontological status of the filmic event. That Trifonova's superb analysis of cinematic time fails to invoke the screenplay as the narration that precedes the filmic event illustrates well the screenplay's general invisibility in critical studies of cinema. Moreover, as we shall now see, even the many attempts to conceive of it as a written text are fraught with difficulty.

2
From Work to Text

A short history of the new

Gilles Deleuze conceives of the human as radically altered by its engagement with machines and technology, and in his writings on cinema emphasises that it changes the human as much as the human changes cinema. Something similar may be said of literature: the coming of film moves writing into a new era, in which previously accepted conventions fall into disuse and new approaches to narrative and image that were previously almost unthinkable become commonplace. Tolstoy recognised this in a startling insight as early as 1908:

> You will see that this little clicking contraption with the revolving handle will make a revolution in our life – in the life of writers. It is a direct attack on the old methods of literary art. We shall have to adapt ourselves to the shadowy screen and to the cold machine. A new form of writing will be necessary. I have thought of that and I can see what is coming.
>
> But I rather like it. This swift change of scene, this blending of emotion and experience – it is much better than the heavy, long-drawn-out kind of writing to which we are accustomed. It is closer to life. In life, too, changes and transitions flash by before our eyes, and emotions of the soul are like a hurricane. The cinema has divined the mystery of motion. And that is its greatness.[1]

If cinema changed writing, it has often been suggested that writing conducted specifically for cinema itself 'introduces a new form of literature', as Ernest Betts suggested in his introduction to the 1934 publication of the screenplay of *The Private Life of Henry VIII* (Alexander

Korda, 1933).[2] If 'literature' here means simply textual documents, without any evaluative criterion, then this was not strictly accurate: several continuities for silent films had previously been published, often in self-help manuals such as those published by the Palmer Photoplay Corporation in the 1920s. The *Henry VIII* script was certainly, however, a very early example of a screenplay written for a sound film finding its way into publication for reasons beyond those of mere instruction for aspiring scenario writers. The corollary implication of Betts's remark is that there may be a literary *value* to the best screenplays that would justify the same kinds of attention to form and style as are routinely applied to novels, poetry, and plays, and not to (for example) journalism or pulp fiction.

In 1943 John Gassner and Dudley Nichols co-edited a collection of *Twenty Best Film Plays*, a title that overtly introduces the issue of evaluation while complicating the relationship to cinema. The suggestion again is that if works for the theatre can merit the status of literature, then so can those written for the screen: both are merely variant forms of 'play'. There is a subtle difference between this and the term most commonly used today, 'screenplay', which appears to relegate the text to an industrial function within the development of a film. Accordingly, the title of Gassner's historically important introductory essay, 'The Screenplay as Literature', has an air of deliberate provocation. Like Betts, however, Gassner was mistaken in thinking that this was the first time such texts had been made available to the public as reading texts in something resembling their original form, rather than rehashed as novels. Once again, what was being presented was 'a new form of literature'.[3]

Gassner's combative phrase would recur thirty years later as the title of the first book-length critical study in English, excepting John Howard Lawson's part-manual of 1949. Douglas Garrett Winston's *The Screenplay as Literature* (1973) intended 'to show that cinema, and especially the screenplay from which it is usually derived, have equalled (if not in some cases surpassed) the subtleties and complexities that we usually associate with outstanding literature'.[4] For reasons considered in the next section, however, what is most valuable about his book is the way in which it goes about arguing that screenplays are *not* literature, in any commonly accepted sense of the term. Possibly in consequence, Winston failed to provoke any conspicuous re-evaluation of the form, leaving others seemingly to blaze a trail through terrain that in fact had been mapped many times already. In 1980, Yaakov Malkin published in Israel a doctoral lecture, *Criticism in Creation and the Screenplay as a New Literary Form*, seeking to engage with 'the definition of a new field of critical inquiry – the screenplay as literature'.[5] In 1984, Gary Davis's short article on this 'rejected offspring' once again considered it a 'new' literary genre.[6] Ten years later the widely used *Norton Anthology of American Literature* included in its fourth edition David Mamet's screenplay for *House of Games*, again as an illustration of what the jacket blurb described as 'an increasingly important literary form'.[7] Typically, however, by the fifth edition, *House of Games* had been replaced by Mamet's stage play *Glengarry Glen Ross*, and the increasingly important screenplay form had vanished without trace.

Given this history of perpetual novelty, the question that immediately needs asking is not whether the screenplay should be regarded as literature, but why attempts to present it as such have repeatedly failed. One answer lies in the general absence of any substantial community, either of scholars or of readers, that would enable the dissemination of ideas and the establishment of significant areas of agreement and contention. For example, the most impressive critical analysis of screenplays to date is arguably Claudia Sternberg's 1997 study *Written for the Screen: The American Motion-Picture Screenplay as Text*, derived from a doctoral dissertation.[8] Unfortunately, it has had little impact: partly perhaps because, although written in English, it appears under the imprint of a German publisher of academic monographs with severely limited distribution. Sternberg's work is cited in another German-authored English language publication, by Barbara Korte and Ralf Schneider, who in 2000 asked the almost inevitable question about 'The Published Screenplay – A New *Literary* Genre?';[9] but neither Sternberg nor any of the other sources cited above is mentioned in Kevin A. Boon's *Script Culture and the American Screenplay*, even though this American study was published as recently as 2008 and offers in one chapter a lengthy account of the marginalisation of the screenplay in film studies and the wider culture.[10]

A second explanation is suggested by Steven Maras's recently published *Screenwriting: History, Theory and Practice* (2009), which is not a study of screenplays but rather of the 'discourse' by which 'screenwriting has been shaped and talked about'. This 'invention' of the screenplay 'articulates a perspective on writing for the screen, a script-centred way of speaking about production, and relations between different crafts'.[11] Maras argues that an understanding of the screenplay has been bedevilled by the overly schematic separation of conception (the writing stage) from execution (the filming) by writers and theorists who are too willing to regard the latter as merely the cinematic realisation of work that has already been mapped out by the screenplay 'blueprint'. Instead, he favours the term 'scripting' as a way of showing how the line between these two practices is less distinct than the blueprint analogy would suggest; moreover, other aspects of the production process, from acting to direction, may themselves be seen as forms of cinematic 'writing'. However we conceive of these matters, it is undoubtedly the case that the discourses surrounding the screenplay are sufficiently problematic that its status as literature will always be open to question, sealing its fate as a form that seems fated forever to disappear and reappear as the return of the repressed in literary studies.

The screenplay and literature

Screenwriting is increasingly popular as a subject at university level, but almost exclusively as a vehicle of 'creative writing', or as a vocational or practical craft, rather than as a subject of scholarly or historical analysis. Consequently, a student researching the screenplay will almost undoubtedly be directed to one of the innumerable self-help manuals on the subject, whereas the same student studying fiction is far more likely to encounter (say) Wayne C. Booth's *The Rhetoric of Fiction* than *How to Write a Novel*. In the scholarly analysis of film, meanwhile, the script tends to be considered one stage (or several stages) within a filmmaking process that ultimately erases it as an object of independent critical inquiry – although Maras rightly questions whether this linear model accurately describes the actual process surrounding most modes of film production. Still more problematic are attempts to situate the screenplay within the field of literary criticism, since it tends to fall victim to the twin problems of defining 'literature' and constructing evaluative criteria that determine whether a given text, or even a whole genre, merits entry to the canon.

Gassner felt that what he called the 'film play' had been excluded from the study of 'dramatic literature' through simple snobbishness, noting that many objections to it – its 'verbal record of enacted events', multiple scenes, use of directions to those working on the production, and prevalent adaptations – actually indicated its proximity to the stage play.[12] He recognised, too, that both collaboration and the screenwriter's relative lack of authorial status in copyright and publishing had contributed to the low regard in which it was held. Although Gassner expresses a preference for single authorship, he notes that this is in fact a frequent occurrence in screenwriting; conversely, collaboration is by no means unusual in other fields of artistic creation. He then enumerates some of the unique stylistic properties of the form, focusing on its often-compressed dialogue and the fluid possibilities of narration presented by montage, counterpoint between dialogue and image or sound, and the removal of boundaries of time and space. Given the prominent role of dialogue in these arguments, it is not surprising that Gassner considers that 'screenplays appreciable as literature came only with the rise of the "talkie"'.[13]

Yet in attempting 'to present the screenplays as an interesting contemporary form of literature', Gassner and Nichols resort to extreme editorial methods. They eliminate the 'technical jargon' and 'broken typography of the shooting script, useful only to the director and the camera-man', producing texts that could be read either as narrative fiction (since 'on the printed page they consist of two basic ingredients, narrative and dialogue'), or as 'plays that happened to be written for the screen rather than for the stage'.[14] We shall consider in Chapter 6 the difficulties that confront editors of published screenplay texts, but it is at least arguable that such radical editorial recasting into textual forms appropriate to entirely different media provides good reason for concluding that screenplays should *not* be considered as literature. As John Howard Lawson pointed out in 1949 in his own book, which passes both for a manual and a theoretical analysis of the screenplay, the text that results from Gassner and Nichols's efforts 'may please the reader, but it is not helpful from the viewpoint of general analysis'.[15] That the screenplays selected by Gassner and Nichols read perfectly easily once supposed distractions are removed suggests that a reader who takes the time to become familiar with the conventions of screenplay format should thereafter be able to appreciate them as written texts, without further difficulty.

Lawson's book itself is something of a historical rarity. Although writing manuals had been widely published during the silent era, the coming of sound, and refinements in the management structure of Hollywood studios with enormous budgets, meant that in the 'classical era', between about 1930 and 1960, there was little prospect of the non-professional writer gaining work for the studios without being trained in-house. Non-specialist publication of such manuals effectively ceased during this period. Nor was the screenplay of any interest in academic circles, since film studies barely existed as a discipline, while departments of literature were largely focused on refining and exploring a canon from which the screenplay was automatically excluded.

The humanities' overwhelming emphasis in the post-war period on canon formation, authorship and auteurism, and related questions of evaluation are evident in Winston's study of 1973. Despite his title and aim, Winston in practice focuses principally on film-making as a continuous process, from writing through shooting and editing, emphasising the film and engaging only intermittently with the written text. For lengthy stretches the screenplay itself largely disappears as the object of study, to the extent that a more accurate title might have been not *The Screenplay as Literature* but *The Director as Auteur*. Winston considers such matters as narrative and stream of consciousness in novels and films, but barely considers their representations in the screenplay itself, which emerges from this study as a distinctly sub-literary form. Screenplays have 'impoverished vocabularies' and 'elliptical sentence structures', are not intended for publication, and are rarely considered examples of the best work of major writers who have also written in other genres.[16] Elsewhere Winston makes the trenchant point that, unlike in the screenplay, '[i]n a great work of literature it is impossible to separate that which the author is describing from the actual words that he uses'.[17] Given his title, the suggestions about 'what makes a good screenplay' are distinctly bathetic:

> First, the scriptwriter should realize that the screenplay represents only the initial stage in the making of a film … Secondly, the writer should not intend that his script be complete in itself – as a full-blown work of art – otherwise, there would be little point in filming it. What the scriptwriter should be particularly concerned with at the writing stage is that his idea be fully thought out, that it can hold up on paper … the action, structure and inner logic of the film should be completely worked out … along with the characters and dialogue – i.e. their purpose and meaning, respectively, but not necessarily their texture or exact details. Finally, the writer, in the final version of his script, should emphasize the depiction and description of the action – although not necessarily all or *any* of the individual shots, camera angles, etc.[18]

Winston characterises 'literature', on the other hand, with lofty vagueness. It is 'universal and limitless', and his favoured directors – Bresson, Bergman, Fellini, Godard, Antonioni, and others long established in the pantheon of post-war European cinema – have produced work of a comparable stature because of their 'increasing concern for the depiction and/or discovery of reality – whereas the directors and writers of Hollywood's Golden Age were primarily concerned with myths … [film] must deal with reality and not abstraction'.[19]

Like Winston's, Richard Corliss's contemporaneous attempt to champion the screenwriter suffers from an inattention to the nuances of textual expression. He does not explore dialogue in any detail, for example, and although his approach is incisive and methodical, it has limited ambitions. His proximity to his mentor Andrew Sarris means that, like Winston, he is trapped in now-dated concerns with authorship and evaluation. Corliss's consideration in *Talking Pictures* (1974) of 100 scripts by 35 writers or teams aims to construct a pantheon of screenwriters to rival that of Sarris's directors, with an apex of 'author-auteurs' – Ben Hecht, Preston Sturges, Norman Krasna, Frank Tashlin, George Axelrod, Peter Stone, Howard Koch, Borden Chase, Abraham Polonsky, and Billy Wilder – whose 'personalities are indelibly stamped on their films. In their fidelity to idiosyncratic themes, plots, characterizations, styles, and moods, they won the right to be called true movie auteurs'.[20] The book becomes little more than a series of sketches of the hundred chosen films, concentrating on themes as they recur between films by the same writer, but with very little analysis of the scripts themselves. For example, 'Borden Chase's story, repeated throughout a decade of films that stretched from *Red River* (1948) to *Night Passage* (1957), was that of the civilising of the American West. His films were miniature epics of westward movement and colonization, with the forces of Good and Evil in an embryonic age often battling within the same person, whether hero or villain.'[21] This is an unpromising basis on which to construct the writer as auteur, because 'theme' is an unconvincing marker of authorial 'personality', being translatable with relative fidelity from source story to screenplay to film. In any case, there is scant justification for arguing that screenwriters are more responsible for themes than are directors, who have the opportunity to introduce their own thematic concerns in the filming. Like Winston, Corliss fails to analyse the specifically textual properties of screenplays themselves that might help to establish the writerly qualities of the form in general or the detailed signifiers of an individual writer's style.

Little further headway was made between the mid-1970s and the early 1990s, possibly because during that time, power in Hollywood shifted decisively from writer-directors such as Francis Ford Coppola, whose screenwriting would certainly repay critical attention, to the producer-driven culture in which the screenplay was merely one element in a modular 'package' of stars, spectacle, and soundtracks. It was not until 1997 that Sternberg published the first genuinely substantial, book-length study of the screenplay as a textual form. She examines briefly but incisively the questions of authorship and production that have been dominant in most discussions of this subject, but more valuably concentrates on defining the distinctive properties of the written screenplay text, largely confining herself to what is often termed the 'master-scene' format that has been conventionally used in Hollywood since the introduction of sound. Although she indicates the potential for discerning the individual style of particular screenwriters, her analysis is principally structural, and concerned with 'text linguistics' – the 'regularities' of the form and its possibilities – taking 43 more or less well-known Hollywood screenplays as a test sample.[22]

The book is derived from her doctoral dissertation, and follows the standard German methodology in the humanities of constructing a taxonomy of discrete textual elements, which can then be subjected to critical analysis. An important principle here is that 'the screenplay has internalized the nature of film as the target medium',[23] and for this reason her study is perhaps best read as a contribution to film rather than literary studies, since the aim is 'to draw attention to the stylistic design of the text as a performance blueprint'. As this comes '[a]t the cost of literary subtlety', there is an apparent contradiction between this cinematic emphasis and the assertion on the same, concluding page of her book that the screenplay is 'a multi-dimensional, multi-functional and independent text deserving of the critical attention that is taken for granted in the study of literary texts'.[24] Although Sternberg's book as a whole is a model of clarity, once again the screenplay appears to be too literary to be cinematic, and too cinematic to be literature.

Generic hybridity

The Russian director Andrey Tarkovsky is troubled by no such confusion. 'I do not look on scenario as a literary genre. Indeed, the more cinematic a script, the less it can claim literary status in its own right, in the way that a play so often can. And we know that in practice no screenplay has ever been on the level of literature.' If the screenwriter is good at his job then he should give it up, because 'someone who thinks in cinematic images should take up directing'.[25] If this is so, then the screenplay is caught in another double bind unique among imaginative forms of writing: the more successfully it achieves its purpose as a text, the less value it will have beyond the narrow sphere of its field of production, and if it aspires to the condition of literature it will have to fail to succeed.

A multitude of assumptions about the screenplay are compressed into Tarkovsky's statements. The screenplay's only function is to assist in the practical realisation of the film, and therefore it only has one real reader: the collaborator in the making of the film. Writer and director should logically be the same person, or if not, the writer 'must share the director's conception, [and] be prepared to be guided by it in every instance'. The writer must either be talking to himself or to a single collaborator who will efface him. In all of these ways, the screenplay appears to lack the aesthetic resonance and openness to multiple interpretations from a varied readership that are inextricable from a commonsense understanding of 'literature'.

Even in such a bleak outlook for the screenwriter, however, at least such arguments imply that it is a unique form – or, rather, set of forms, since there are significant differences between different kinds of screenplay. The screenplay might, then, at least hope to benefit from the same kind of 'specificity thesis' that early film theoreticians attempted to use to validate that medium. Here too, however, it finds itself in a double bind. On the one hand, the 'specificity thesis' appears to work all too well with regard to the screenplay: in particular, the 'slug lines' that commence a scene with indications of location and time are unique to the form, but being purely functional have no 'literary' quality. On the other hand, the slug line refers beyond itself to another medium, that of the film, that will supersede it. Perhaps the screenplay thereby contains within itself the seeds of its own destruction.

In practice, those who have attempted to validate the literary quality of the screenplay have almost invariably done so by comparing it to other forms, running the risk that it will appear merely a shadow of them rather than an object worthy of study in itself. A glance at any screenplay immediately suggests relationships to drama, because (albeit in different proportions) both offer a combination of description and dialogue, and invite discussion of the relationship between the written text and the realisation of that text in performance. The same glance, however, may well prompt a comparison to certain forms of poetry, due to the compressed nature of the descriptions, indicating a succession of images rather than the relatively prolix quality of most prose fiction. And yet, of course, it is narrative fiction itself that in some respects appears most closely analogous, in that both are storytelling forms, with narrative elements frequently being adaptable from one form to the other.

Most worthwhile studies of the screenplay along these lines have tended to argue that it possesses both certain unique features, and a generic hybridity that demands some consideration of its relationships to other kinds of text. Gassner felt that, after he and Nichols had drastically reconfigured the form of the screenplays their collection of *Twenty Best Film Plays*, the reader could now choose whether to read them as narrative fiction (since 'on the printed page they consist of two basic ingredients, narrative and dialogue'), or as 'plays that happened to be written for the screen rather than for the stage'.[26] For Sternberg, film has a 'hybrid position ... between theatre and narrative prose': like theatre it is often dialogue-intensive, but it is distinct from theatre in the operations of the camera. Moreover, 'both prose and film' have 'independence from the space/time continuum that determines many theatrical works'.[27] The screenplay, as the text from which film is adapted, by inference possesses similar qualities. For Malkin, it is 'a new and independent literary form', yet also an amalgamation of old forms on which it seems to be dependent, since it 'combines the *epic* mode of observation through narration and the *dramatic* mode of presentation through action and dialogue'.[28]

It is in the comparison to poetry, however, that the most provocative claims have been made for the literary status of the screenplay. Screenwriter Abraham Polonsky, for example, recommends that the writer should in effect direct the work while writing. This will move the writing 'in a direction away from technology, away from the exhaustive analysis and description of the shots', and 'toward compression, density, structure, elegance, metaphor, synthesis, magnitude and variety, all held within a unified verbal structure'. Consequently,

> the literary form I have in mind for the screenplay is the poem. I am using the terms *poetry* and *poem* to characterise a screenplay which instead of conventional camera angles would guide the attention through concrete images (as in metaphor); which instead of stage directing the action would express it; which instead of summarizing character and motive would actually present them as data; which instead of dialogue that carries meaning where the film image fails, would be the meaning that completes the film image.[29]

In general, cinematic dialogue tends to be spare, and Sarah Kozloff compares it to the 'many verbal forms – haiku, sonnets, limericks – [that] draw their power from extreme condensation'.[30]

More than one recent critic has observed connections between the studio script and Imagist poetry. Gary Davis offers a suggestive qualification of screenwriting guru Syd Field's well-known definition of a screenplay as 'a story told with pictures'; as Davis notes, it would be more accurate to describe it as 'a story told with word-pictures', and he quotes Ezra Pound's definition of an image as 'that which presents an intellectual and emotional complex in an instant of time'. Developing the very familiar Aristotelian argument that a creative writer should present a story by showing rather than telling, Davis compares the screenplay to Imagist poems such as Wallace Stevens's 'Peter Quince at the Clavier' (1915) and William Carlos Williams's 'The Red Wheelbarrow' (1923), concluding that the formal concerns of contemporary literature are 'fully realized, perhaps more fully than anywhere else, in the form of the screenplay'.[31] Similar ideas are developed at greater length, and placed in a broader historical context, in Julian Murphet and Lydia Rainford's introduction to their edited collection of essays on *Literature and Visual Technologies*. Here they survey the effects upon literature of the invention of cinema and its associated forms of writing, noting in particular that it eased or eliminated the narrative transitions that are often cumbersome in realist fiction, stimulated corresponding effects of montage in literature, and necessitated a paring away of rhetoric in narration that Murphet and Rainford align with the Imagism of Pound and the literary ideas and prose styles of Gertrude Stein, Virginia Woolf, and Ernest Hemingway.

A similar set of connections has been traced independently and still more recently by Kevin Boon, who abstracts seven principles that he regards as foundational characteristics of Imagist poetry. He recasts a few lines of William Carlos Williams's 'The Young Housewife' (1916) in screenplay form, and, for comparison, sets the opening sentences of the screenplay for *Salt of the Earth* (1954), by Michael Biberman and Michael Wilson, as poetry, in order to show that they have a 'mutual relationship to literature', and that '[t]he only rhetorical distinctions between the two are context and layout'.[32]

Boon is surely right to emphasise that compacted syntax and the presentation of concrete images without overt narration are qualities of both forms. He also makes much of the 'compression and connotation through color' in the descriptions that commence two screenplay drafts. That for *Total Recall* (Paul Verhoeven, 1990; screenplay by Ronald Shusett, Steven Pressfield, and Gary Goldman), revised from a more prolix draft, dramatically opens with 'RED! A vacant, epic expanse of glowing crimson'.[33] *Fargo* (Joel Coen, 1996; written and directed by Ethan and Joel Coen) similarly emphasises colour, or perhaps the lack of it:

FLARE TO WHITE
FADE IN FROM WHITE

Slowly the white become[s] a barely perceptible image: white particles
wave over a white background. A snowfall.

A car bursts through the curtain of snow.[34]

Boon discovers five of the seven 'principles' of Imagism in these examples: 'a privileging of concrete images, a practical aversion to abstract
and indefinite descriptions, the excising of unnecessary words to arrive
at an efficient use of language, the use of poetic compression as a
strategy for suggesting more than literally stated, and the avoidance of
vague generalities'.

The remaining two Imagist 'principles' are 'the establishing of new
rhythms' and 'a focus on common speech'.[35] These Boon also connects
to the screenplay, as well as to 'the plain writing of modernist prose styl-
ists' such as Hemingway, Gertrude Stein, and the 'hard-boiled' writers of
crime fiction such as James M. Cain, Dashiell Hammett, and Raymond
Chandler.[36] It is no coincidence that the stories of the latter three
helped to shape the development of *film noir*, to the point at which that
genre is inextricable from these prose writers, even though none can be
said to have had a successful Hollywood career. Boon concludes that the
screenplay represents a conjunction of Imagist poetics and modernist
fiction of the 'plain' style.

All of these local comparisons are eminently valid, recur in defences of
the screenplay as a literary form, and will be the subject of more detailed
scrutiny in Chapters 7 and 8. Yet the argument that the screenplay
resembles both Imagist form and modernist prose narratives immediately presents a problem. The passages that Boon excerpts from *Salt of the
Earth*, *Total Recall*, and *Fargo* are all taken from the very beginnings of the
respective scripts, and one can find similar descriptions on the first page
of, very possibly, the majority of screenplays. Here are two more examples, taken almost literally at random. The first is the opening image of
Frank S. Nugent's screenplay for *The Searchers* (John Ford, 1956):

EXT. PLAINS COUNTRY – CLOSE SHOT – MOVING JUST ABOVE
GROUND LEVEL – A STUDY OF HOOFPRINTS – LATE AFTERNOON
The hoofprints are deeply etched in the ground, picking their way
through scrubby desert growth. An occasional tumbleweed drifts

with the light breeze across the pattern of prints; and lightly blown soil and sand begin the work of erasing them.[37]

The second is a montage intended to accompany the titles at the beginning of *Don't Look Now* (Nicolas Roeg, 1973):

> A series of stylised images – Escher, Magritte – that are disturbing, disorientating[.] Figures, insects, impossible buildings, reflected images. All should convey a sense of foreboding – of things not being as they seem. A momentary impression of a small, distorted, gargoyle-like creature. Vivid red. And then a strange, reflective pond of water that ripples and sears in the mind a moment.[38]

Each of these opening images contains similar qualities to those identified by Boon, which tends to confirm that they are in the nature of screenwriting in general, and not simply peculiar to the examples he gives. Yet this in itself tends to undermine his corollary, evaluative argument for the screenplay as a 'literary' form, since these illustrations are drawn from a range of screenplays widely diverse in time, production context, and genre: *Salt of the Earth* (1954) is a social issue-based drama written by members of the 'Hollywood Ten', *The Searchers* (1956) is a big-budget Western directed by John Ford and starring John Wayne, *Don't Look Now* (1973) might loosely be described as a British art-house movie, *Total Recall* (1990) is a science-fiction blockbuster vehicle for Arnold Schwarzenegger, and *Fargo* (1996) is what is often termed an 'American Independent' movie.

That the technique of beginning a screenplay by way of a compressed, striking, and ambiguous image is so widespread certainly suggests much about the screenplay as a form, but otherwise indicates not that the device itself is 'literary' in the sense of having a peculiar textual value, but simply that it is commonplace in this kind of writing. The reason for this is that the image is invariably positioned within a narrative structure that will cause it to be read completely differently from an Imagist poem. For instance, in both the film and the published text of *Fargo*, the first thing that appears is not the picture cited by Boon, but a legend: 'This is a true story. The events depicted in this film took place in Minnesota in 1987. At the request of the survivors, the names have been changed. Out of respect for the dead, the rest has been told exactly as it occurred'.[39] The shot that immediately follows therefore becomes part of a story, and the interest of both spectator and reader moves beyond the image to questions of narrative ('what kind of story might begin with this image?'), structure ('what will be the relationship between this image and others within the story?'), and ontology ('did these events really happen? If they did, is it possible to give an unmediated representation of them? Even if it is, do I think the Coen brothers are likely to give it to me?')

Similar questions would arise independently of the legend. The montage commencing *Don't Look Now* introduces a question – who or what is the fleetingly glimpsed figure in red? – that will be answered by the end of the story. The questions posed by the Imagistic nature of the screenplay text are, therefore, less to do with poetic form than with the kinds of narrative code theorised perhaps most prominently by Roland Barthes in his 'Introduction to the Structural Analysis of Narratives' (1966) and, in particular, *S/Z* (1970). The image from *Fargo* illustrates *S/Z*'s 'proairetic' code, whereby one signifier prompts the reader to expect a second that will place the first in a temporal sequence. The flash of the red gargoyle in *Don't Look Now* belongs to the 'hermeneutic' code, which poses a mystery to which the reader expects an eventual solution. In each case the shot is tied to a specifically temporal code that encourages the reader to see it as part of a linear sequence, and this expectation is automatically built into the dominant, narrative forms of Western cinema of which both of these films are excellent examples.

This narrative function of the image causes it to appear different in kind from that in the Imagist poem, at least as Boon describes it. The script examples he gives are not 'concrete' but rather abstract, indefinite, and vague. The red of *Total Recall* is 'a vacant, epic expanse'; the white of *Fargo* gives way to 'a barely perceptible image'. That these shadows will in time develop into something more concrete is due to the narrative nature of the form: it is a function of the story, in these examples at least, to resolve the indeterminacy with which it begins.

Although this is true of most screenwriting, it does not mean either that Boon and others are mistaken in stressing its Imagistic style, or that it is merely an inferior mode of narrative fiction. On the contrary, this style, combined with the fact that the screenplay by its nature enters into problematic relationships with both cinema and other modes of writing, arguably exemplifies the post-1968 critical reorientation away from notions of the literary work and towards an idea of the 'text', a word that can be used productively in this context in at least three ways. First, 'text' tends to sidestep the question of evaluation that is inextricable from the word 'literature', which always invokes an opposition to the non-literary. Second, therefore, 'text' broadens the object of study to include, potentially, more or less any written material (and indeed non-written ones, as the widespread use of terms such as 'film text' or 'theatrical text' illustrate). Third, the opposition between 'work' and 'text' acquires more specific but also more slippery meanings as a result of Barthes's work in theorising the distinction between them.

From Work to Text

In his essay 'From Work to Text', Barthes outlines seven 'propositions' concerning 'methods, genres, signs, plurality, filiation, reading and pleasure',[40] by means of which he contrasts existing conceptions of the 'work' – which in his usage has clear associations with 'literature' – with his proposed alternative, the 'text'. There is a typically fluid and dynamic – indeed, textual – play in Barthes's essay that prohibits simple paraphrase and summary. Nevertheless, the seven propositions clearly distinguish the Barthesian from the conventionally 'literary' text, and from the present perspective consistently suggest associations with the screenplay.

1   The work is a material artefact, such as a book in a library. The text, by contrast, 'is a methodological field', and 'only exists in the move-ment of a discourse … or, again, *the Text is experienced only in an activity of production*' (p. 157). One of the most persistent objections to the screenplay is that it lacks the fixed form of a published work, and instead is open to constant change as a result of its status as a text to be reworked in the process of film production.

2   'In the same way, the Text does not stop at (good) Literature' (p. 157). Put as baldly as this, 'text' simply makes available for analysis a range of materials conventionally excluded from literary analysis, while also anticipating some of the methodological approaches of New Historicism. This being Barthes, however, the matter is not quite so simple:

3   'The work closes on a signified', which is either evident or secret, and therefore to be investigated and interpreted; whereas the Text 'practises the infinite deferment of the signified, is dilatory; its field is that of the signifier and the signifier must not be conceived of as "the first stage of meaning", its material vestibule, but, in complete opposition to this, as its *deferred action*' (p. 158). This is a typically elusive Barthesian construction, but conceived in such binary terms, the screenplay appears to be a 'work', because, as noted above, it tends towards nar-rative closure. On the other hand, in a very literal sense its textual sign-system does involve deferral of action and closure, because it invokes a potential but as yet hypothetical realisation within a second,

cinematic sign-system. Put more simply, and contrary to the conventional view that the screenplay exists purely to effect a single realisation only to die like a bee spending its sting, it is purposely vague in those areas that invite the collaborative interpretive strategies of its readers, industrial or otherwise. In this way, it inhibits the security of interpretive closure offered by the realistic 'work'.

4 'The Text is plural' (p. 159); that is, intertextual, 'woven entirely with citations, references, echoes, cultural languages', and 'the citations which go to make up a text are anonymous, untraceable, and yet *already read*: they are quotations without inverted commas' (p. 160). In many ways this looks more like a reorientation at the level of theory rather than a distinction between different kinds of writing. Literary scholarship has traditionally been concerned with sources, influences, and origins; but post-structuralist writers like Barthes, Julia Kristeva, Jacques Derrida, and others question whether textual utterances can ever be traced back to a single source, partly because language itself always precedes and informs a given utterance. Instead, a text is, in the words of Barthes's even more influential essay 'The Death of the Author', 'a multi-dimensional space in which a variety of writings, none of them original, blend and clash'.[41] If one accepts the theoretical justification for the argument, then *all* texts are 'plural' in this respect, and there is little here to distinguish the screenplay from other kinds of text.

The screenplay is, however, 'plural' in at least one specific sense, in that, as noted above, it participates within two different sign-systems. In this respect, the constant referencing of a cinematic discourse by means of slug lines and other textual elements, which are commonly held to reveal the screenplay as an industrial rather than a literary document, makes it a peculiarly rich verbal structure. Because the large majority of Hollywood screenplays, at least, are genre pieces (another 'unliterary' quality), it is also an uncommonly self-referential document, in the sense that it repeatedly quotes its own conventions, 'without inverted commas'.

This is also, arguably, a quality of much screenplay dialogue. Philip Brophy has observed of film dialogue that 'the role of "quoting" when voiced becomes more complex than the linear text-referencing invoked by literary discourse. When the written becomes spoken, a whole range of potential clashes arise between the act of enunciation, the role of recitation and the effect of utterance, in that, for example, one can vocally "italicize" an earnest statement, just as one can compassionately "underline" a self-deprecating quip'.[42]

Arguably, this is also a quality of written screenplay dialogue, which contains far fewer parenthetical directions as to how it is to be spoken than the average play text, while also lacking the narrational voice that often performs a similar role in the novel.

5 As in 'The Death of the Author', intertextuality undermines what in 'From Work to Text' Barthes describes as 'filiation': that is, authorship. Much as Foucault observes that ownership is one means of defining the author function, Barthes notes that '[t]he author is reputed the father and owner of his work ... society asserts the legality of the relation of author to work'. The text, by contrast, 'reads without the inscription of the Father.... Hence no vital 'respect' is due to the Text' (pp. 160–1). This describes quite precisely the role of the screenwriter in relation to authorship.

6 'The work is normally the object of a consumption' that is characterised by 'quality' and 'taste' (p. 161). The text, by contrast, 'decants the work ... from its consumption and gathers it up as play, activity, production, practice. This means that the Text requires that one try to abolish (or at the very least to diminish) the distance between writing and reading, in no way by intensifying the projection of the reader into the work but by joining them in a single signifying practice' (pp. 161–2). Again, this functions as an accurate summary of many accounts of the screenplay text, particularly those which tend to regard directing as an extension of writing in 'a single signifying practice'.

7 The work is associated with a rather depressing 'pleasure' of consumption, since 'I cannot *re-write* them', whereas the text 'is bound to *jouissance*, that is to a pleasure without separation ... the Text achieves, if not the transparence of social relations, that at least of language relations: the Text is that space where no language has a hold over any other, where languages circulate (keeping the circular sense of the term)' (pp. 163–4). In another characteristically difficult opposition, Barthes here invokes notions of the text as the kind of 'readerly' material he associates with the avant-garde, while the work merely follows the easily-decoded 'readerly' conventions of literary form. From this point of view, the screenplay, which is forced to adhere very closely to established conventions of format, is unpromising material. And yet, from a more literal-minded perspective, the screenplay is routinely rewritten – another familiar objection to its claims to literary status – since the screenwriter relinquishes authority and ownership. Its two competing sign-systems offer a very clear illustration of the engagement of multiple 'languages', and despite

the industrial requirement of readability, the competition between these two sign-systems can make it literally impossible to read conventionally, as we shall see in Chapters 7 and 8.

It would, of course, be absurd to suggest that the screenplay exhibits all of the qualities Barthes associates with 'text'. Indeed, the Barthesian text is less an artefact than an ideal, a dream of a language liberated from convention. The above is a deliberately literal-minded reading of some of Barthes's terms, and simplifies what are often slippery and elusive concepts and turns of phrase. For example, when Barthes writes that 'the Text does not stop at (good) Literature', he is not simply opening the door to that view of the screenplay which sees it as an industrial planning document that must meet criteria of comprehensibility and ease of reading. Nor is the Text defined by the conventional kinds of readerly 'pleasure' offered by the 'Work'. On the contrary, the Barthesian reader prefers to experience a quasi-sexual 'jouissance' in engaging with the radical disturbances of the Text, which appears to be defined by a particular kind of difficulty. In a very Foucauldian expression, Barthes considers the Text a kind of 'limit-work ... which goes to the limit of the rules of enunciation (rationality, readability, etc.)' (p. 157). In this respect it represents the polar opposite of the screenplay text, which ordinarily prioritises ready comprehensibility because of the collaborative nature of film production.

Nonetheless, conceiving of the screenplay in the ways prompted by Barthes's essay helps to explain its exclusion from the canons of literature. Although it is clearly to be differentiated from the Barthesian text, it is still in many respects the contemporary text *par excellence*, and at the very least this essay can take us further in distinguishing the screenplay from literature (or 'work'). It clearly functions within 'the activity of production' rather than as a closed work; it is not concerned with validating itself as 'literature'; its meaning is deferred, since it is a text of suggestive incompletion that demands the writerly activity of others; it is markedly intertextual, participating within the general fields of cinema and literature, but – other than in adaptation or historical drama – rarely concerning itself with 'source' materials; it is indisputably severed from the legal conceptions of authorship outlined by both Barthes and Foucault; and the reader of the screenplay, at least in its industrial context, directly participates in the activity of production and, metaphorically and very often literally, in the 're-writing' of the text.

Indeed, the problem lies not with the screenplay as literature, but in the persistent failure to recognise it even as a text, in the broadest cultural sense of that word. The radical reconception of the text by Barthes, Foucault, and others has ostensibly led to the postmodernist rethinking, if not outright abolition, of distinctions between 'high' and 'low' culture. Yet the theoretical assault on the canon and on established practices in criticism since the mid-1960s has had little effect on the status of the screenplay, which remains largely invisible. Perhaps not surprisingly, then, Ian W. MacDonald's comparable discussion of Barthes and screenwriting makes no direct reference to 'From Work to Text', but instead examines 'The Death of the Author' and *S/Z* in the course of considering 'the screen idea'. By this, MacDonald means 'any notion of a potential screenwork held by one or more people, whether or not it is possible to describe it on paper or by other means'.[43] As such, his essay not only helps to explain why arguments for the screenplay as literature have repeatedly failed, but also is another lucid contribution to the critical discourses, concepts, and metaphors which, as we shall now see, have persistently pushed the screenplay text into a peculiar ontological state of non-being.

3
Ontology of the Screenplay

William Horne begins his essay 'See Shooting Script: Reflections on the Ontology of the Screenplay' by citing a salient fact. The third edition of Leslie Halliwell's *Filmgoer's Companion* contains an entry on '*screenplay*', but the entry is: 'see *shooting script*'. The entry for 'scenario', which was the term given in the silent period to what we would now call the screenplay, is also 'see *shooting script*'. There is, of course, no entry for 'shooting script'. It is, as Horne drily remarks, 'a fitting index to the general lack of visibility of the screenplay, both in film production and in film theory and criticism'.[1]

While this 'lack of visibility' is partly a consequence of processes of academic and industrial marginalisation, it is also very frequently the effect of an act of rhetorical conjuring in which the screenplay and its writer are *made to disappear.* Jean-Luc Godard contends that 'to make a film is to superimpose three operations: thinking, shooting, editing'.[2] An earlier example is Alexandre Astruc's metaphor of the 'caméra-stylo', in which '[t]he filmmaker/author writes with his camera as a writer writes with his pen', so that 'the distinction between author and director loses all meaning'.[3]

In each case, however, the writing stage vanishes only through an act of rhetoric or figuration. Godard's account subordinates 'writing' to 'thinking', but the two are clearly interconnected, as we shall see in the comparable formulations of other directors. The metaphor of the 'caméra-stylo', meanwhile, has an inherent instability that is historically tied to the early years of cinema. Elizabeth Ezra argues that Georges Méliès's sequence of eleven one-minute films re-enacting the Dreyfus case reveals a

nostalgia for writing [that] was reflected in film generally, which retained the ghostly presence of writing as an afterimage. The first newsreels, created in 1908, were given names like the *Pathé-Journal* and the *Éclair-Journal* ... names that evoked film's writerly origins, as did the term for the Lumières's invention, the *cinématographe*, literally writer of motion, and later expressions such as *camera-stylo*, cinematic *écriture*, and the *auteur* theory of cinema.[4]

Yet in the *politique des auteurs* such terms are used to displace a writer who keeps on returning, not least in the language that attempts to efface him. The homicidal impulse behind such tropes is apparent in Astruc's attempt to resolve any ambiguity in his metaphor by contending that 'the scriptwriter ceases to exist'.[5]

When not simply erased, the screenplay is frequently described in terms of its relationship to other texts, and in particular in terms of what it is not: it is not a novel, stage play, or poetry, but instead merely a stage in the creation of another artefact in a different medium. It is not a thing-in-itself, it has no innate qualities; its formal properties are either the result of the managerial organisation that necessitates its creation, or mere shadows of other kinds of text: narrative fiction, theatrical dialogue. The cause and result of this tendency is the definition of the screenplay as not-literature. Analysis of the screenplay therefore finds it difficult to imagine as a stable text: instead, in the words of one its most sympathetic and lucid scholars, it is '*literature in flux*'.[6] Although developments in textual editing in the work of Jerome McGann and others have relatively recently begun to move the study of more 'literary' texts in the same direction, it is nonetheless a necessary assumption of textual analysis that *a* text is available, and rewards close scrutiny. But most screenplays are *not* readily available to a wide readership, other than via often suspect online sources. Even those that have been published, aside from the very few that have not been filmed (Harold Pinter's *The Proust Screenplay* is the unavoidably best example), almost invariably suffer, by comparison to a stage play, from the unique ontological relationship to the film as a parallel and detectable presence. Because it is so difficult to grasp the screenplay as a text, the study of it tends towards metaphor, almost by default: metaphors of industry, but also those of loss, absence, erasure, and death.

The blueprint metaphor

The most familiar and insidious argument against the literary status of the screenplay is that it is nothing more than a planning document. Hence the metaphor that is pervasive to the point of near-ubiquity: it is a 'blueprint'.[7] In 1943 Dudley Nichols, a screenwriter himself and a pioneer in the serious critical analysis of the form, argued that screenplays 'are not complete in themselves, they are blueprints of projected films'.[8] Janet Staiger, one of screenwriting's foremost historians, titled her contribution to Tino Balio's influential anthology of essays on *The American Film Industry* 'Blueprints for Feature Films: Hollywood's Continuity Scripts'.[9] The equally eminent Kristin Thompson, in arguing that classical norms are preserved in contemporary Hollywood to a greater degree than is generally acknowledged, notes that '[t]he tasks of the various filmmakers are still coordinated from development to post-production via the use of a numbered continuity script used as a blueprint'.[10] A recent book that seeks to analyse film construction finds it more helpful to 'describe what actually happens on screen, rather than using the original screenplays. This is because screenplays are blueprints for a film and don't include all the elements of screen language which we want to learn about here'.[11] And if the screenplay is a blueprint for a film, 'a model screenplay ... can be used as a guide or blueprint' for other screenplays, as perhaps the most widely read writer of screenwriting manuals, Syd Field, recommends.[12]

Claudia Sternberg also adopts 'classic metaphor' of the 'blueprint',[13] but in a more nuanced and discriminating way that clarifies and expands the usefulness of the term. In her account, it refers only to the second, intermediate 'stage' through which the screenplay passes. This comes between the first or 'property' stage (when a writer, agent, or producer attempts to market what is often termed a 'selling script' to a readership of pre-production industry insiders, such as story analysts), and the third, 'reading material stage', when it may be read by 'critics, (film) scholars and the public who see and read the (published) screenplay as written literature'.[14] The intermediate 'blueprint' stage designates 'the screenplay during the production process'.[15] This crucial qualification helps to establish that the 'blueprint' analogy only makes sense in an industrial context, and cannot define all of the various kinds of text that circulate as 'screenplays'.

Not only is the blueprint just one of Sternberg's stages, it is also, as she notes, a metaphor. A blueprint is 'a photographic print of the final stage of engineering or other plans in white on a blue background', or 'a detailed plan, esp. in the early stages of a project or idea' (*OED*). The first of these definitions is literal; the second is a metaphorical extension of the first. In its literal sense, a blueprint is a projection of a design for a material object. For this reason, an industrial blueprint will ordinarily have an arithmetical precision that allows for the precise visualisation of size and volume. Screenplays almost by definition are vague in such matters. Exactly how big is the 'coffee shop somewhere in New Mexico' that is the first location in Quentin Tarantino's screenplay *Natural Born Killers*?[16] It is a question that probably a director, and certainly a set designer or location manager, would ask – but not a reader, and probably not a writer either.[17]

As for dialogue, the translation of the written words of the script into the spoken words of the actors involves a process of mediation, but one that is less radical than the rendition of lines and numbers into volume and mass. Still, as the Italian director Michelangelo Antonioni observed, 'a line spoken by an actor in profile doesn't have the same meaning as one given in full-face. Likewise, a phrase addressed to the camera placed above the actor doesn't have the same meaning it would if the camera were placed below him'.[18] The director may have to think of the relation of dialogue to image in such geometrical terms, but the general screenplay reader is unlikely constantly to be framing the dialogue within a precisely imagined diegetic world, just as the reader of *Hamlet* will ordinarily be concentrating more on the words of the speakers than on the architectural design of Elsinore or the theatre.

The blueprint metaphor compromises the aesthetic and thematic seriousness of the text, because it ascribes to the screenwriter a bathetic non-imagination akin to that of the narrator of Wordsworth's ballad 'The Thorn'. In a notorious description of a pond in the 1798 version, the narrator reports that 'I've measured it from side to side: / 'Tis three feet long, and two feet wide'. Although he is clearly characterised as excessively prosaic, lacking the verbal sophistication to articulate his response to an encounter with human tragedy, the register still seems shockingly inappropriate, and Wordsworth removed the lines in a later revision.

Although it is only the metaphorical usage of the blueprint figure that can properly be applied to the screenplay, the insidious connotations of the literal meaning have proved persistently damaging. It implies that the screenplay is of value only as a set of practical guidelines to be followed by others who will make the finished product; that it is, in effect, erased in the creation of the film, remaining of value thereafter only as a record of planning; that it can only be a model of structure rather than a work of aesthetic interest; and that the screenwriter is, like Melville's Bartleby, essentially a drawer-up of recondite documents, rather than an artist in his or her own right.

Jean Renoir detested the word, because it represses the creativity, improvisation, and dynamic collaborative relationships of the film-making process.[19] Sternberg rightly insists that the 'craftsmen' involved in transforming the screenplay into the film 'work to change and improve a "structure" that is not identical to the blueprint'. Quoting Lienhard Wawrzyn, she argues that the screenplay 'has a "serving function" in creating a "desire to take over the design provided"'.[20] The craftsmen, then, are not slavishly following a blueprint, just as it is impossible for the writer of a screenplay adaptation slavishly to follow a source text. In each case, the process involves the imaginative transformation of a work in one medium into a work in a different medium.

Producer Dore Schary comments that writing the screenplay 'call[s] not only for creative writing talent, but for a technique equivalent to that possessed by an architect, attorney, or other professional practitioner',[21] but as Carl Foreman, writer of *High Noon*, noted apropos of the blueprint metaphor: 'This kudos writers have received many times ... and have then wondered why the architects were barred from the building site'.[22] Peter Wollen, however, in discussing the distinction between composition and performance in the arts generally, suggests that the screenplay text is only brought to life by the interpretive skills of the director. Far from granting the screenwriter the status of the musical composer, Wollen considers the script 'only a pretext, which provides catalysts, scenes which fuse with [the director's] own preoccupations to produce a radically new work'.[23] Douglas Garrett Winston puts it simply: 'Just as no one would claim that reading an orchestral score is as satisfying as hearing it performed, equally no one would claim that a script or synopsis is an adequate substitute for a completed motion picture: both the script and the score are only the first steps, albeit very important ones, in the creative acts of music and cinema.'[24]

Origins and destinations

Yet the differences between a verbal text and musical notation, between the readerships of a screenplay and a musical score, and between the spectator at a film and the audience at a concert are almost too numerous to be worth unpacking. Nor is readership the only difficulty here. Winston's apparently unexceptional metaphor of the 'first steps' is still more problematic, though again he is not the first to make it. Dudley Nichols similarly considers that a screenplay 'is a step, the first and most important step, in the process of making a film'.[25] But is it the first step? The first step to where? And where does a screenplay come from? Until the reorientation in theories of textual editing in the work of Jerome J. McGann and others (see Chapter 6), the problem of intentions in literary criticism had tended to be confined to what a writer's intentions were: whether they can successfully be recuperated, and, if so, to what extent a knowledge of them should influence interpretation of the text. These have been fraught issues in literary theory and criticism at least since W. K. Wimsatt and Monroe C. Beardsley identified what they saw as the 'intentional fallacy', whereby 'the design or intention of the author is neither available nor desirable as a standard for judging the success of a work of literary art'.[26] As noted in Chapter 1, however, there is no shortage of critics who argue that knowledge or inference of an author's intentions furnishes a valuable set of intertexts that in any case cannot simply be wished away.

A more pertinent question in the case of many screenplays, meanwhile, is whether a writer necessarily has any intentions *at all*. For *North by Northwest*, Alfred Hitchcock and writer Ernest Lehman began with ideas for particular scenes, notably the assassination at the United Nations that begins the film and the climax at Mount Rushmore, and then constructed a storyline to incorporate these spectacular events. Similarly, when Robert Towne was engaged to work on *Mission Impossible II*, 'the whammos had already been worked out in detail; all that remained was for him to add such minor touches as characters, dialogue, and plot'. According to Towne, the producers presented him with 'six big action sequences' and asked if he could 'write a movie connecting them'.[27] The resulting screenplays may be perfectly good pieces of work without the writer having any particular 'intentions', whether 'original' or 'final', other than to join the dots in a satisfyingly professional manner. 'Intention' in literary studies seems to presuppose an individual subject that does the intending; it is therefore bound up with the Romantic notions of authorship considered in Chapter 1. But because many screenplays are written to order after a 'package' of ideas and talent has been put together, there are ordinarily – and, in the case of adaptations, necessarily – important textual stages prior to the writing of the screenplay.

If origins need to be disentangled from notions of intention, it is equally questionable whether a screenplay's final destination is quite as obvious as it seems. In many, indeed most, cases a screenplay will be written from which no film is actually made. The readability of Harold Pinter's unfilmed *Proust Screenplay* is a reminder that, at most, the screenplay is a textual invocation of *a* film; never *the* film. As Sternberg observes, in the transition from text to screen there is, ordinarily, 'only one performance', but crucially 'the potential for multiple interpretations exists when the screenplay text is first approached'.[28] As we shall see in the later discussion of *The Birds* (Alfred Hitchcock, 1963), Hitchcock and his writer, Evan Hunter, disagreed radically about the meaning of the script on which they had closely collaborated. This was not just a matter of thematic interpretation. One of the ways in which Hitchcock radically reconfigured his writer's final draft was to work out with his technical assistants a detailed study of the matte shots of the birds. These tend to imply that the bird attacks are in some way invoked by the humans, whereas Hunter felt he had shown the humans reacting to the birds. These represent two different visualisations of the same events, indicating that the two men were mentally seeing two different films – if, indeed, they were seeing a film at all.

Moreover, there are multiple readerships, as Sternberg points out in identifying the 'blueprint reader' as merely one target audience. She cites several sources who argue that screenplays cannot – and should not – be 'readable' other than to industry insiders. For example, John Paxton, in a 1947 review of one of the Gassner and Nichols anthologies, dismissed it as 'Collected Blueprints Vol. III', and advanced the Catch-22 argument that '[t]he fact that some of them sound better on paper than others is a trap'. Once again, the blueprint metaphor had done its work. Conversely, Sternberg cites other sources who felt that viewing two highly acclaimed films, *M*A*S*H* (Robert Altman, 1970) and *Wild Strawberries* (Ingmar Bergman, 1957) was less rewarding than the experience of reading the screenplays (by Ring Lardner and Bergman, respectively).[29]

If Ezra Pound could propose that anyone who lacked the initiative to learn to read Chaucer in the original should forever be barred from the reading of literature, a worse fate should befall those who cannot spend the small amount of time required to gain the necessary understanding of screenplay form. In any case, the multiple versions of screenplay texts are in part created to meet the needs of different readerships. Publication represents merely one more transformation, and the copy text chosen for publication may be derived from any of the stages identified in Chapter 4, or be a new construction compiled with the needs of another target audience in mind. The 'real' or 'authentic' screenplay is a chimera. Just as students of drama are familiar with the idea of a 'theatre of the mind', so the screenplay will always be realised first in the mind of whoever reads it. Indeed, John Collier has attempted to create a 'cinema of the mind' in writing an adaptation of *Paradise Lost* in screenplay form, just as Shelley's *Prometheus Unbound* and Byron's *Manfred* were written in dramatic form but with no presumption that the texts would be amenable to theatrical staging.[30]

The problem of origins and destinations is perhaps unconsciously signalled in the temporal confusion that bedevils certain teleological arguments, whereby the existence of a film provokes a reading of the screenplay as simply an anticipation of it. Andrey Tarkovsky, like many directors, sees the script as mere preparation for the production; after that point it can be of interest only to scholars. Yet as Ian W. MacDonald points out, '[a]t no point in its development can the screenplay be said to truly reflect the final screenwork'.[31] The two media are simply different in kind, with the images in a screenplay possessing a textual rather than a visual or synaesthetic form. There is something indigestible about it, prompting the temporal paradoxes and impossibilities that haunt the attempt to think through the relationship between the script and its cinematic realisation. For example, Tarkovsky affirms that the screenplay is 'a kind of prescient transcript of the finished film'.[32] A still greater degree of uncanny temporal slippage emerges in Eisenstein's much more favourable view of the pre-production 'film novella', which, unlike the hack work of the numbered script, 'is essentially a future audience's anticipated story of the film that has captivated it'.[33] Something of the same difficulty emerges in Pier Paulo Pasolini's argument that the reader, whom he regards as a kind of collaborator with the screenwriter, is compelled '*to think in images, reconstructing in his own head the film to which the screenplay alludes as a potential work*'.[34]

John Ellis states more crisply and simply that there is a 'difference between *mise-en-page* and *mise-en-scène*', and the 'terrain' between them remains 'vague' in the absence of 'research which examines what readers do with what they read: whether words remain as words or form into various kinds of "mental images"'.[35] That the cinematic realisation of a screenplay is a uniquely privileged interpretation of it has tended to lead to the assumption that the script can be simply forgotten for most purposes once the film has been released. Yet the same observation may prompt an argument in favour of revisiting the written text, a reading of which may indicate qualities and possibilities obscured in the final cut. The ideological transformation brought about by imposing a frame story on *The Cabinet of Dr Caligari* (Robert Wiene, 1919), completely changing the meaning of the story, is but an extreme instance of a general condition afflicting the written text.

Ghost writing: The screenplay and death

The strange, convoluted constructions of Tarkovsky, Eisenstein, and Pasolini seem to be struggling with a text that is both inside and outside the film, temporally preceding it yet enunciated from within it, like the voice issuing from the mouth of a corpse in Poe's story 'The Facts in the Case of M. Valdemar'. This presents a problem for the ontological status of cinema as the realistic medium it appeared to be at its invention. Cesare Zavattini, the brilliant writer who was as responsible as any director for the achievements of Italian neo-realism, once remarked that 'the ideal film would be ninety minutes in the life of a man to whom nothing happens'.[36] Instead, Zavattini played a significant role in constructing the tight, carefully shaped stories that give films like *Bicycle Thieves* and *Umberto D* their structure. His 'ideal film' is a dream of realism, of life without structure, of a film without a script. Design is suspect, because the more carefully plotted the events, the more certain it is that they have been worked out on paper in advance.

Truffaut revealingly illustrates this prejudice against the script during a conversation with Hitchcock about *The Thirty-Nine Steps*, a film in which Hitchcock keeps the pace moving swiftly by eliminating tiresome exposition and transitions. The French director observes,

> It's a style that tends to do away with anything that is merely utilitarian, so as to retain only those scenes that are fun to shoot and to watch. It's the kind of cinema that's extremely satisfying to audiences and yet often irritates the critics. While looking at the movie, or after seeing it, they will analyze the script, which, of course, doesn't stand up to logical analysis. So they will single out as weaknesses those aspects that are the very essence of this film genre, as, for instance, a thoroughly casual approach to the plausible.[37]

Logically, however, the script is the one thing that critics *cannot* analyze from a viewing of the film: its existence can be deduced, but its text cannot be scrutinised. That Truffaut phrases the issue in this way on the one hand unfairly attributes to the screenplay a problem with the film or its genre, but on the other hand accurately and acutely senses the difficulty posed by the script as something troublingly both inside and outside the film.

Such views seem to be prompted by the belief that whereas both literature and film have an intrinsic significance and are ultimately self-sufficient, the screenplay acquires meaning only in relation to something outside itself. As Sternberg puts it, '[t]he screenplay text must ... be written and read with the notion that the transposition process from the written to the filmed text is already inherent in the script pages.'[38] For the cinema spectator, however, the screenplay is an ur-text that is detectable not as the cause of the movie, but as an effect of it. Certain kinds of establishing shot can indicate its presence: the prominent display of the name of a character ('Sam Spade' etched on an office window at the start of *The Maltese Falcon*, for instance) or place (the multiple textual indicators of location in the introductory sequence of *Casablanca*) draws attention not just to the prearrangement of scenes, but to their prior existence in the medium of writing. Somebody, somewhere, must have committed the words to paper, knowing that they will reappear on the screen. The momentary destabilisation of the sense of diegetic realism that such shots provoke tends to lessen once action or speech begins.

Yet it is in speech that the most visible – or audible – traces of the screenplay are to be found. Sternberg proposes that, of all the elements in a screenplay, 'only the dialogue text – in the form of "spoken text" – reaches the spectator directly'.[39] While textual inserts and certain other elements are also transmissible more or less directly from the script, dialogue is certainly the most significant. Improvised speech is often mentioned as a possibility by critics wishing to minimise the significance of writing, but is a relative rarity other than in the films of a few directors such as John Cassavetes and Mike Leigh, who habitually use it as part of the rehearsal process. More significantly, there is a difference between dialogue as it appears in the text, and dialogue as spoken: at the very least, the latter always represents a particular interpretation by actor or director of the words written by the screenwriter. The words of the screenplay, then, are not *simply* reproduced, and their transmission is not direct; they are subject to interference from the various kinds of noise generated by the filming process. Their textual form is glimpsed through a veil; their existence in that prior medium is suggested rather than demonstrated. This is one illustration of a general condition: the screenplay is erased in the process of production, but only partially, and it emerges as a ghostly presence to trouble the illusion of realism. For all of these reasons, it is the subject of a variety of metaphors in film theory and criticism that seek to grasp its peculiar ontological status.

While conceding that 'dialogue is always literary', Tarkovsky liquidates it in an image that neatly combines the industrial and the homicidal: 'The scenario dies in the film.... The literary element in a film is *smelted*; it ceases to be literature once the film has been made'.[40] For the picture to exist, then, the screenplay must be killed and the body made to disappear. Yet although dead, it continues to speak: the words of Tarkovsky's screenplays are heard in his films, and in a supreme irony, were published after his death.[41]

As Godard's term 'superimposition' suggests, the best literary analogy is that of the palimpsest: one text (the screenplay) is apparently erased by another (the film), but parts of the prior script remain faintly detectable, never recoverable in their original form yet retaining a ghostly aura that participates in the general play of presence and absence that is a preoccupation of cinema. As Jacques Derrida remarks, '[W]hen the very *first* perception of an image is linked to a structure of reproduction, then we are dealing with the realm of phantoms.'[42] Indeed, much of Derrida's work explores problematic expressions of the ghostly interplay of interiority and exteriority in ways that prove highly illuminating in the present context. Kevin Boon observes that Peter Brunette and David Wills's 1989 book on Derrida and film theory, despite being titled *Screen/Play*, makes no mention of screenplays at all, even though 'Derrida's concept of invagination, for example ... could have been used ... to show how the screenplay is both internal and external to the film'.[43]

Boon takes this no further, yet it captures the relationship quite precisely. Death-metaphors seek to establish precise boundaries between the screenplay and the film, both temporally (the screenplay dies, then the film is born) and textually (no trace of the screenplay remains in the film, both because the text has evaporated and because the difference between film and screenplay is one of kind and not of degree). Yet this cannot do justice to the complexity of the relationship; in all of the ways noted above, the film refers back to the screenplay without incorporating it, just as the screenplay looks forward to a film without becoming it. The screenplay is a kind of doppelgänger of the film, seemingly physically separate and yet operating as a second, parallel form that can never wholly be repressed.

For these reasons, Robert Bresson's description of the tripartite production process of which so many directors have spoken is the most persuasive as well as the most poetic: 'My movie is born first in my head, dies on paper; is resuscitated by the living persons and real objects I use, which are killed on film but, placed in a certain order and projected on to a screen, come to life again like flowers in water'.[44] Death is not the end, but instead is followed by resurrection, transformation, and adaptation.

Adaptation

Adaptation offers the most familiar illustration of the play of presence, absence, and ghostliness that surrounds film and screenplay alike. The source text is sometimes said to exist in 'a transcendent relation to any and all films that adapt it'.[45] On the other hand, in a certain way it exists within the film, speaking from inside it, as one more repressed layer in its palimpsestic structure. And there are also films in which the seemingly adapted text can at best be regarded as merely one among several motivations coinciding to produce a film that largely dispenses with the source story along the way: *The Killers* (Robert Siodmak, 1946), *Homicide* (David Mamet, 1991), *Adaptation* (Spike Jonze, 2002), among many others.

Thomas Leitch sees adaptation as the norm in film-making. Each version of a screenplay adapts a previous one; similarly, a film is an adaptation of the screenplay, while every adaptation is also an interpretation of one or more source texts that are amenable to other interpretations. Seen in this light, 'the adapter is the paradigmatic collaborator' because 'all filmmakers are collaborators', and with the era of 'romantic expressionism' in film studies at an end, 'it is time for the adapter to replace the director as the paradigm for all filmmakers'.[46] This is likely to prove a much more fruitful approach than regarding the film as the creation of a single auteur, although the question of precisely what it is that is adapted is not always easily answered. It is possible for a film neither to allude to nor to signify a source, in the case of invented characters for instance; and there is also the possibility of false attribution, as in the Coens' mischievous title card at the beginning of *Fargo* claiming it to be 'based on a true story'. Adaptation would have to expand to include consideration of the ways in which a given text intervenes within a genre or convention, without being tied to the adaptation of verifiable sources.

The vast majority of Hollywood scripts are 'adaptations', of one sort or another. They account for more than four-fifths of Academy Awards for Best Picture, and for fourteen out of the twenty highest-grossing pictures of the twentieth century.[47] By contrast, 'original' screenplays are more frequently associated with 'independent' films and/or those of the writer-director – although here too, of course, adaptations are commonplace – and originality has long been regarded as signifying a higher level of creativity in both Romantic and Modernist thought. The screenplay adapted from the literary work can thereby seem doubly inferior, being both derivative and (usually) translated into a form that carries less literary value than the source story.

Recent adaptation theory has had little difficulty in demonstrating that such evaluations derive from very tenuous assumptions. Deborah Cartmell, after noting previous critics' attempts to distinguish between different kinds of adaptation and degrees of fidelity to the original (in relationships of 'transposition', 'commentary', or 'analogy', for example), suggests that 'the categories are limitless';[48] and as Leitch drily remarks, there is little point in aiming for fidelity, since 'the source texts will always be better at being themselves'.[49] More useful in practice has been Brian McFarlane's attempt to establish 'procedures for distinguishing between that which can be transferred from one medium to another (essentially, narrative) and that which, being dependent on different signifying systems, cannot be transferred (essentially, enunciation)'.[50] What connects novel and film most closely is narrative, but 'there is a distinction to be made between what may be *transferred* from one narrative medium to another and what necessarily requires *adaptation proper*', that is, 'the processes by which other [less amenable] novelistic elements must find quite different equivalences in the film medium'.[51]

As McFarlane points out, 'transferable' properties resemble what Roland Barthes, in his influential 1966 essay 'Introduction to the Structural Analysis of Narratives', calls 'distributional' functions, namely actions and events that form a horizontal sequence and have a 'functionality of *doing*'. The most significant are 'cardinal functions' or 'nuclei', which open up crucial alternative possibilities in the narrative, thus providing its skeletal structure. This, McFarlane argues, cannot be altered in the translation from one narrative medium to another without suggesting infidelity. The subordinate group of distributional functions are 'catalysers': smaller, complementary actions that establish the world of the story. By contrast, 'adaptation proper' engages Barthes's 'integrational' functions or 'indices'. These include psychological and other information about characters, place, and atmosphere; they 'do not refer to operations but to a functionality of *being*'.[52] The sub-category of 'informants', which include such data as names and ages and details of the setting, may be transferred as readily as distributional functions. The vaguer 'indices proper', for example those involved in creating the illusion of character and atmosphere, are less readily transferable and therefore, in McFarlane's terms, must be subjected to the processes of adaptation proper.

McFarlane's approach to the study of adaptation provides a helpful framework for studying what is peculiar to the screenplay as opposed to either the source text or the completed film. In particular, the notion of transferable materials applies equally to all three narrative media: the prose fiction source, the screenplay adaptation, and the film developed from the screenplay. It suggests that the study of story itself is likely to reveal relatively little about the nature of the screenplay, unless it can be shown to take structural forms distinct from those either of novels (which is possibly the case) or of films (which by definition is unlikely). The extreme emphasis on structure in screenplay-specific discourses such as writing manuals and the credit system, and the concomitant devaluation of enunciation (which, as far as the cinematic spectator is concerned, essentially means dialogue), therefore contributes materially to the perception of the screenplay as non-literature. If the screenplay adaptation represents an intermediate stage in the translation of the precursor text into film – a kind of midwifery – then any distinctive properties it may possess are liable to evaporate. Instead, it becomes little more than a mediating device, a mechanism for both 'transferring' the narrative structure from source text to film, and developing some aspects of 'adaptation proper' that cannot be peculiar to the screenplay, but must instead be realisable within a cinematic text that has richer resources than those of the screenplay alone. At best (or worst), anything that remains in the screenplay but is not found in the film has the status of an indigestible residue, and nobody wants to write about shit. Consequently, while book-length 'case studies' of films in production form one of the relatively few areas in which screenplays are discussed as a matter of course, the chapter on the script will typically feature early in the study, with variant ideas raised in the screenwriting process tending to fall by the wayside once the study of pre-production gets underway. The discussion of *The Birds* in Chapter 5 of this book deliberately has a different emphasis.

The screenplay shares with the source text the fact that both are purely textual (or in McFarlane's term '*verbal*') forms, unlike the film, which contains '*visual, aural,* and *verbal* signifiers'.[53] As he also notes, the written text unfolds in a linear sequence, whereas the visual image draws on a sense of spatial awareness of what lies beyond the limits of the frame. At the very least, therefore, the effect of reading a screenplay is very different to that of watching a film derived from it. It also, ordinarily, provides a very different experience from reading the precursor text. Both Leitch and Boon have recently focused on John Huston's 1941 film of *The Maltese Falcon* to illustrate such differences. Pauline Kael remarks that 'Huston was a good enough screenwriter to see that [Dashiell] Hammett had already written the scenario':[54] Huston invented no new scenes, rearranged only slightly, and diverged from the novel mainly through cutting, at times apparently prompted by the demands of the Production Code. Boon accepts the commonplace argument that unlike the novel, the depiction of 'psychological states' and 'extensive use of metaphor and figurative language ... are difficult, if not impossible, in film', which 'cannot provide access into a character's mind except through action and dialogue; that is, except through implication'.[55] Nevertheless, that *The Maltese Falcon* lent itself so readily to adaptation suggests that Hammett is a prose writer thinking and writing cinematically. It is notable that many of the most impressive Hollywood adaptations, especially the *films noirs* of the 1940s, are derived from the works of Hammett and other 'hard-boiled' writers such as Raymond Chandler and James M. Cain.

However, Leitch focuses on a descriptive passage in Hammett's novel that Huston makes no attempt to represent:

> Spade's thick fingers made a cigarette with deliberate care, sifting a measured quantity of tan flakes down into curved paper, spreading the flakes so that they lay equal at the ends with a slight depression in the middle, thumbs rolling the paper's inner edge down and up under the outer edge as forefingers pressed it over, thumbs and fingers sliding to the paper cylinder's ends to hold it even while tongue licked the flap, left forefinger and thumb pinching their end while right forefinger and thumb smoothed the damp seam, right forefinger and thumb twisting their end and lifting the other to Spade's mouth.

Leitch notes that in Hammett's prose the scene is not neutral but disturbing, 'because readers of novels, unlike viewers of movies, expect a certain amount of psychological description and are troubled, even if they do not know why, if it is suppressed'.[56] This is a fine insight, but it is characteristic of Leitch's approach, and indeed of adaptation studies in general, that the argument is conducted in relation to films and prose fiction but without consideration of the readerly affects that a comparably paratactic style of writing generates in the screenplay text.

Leitch pays little attention to screenplays because he conceives of them not as literary but as performance texts; 'their gaps are designed to be filled once and for all by the cast and crew'. Yet this argument is itself fallacious, because to conceive of screenplays *only* as performance texts erases the unquestionable fact that many of them circulate in other forms and to other readerships than the immediate production team. Only a highly restrictive conception of what a text can be could have led Leitch to the assertion that Shakespeare's plays 'are nothing more than performance texts whose verbal texture happens to support an incomparably richer sense of reality than that of any screenplay to date'. Even in the field of adaptation, then, the screenplay tends to disappear because of a tendency to compare the film to the source text in far greater detail than to the text that mediates between them. This is curious, because elsewhere Leitch rightly stresses that '[a]daptation study requires ... sensitive and rigorous attention to the widest possible array of a film's precursor texts', which should surely include its own screenplay. Even confining such study to strictly textual materials outside the production process, it makes little sense to restrict consideration to a single privileged source. Like any film, a screenplay will draw on multiple influences, often to the point at which the distinction between the original and the adapted screenplay becomes tenuous. For example, the screenplay for Hitchcock's film of *The Birds* is nominally adapted from Daphne du Maurier's short story of the same name. Yet Hitchcock habitually adapted his sources in much the same spirit as Gene Gauntier, a prolific writer for the early silent cinema, whose cavalier approach to adaptation entailed the polar opposite of fidelity:

> I learned to dip into books, read a page almost at a glance, disentangle the plot in an hour; then lying face downward on the bed compel my mind to shoot off into the byways, twisting and turning the idea until it was as different as possible from the one that suggested it. Then to the typewriter to embroider the bare plot with details of 'business', scenic suggestions and original personalities.[57]

Hitchcock and his screenwriter Evan Hunter retained only the seed idea of birds attacking people; otherwise, neither the story nor its characters are derived from the putative source, and the isolated setting is transposed from Cornwall to California. Does it make sense to consider this an adapted screenplay, when that for an undistinguished genre piece may be 'original'?

What *is* the source of *The Birds*? The only answer that would satisfy a Hollywood lawyer is 'Daphne du Maurier's story'. Yet if the question were phrased slightly differently – 'where did Hitchcock's film come from?' – the range of contributory factors suddenly becomes almost limitless. Going no further than the director himself, one could begin by citing Hitchcock's position in the Hollywood studio system, his apparent desire to compete with his European rivals by making an 'art movie', his allegedly cruel fascination with Tippi Hedren, the script conferences with Hunter, the contributions of several other writers he brought on board, and so on. Immediately, the precursor story becomes of relatively minor significance – and we haven't even stepped out of the studio yet, into the wider arena of the dominant ideology and Cold War politics that undoubtedly trouble the world of *The Birds*. The film and its screenplay will acquire different meanings depending on which of these, or other, intertexts receives attention. As Jonathan Culler put it in *On Deconstruction*, 'Meaning is context-bound, but context is boundless'.[58] Or as Hitchcock stated to a collaborator apropos of a source novel, in a remark that should long ago have put to bed the insistence on fidelity to an individual precursor text: 'I don't have any regard for the book. It's *our* story, not the book's'.[59]

The real McKee: *Adaptation*

No screenplay better illustrates the impoverishment of the idea that adaptation is a linear process of textual transmission, more inventively grapples with its alleged source, or more richly demonstrates the imaginative potential of the form than Charlie Kaufman's script for *Adaptation*. This is, indeed, ostensibly an adaptation of the journalist Susan Orlean's non-fiction work *The Orchid Thief*, which describes her encounters with the title character John Laroche. Kaufman – and, astonishingly, his fictional brother Donald – won an Academy Award in the adaptation category.

From the beginning, the screenplay is concerned less with fidelity than with the question of what lies inside and outside the script. The opening scene purports to record behind-the-scenes events on the set of Kaufman and Jonze's previous movie, *Being John Malkovich* (1999). But what is the relationship between Malkovich the actor, Malkovich the character in *Being John Malkovich*, and Malkovich the actor/character from *Being John Malkovich* as he now appears in *Adaptation*? And what is the correlation between the screenplay of *Adaptation* and any of these Malkoviches, especially as, in this scene, '[t]here are many extras dressed in rubber over-the-head John Malkovich masks. The actual John Malkovich sits at one of the tables. He is dressed as a woman'?[60] What is the relationship to this film-within-the-film of its writer, Charlie Kaufman, who (as played by Nicolas Cage) is literally on the margins of the set and summarily dismissed from the stage? Does the fact that Kaufman (as Cage) narrates the voice-over and is known to be the writer of *Being John Malkovich* ironically locate him as the centre of consciousness within the film, or does he only have that status within his screenplay? In what ways is this Kaufman related to the 'real' Kaufman? Did he, in fact, write this part of the screenplay, or is much of it a transcription of dialogue that was spoken during the filming of *Being*

John Malkovich? If so, was that dialogue scripted, improvised, or merely spoken with no intention that it form any part of any text? Would consulting the screenplay of either film answer any of these questions? Is *Adaptation* a single-authored screenplay or is it really, as the cover and title page proclaim, written by Charlie Kaufman and Donald Kaufman? Does Donald Kaufman even exist? Under normal circumstances a glance at the copyright page would answer that question, but, this being a Hollywood screenplay, normal circumstances do not apply, and the copyright holder is neither Charlie Kaufman, nor Charlie Kaufman and Donald Kaufman, but Columbia Pictures Industries, Inc.

What is the relationship between the screenplay and the paratextual elements of the published text – the cover, title page, copyright page, foreword by Susan Orlean, interview with Kaufman and Jonze, and critical commentary by Robert McKee? Donald Kaufman, in fact, is simply a character created by Charlie Kaufman, but these paratexts have eased him out of the pages of the book and into the real world, in which he is the Oscar-winning co-writer of *Adaptation*, credited as such in library catalogues. If we have discovered that Donald Kaufman does not exist, does that knowledge subsequently belong inside or outside the text? What about McKee? He, too, appears as a character (played by Brian Cox) in *Adaptation*. Are the words that he speaks at the writing seminar in *Adaptation* his own words, as spoken at seminars given by the 'real' McKee, or have they been written for the fictional McKee by Kaufman? What about his 'commentary' that appears in the published text? With doubts crowding in about the 'authenticity' of anything in that book, McKee's opening paragraph reads like self-parody:

> Charlie Kaufman is an old-fashioned Modernist. He writes in the palaeo-*avant-garde* tradition that runs from the dream plays of Strindberg and inner monologues of Proust through the tortured identities in Pirandello and the paranoia of Kafka to the rush of subjectivities in Wolfe, Joyce, Faulkner, Beckett, and Bergman – that grand twentieth-century preoccupation with the Self.
>
> (p. 131)

Did McKee really write this? If he did, was he put up to it by Kaufman, or Jonze? Whoever is responsible, did he really mean Wolfe, or could he have meant Woolf? If the latter, is that a mistake, or another joke?

McKee's presence attracts attention not just because of the audacious conceit of placing the best-known Hollywood screenwriting guru inside a fictional film about Hollywood screenwriting, but because it raises the question of exactly what it is that *Adaptation* is adapting. The film is not an adaptation of *The Orchid Thief* in any conventional sense, as it obsessively points out. Other precursor texts are, arguably, equally important, most notably *Being John Malkovich*, McKee's screenwriting manual *Story*, and McKee's writing seminars, which Donald discusses at length and which both brothers separately attend.

In an important sense, the 'real' Robert McKee is an active collaborator in the script, and not just for these reasons, or because Cox has clearly based his performance on a close study of McKee's persona. More importantly, McKee's strictures concerning screenplay form directly shape the development of *Adaptation* itself. As in *The Usual Suspects* (Bryan Singer, 1995), the development of the story is prompted by events within its own narration. The 'fictional' Charlie Kaufman is stymied because he feels a sense of responsibility to Susan Orlean's book, but as the narrative develops he realises that he has to abandon any notion of fidelity, the eureka moment coming when he realises he can write about not Susan but himself. The driving force behind the adaptation now becomes neither Orlean nor Kaufman but the advice McKee dispenses during and after the seminar. From this point, the story develops towards the kind of explosive ending that McKee has told Kaufman can compensate for earlier weaknesses. In place of the thematic and self-reflexive struggle to adapt the intractable source material, Kaufman creates a firmer, goal-oriented structure of desire and opposition that superficially follows some of the basic precepts of *Story*.

Yet it's too good to be true. The real McKee, whose voice sounds very clearly in the dialogue given by the real Kaufman to the fictional McKee, is a sharp and even profound story analyst, and would have dismissed out of hand *Adaptation*'s climax: Susan and Laroche become sex-mad, drug-crazed criminals in a cat-and-mouse pursuit by, and of, the emotionally reunited Kaufman brothers, Donald dying heroically in the arms of Charlie, who (as the script ends) may finally be about to discover true love and happiness. In these sequences, *Adaptation* also sends up the expressive verbiage that passes for significant dialogue in the worst Hollywood blockbusters: the brothers take time out from their escape from Laroche to reminisce about girls, and Donald delivers a thematic one-liner ('You are what you love, not what loves you' [p. 93]), shortly before delivering his equally glib dying words. In these climactic sequences Kaufman is adapting neither Orlean nor McKee, but instead is engaging through parody with a wider debate about Hollywood conventions that shapes the conversations of the brothers and accounts for the multiple genres and structures that give the screenplay, and the film, their final shape.

The 'real' Charlie Kaufman's invention of the fictional brother Donald brilliantly dramatises the screenplay's profound ontological uncertainty about adaptation and authorship. Donald asks Charlie if he (Donald) is in the script: but not only is he in it, he appears to have written it. Both the real and the fictional Charlie play with the conceit that Donald, the untalented writer who is nevertheless 'amazing at structure' (p. 65), may have silently taken over the screenplay and turned it into a commercially viable project. The division of the self into multiple personae is the subject of Donald's own script, but that is itself just another convention, as Charlie points out. So is the story about a battle between two Hollywood screenplays, in which the writer of the more 'artistic' script eventually accepts that the more commercial product is better – more authentic, even – because that is what a Hollywood script should be. It is the story of *Sullivan's Travels* (Preston Sturges, 1941), *Sweet Liberty* (Alan Alda, 1986), *State and Main* (David Mamet, 2000), the stage plays *True West* (Sam Shepard, 1980) and *Speed-the-Plow* (Mamet, 1988), and many more. And if Kaufman is adapting conventions, he is also adapting himself: adapting *Being John Malkovich*, adapting and rewriting and abandoning pieces of text, adapting Charlie Kaufman into Donald Kaufman and back again, to the point at which he has the 'multiple personality disorder' that his fictitious brother wants to write about.

Just as the living organism adapts to its environment, so the process of textual adaptation is directed not by notions of responsible fidelity but by the cultural environment of Hollywood. The title of *Adaptation* refers not to Orlean's source text, but to the screenplay itself. The double meaning of the abstract noun, designating both biological evolution and the process of transforming one text into another, are played upon throughout the script. The dejected Charlie asks what he is doing on the planet; the succeeding montage shows the process of evolution from the primordial swamp to Charlie's birth. The baby and the single-cell organism bear no physical resemblance, and that, Kaufman seems to be saying, is the real nature of the relationship between his source material and that into which it finally evolves.

4
Stages in Screenplay Development

The frequent absence of any 'final' textual form, and the widespread and sometimes inevitable practices of collaboration, often make the preparation of the screenplay text a chaotic affair that removes any sense of authorial control and structure. In the classical Hollywood studio system, this is one result of industrial procedures imposed by authoritarian producers; in the post-classical cinema, the 'packaged' nature of production mean that directors, stars, or others might also demand changes. The ongoing nature of revision during production calls into question the belief that the script is a completed conception awaiting execution at the filming stage. Several historians now contend it is a 'myth' that scripts at the Thomas Ince studio in the 1910s were marked 'Shoot as Written', and from different theoretical, historical, and practical perspectives the separation of written conception and filmed execution is better regarded as a relatively rare exception rather than a general condition of the relationship between writing and other aspects of film production.[1]

On the other hand, the screenplay does commonly proceed through several more or less formal stages of development corresponding to the input of various members of a production team. The initial idea will be pitched, more or less informally, to a producer or executive; a treatment may be developed to tell the story in the form of a prose narrative; the script will then proceed through however many drafts are necessary to produce the 'final' version; a shooting script will be prepared to include additional technical detail required by the director and others working on the production; further material will be written or edited during filming in response to the inevitable discrepancies between conception and execution; a post-production cutting continuity, essentially a description of the final cut, is drawn up by editorial assistants or other studio staff;

and in rare cases, a version of the script will be published. Some scripts will develop through many more phases than this (especially if one considers storyboarding a form of writing), and others through fewer. Although, as we shall see Chapter 5, the process of script development in a single film is likely to blur the distinction between some of these stages, it is both empirically possible and practically useful to begin the consideration of script development by identifying the different kinds of text that may be generated by the production process.

Terminology

The critical discussion of the stages of screenplay composition can be hampered by inconsistency both in the development process of different scripts, and in the terminology used to describe each kind of text. The two-page 'GMD [Getty Museum Database] Thesaurus List' used by archivists at the Academy of Motion Picture Arts and Sciences to describe their holdings indicates the range of usage of some terms, and the problems faced even by professional librarians and archivists. Several terms are derived from the 'Art and Architecture Thesaurus' [AAT] used by the Getty libraries and archives, but others are noted as 'local Special Collections terms' and 'AAT terms modified for local use'.

The GMD Thesaurus list contains entries for the following:

Continuities. The 'scope' of this term is defined in the GMD Thesaurus as 'Screenplays that contain all necessary visual and audio instructions in the final pre-shooting phase, including dialogue, sound effects, shots, and basic editing for all scenes in the order in which they are to be shown on the screen, subject to change only by the director'. A variant, described as a 'one-line continuity', is a local Special Collections term. The word 'continuity', however, has other more specific meanings. Film historians generally use the term to refer to the silent, often feature-length script that came into being around 1912 to accommodate the growing industrialisation and specialisation of labour within film production. 'Continuity' and 'scenario' superseded the terms 'photo play' and 'photo drama' that in the teens were used variously to describe either the film or the script. In turn, 'continuity' and 'scenario' became outmoded shortly after the introduction of sound. The term 'cutting continuity' was retained into the sound era to describe the textual transcription of the release print used for legal purposes and to facilitate communication between studio and theatres.

Outlines. Among the variants of this term are the sequence outline, 'covering the main points for a series of related shots or scenes'; the step outline, which is a 'Point-by-point plot summary, frequently as a numbered list'; and the story outline, used as a synopsis of original stories.

Screenplays. Seven variants are listed. The potential for confusion is indicated by the fact that no definition is provided for 'shooting script', which is here an 'AAT term modified for local use'.

Synopsis. Six variant kinds of synopsis are listed.

Clearly, there is much scope for error: terms are not used consistently, and a single script may be categorised in different ways. The kinds of text that a given project will generate will depend not only on the proclivities of the writer(s) and other collaborators, but on studio conventions, budget, and other variables. Nevertheless, it is possible to outline with some degree of specificity the types of script likely to be written for a film made according to the conventions most commonly followed within Western studio systems.

The pitch

The *story idea*, or the *pitch*, is essential, yet may not even exist in textual form. It is not so much a document as an encapsulation of a story concept, often in a single arresting phrase, for the purposes of selling the idea. By the 1980s, the pitch had, within Hollywood, become synonymous with the development of the 'high concept' movie, with the producer replacing the director, let alone the writer, as the primary force in the film-making process. In Charles Fleming's vivid assertion, the high concept idea 'was a monster ... a supercharged, simpleminded creature, an Aesop's fable on crystal meth, a movie that any producer could pitch in thirty seconds and any audience could understand without even thinking'.[2] High concept formalised the story idea as a conflation of two pre-existing elements to produce a 'new' idea: *Alien*, for example, could be pitched as '*Jaws* in a spaceship'.[3]

In spite of this, and even though the idea for a film need not exist either orally or as a written text, the pitch requires identification as a particular stage in the film-making process because there need not be an intermediate textual stage between it and the making of the film. In the earliest years of cinema, between 1895 and 1905, many, if not most, films were made without any written preparation at all. The script only became necessary with the coming of narrative film at the beginning

of the twentieth century, around 1903. With today's increasingly prevalent use of relatively inexpensive and very portable digital cameras, it is
quite likely that something resembling the pre-industrial conditions of
early film-making will once again come to play a significant role in film
culture, and that an increasing number of movies will resemble filmed
events rather than pre-scripted narratives. In any event, the recognition
that a film may be made without a script contributes to the primacy of
the visual within film studies.

The outline

Within the Hollywood studio system the *synopsis* or *outline* represents
an early stage in the production process. In the case of original stories
it may be more appropriate to use Edward Dmytryk's term *short treatment*, which can be anywhere from two to fifteen pages in length;[4]
'synopsis' is more likely to imply a condensation of prior material, to
be considered for adaptation, and may be as brief as a single page. It is
a continuous prose text, often generated by a story editor who distils a
promising source story into a summary to be digested by the producer.
Those outside the industry often regard the reliance on synopses as
a sign of philistinism. However, producer Dore Schary noted in 1950
that '[o]ften our reader's synopsis, particularly of a long novel, is better
than the original for our purposes; crisper, the story line cleaner, and
the characters standing out in sharper relief'.[5] More recently, another
prominent producer, Art Linson, has elucidated in characteristically
laconic style the function of pitches and outlines:

> You must convince the guy with the checkbook that he *needs* what-
> ever soap you are selling. I'm not sure anyone actually *needs* to buy
> an idea for a movie. If you buy an idea, you have to pay to have the
> script written. Writers are expensive. In most instances the scripts
> are badly done and only a small percentage ever get filmed. Because
> of the high turnover factor, the executive who winds up buying the
> script probably won't even have his job by the time the wretched
> thing gets made and is ready for release.[6]

The step outline

The less common *step outline* is perhaps best thought of as both an alternative kind of short treatment, and an intermediate stage between it
and either the full treatment or the first draft of the screenplay. Usually

up to ten pages in length, it breaks the action down into a numbered series of sequences and scenes. Each numbered element is headed by a basic description of scene or character involvement, and contains a short paragraph describing the essential action, the subject of conversation (rather than the dialogue itself), and an indication of how the action and dialogue develop. Carl Foreman, screenwriter of *High Noon* and *Bridge on the River Kwai*, habitually wrote a kind of step outline to provide himself with a synopsis of, and direction to, the story. The numbered sequences varied in approximate length between one and five sentences. This process provided him with such a clear grasp of *High Noon* that the first draft did not, in his view, differ significantly from the outline. Presumably this observation pertains purely to the story structure, as opposed to the textural detail that would be found in a draft or treatment.[7]

The treatment

The *treatment*, if it is written at all, may be constructed after extensive story conferences between producer, director, and possibly writer. The treatment is a preliminary version of the story in the form of a prose narrative. Dore Schary reported in 1950 that 'most screen originals which we buy for filming are in treatment form', although

> there is no [standard] form: you simply tell the story; who the characters are, what they want, what's blocking the way, and how they go about achieving their goal. The proper length is the fewest number of pages needed to make the essence of the story clear and interesting – and to bring out unmistakably the essential 'kernel of appeal' which is going to make those millions of people hurry to the theatre to see this particular picture. And it's expected that the action will be 'in the medium', thought out with an eye to how it will look and sound on the screen, and practical to shoot.[8]

The existence of treatments is a powerful reminder that the screenplay is much closer in narrative construction and development to the short story than to the novel. Because it is essentially a preparatory document, however, the treatment differs from the short story proper in its functional prose and use of the present tense, anticipating in this respect the screenplay itself. A treatment might be anywhere between thirty and three hundred pages long, although nowadays it is likely to be towards the shorter end of the spectrum. It helps to sharpen the focus on particular themes and characters, and directs the emotional focus of the action.

Still, their usefulness is moot. Hollywood screenwriter Scott Frank argues that treatments simply describe a film without adding anything helpful to the process.[9] Those who defend them note that treatments allow for a more imaginative, dramatised handling of source material than a mere prose synopsis, while saving time during the script-writing itself by eliminating narrative problems at an early stage. There are many cases, including Schary's primary example, in which the writer of the treatment proceeds to write the screenplay, and feels that he or she has benefited from consolidating the story in prose form before proceeding to the more complex technical process of dividing the action into scenes and writing dialogue. Alternatively, the treatment provides a solid structural outline from which subsequent writers can develop the screenplay, although this function is a product of a division of labour that arguably weakens rather than strengthens the majority of Hollywood films.

There is also a distinction between the treatment that simply details the development of the plot, incorporating perhaps some sample dialogue, and the kind that digresses into the development of extensive character analysis, including the provision of a 'backstory'. These descriptive passages are ordinarily presented separately, in material prefacing the treatment of the story itself. Foreman's *High Noon*, Graham Greene's *The Third Man*, and the final draft of the multiply authored script for Alfred Hitchcock's *Strangers on a Train* are unusual examples of *screenplays* that include this kind of backstory material as a preface to the screenplay proper.

The term 'backstory' in the description of character and plot within the screenplay itself is arguably a logical absurdity, analogous to the term 'subtext' in the description of dialogue. Austin E. Quigley established the methodological weakness of the concept of subtext in an analysis of stage plays many years ago: the word implies that something is hidden underneath the text, yet if this is the case, then that something cannot also be revealed within the text.[10] David Mamet rejects altogether such staples as 'exposition', 'backstory', and even 'character'.[11] Backstory 'seems to mean "narration"', and is 'gobbledegook' because 'all that we, the audience, want to know is "what happens next"'.[12]

Backstory material is, therefore, only rarely incorporated within the 'comment' mode of the screenplay itself, in keeping with the common (although highly questionable) view that one of the things that distinguishes the screenplay from prose fiction is the absence of narration. As we shall see in Chapter 7, however, several eminent screenplays, including most notably perhaps that for *Citizen Kane*, contain substantial amounts of narratorial commentary of this kind. In general, backstory is mainly used as a writing tool in the creation of treatments so that the writer will gain a stronger imaginative grasp of the character or aspects of the story. As such, the term 'backstory' indicates a clear distinction between the naïve reading (that is, a reading that blurs the distinction between characters and 'real people') that is often necessary to literary creation, or to the enjoyment of a work of fiction on first reading, and the properly critical reading of the text in the kinds of retrospective analysis practised in literary study.

The screenplay

'Screenplay' itself, like the now defunct 'scenario', is a nebulous word that can refer to several different things. The term itself seems not to have been used as a single-word, compound noun (as distinct from 'screen play') until around 1940.[13] David Bordwell, Janet Staiger, and Kristin Thompson, in *The Classical Hollywood Cinema: Film Style and Mode of Production to 1960*, detail a series of changes in format, beginning with the 'outline script' in the early years of narrative film, and then proceeding, by way of the 'scenario' and 'continuity' scripts in the silent period, to the master-scene format that was initially introduced to meet the demands of sound and became standardised across the Hollywood studios around 1933.[14] These changes in nomenclature correspond not just to changing industrial conditions but to different ideological conceptions of film writing and film culture more generally.[15]

Unlike the theatre script, over which the playwright retains legal authority regardless of the interventions of others, in the Hollywood system the screenplay is the property of the studio, whose power to authorise revisions is a matter of contractual right. The process of revision is potentially infinite, generating many different kinds of text, and the term 'screenplay' is insufficiently precise to enable easy identification of which of these textual forms is being referred to. As we shall see in Chapter 6, this problem has bedevilled the history of screenplay publication. For practical purposes we shall here provisionally follow James F. Boyle in identifying six materially different textual stages through which the screenplay may proceed.[16]

1   The 'author's version', either in a single completed version or in several, all of which are the work of the writer(s) employed on the project. The matter is complicated by the possibility that the studio may employ several writers simultaneously, or engage one writer or

team to rewrite the work of the first; nevertheless, the script that is sold or that completes the writer's initial contractual obligation to produce a script may be considered the author's version. This will usually be written in master-scene format, although not always: Evan Hunter's drafts for *The Birds*, discussed in Chapter 5, are also segmented by means of numbered shots. In master-scene format the writer omits shot numbers and instead breaks the story into individual scenes, each commencing with a 'slug line' giving indications of time and place. Any change of time or location triggers a new scene; intercutting back and forth between events taking place in two different locations, for example, will therefore generate a large number of separate scenes. The sample from a professionally written screenplay reproduced in the Appendix is written in master-scene format.

In the classical Hollywood studio system the screenplay would also have to pass through several departments that would check for problems: the Legal Research Department; the Censorship Department, which in the classical era would liaise with Joseph Breen, the Head of the Production ('Hays') Code; and the International Department, which would suggest ways of clarifying any Americanisms for markets outside the United States, and deal with worldwide censorship issues.[17] Frequently a script would be returned to departments – particularly the censorship department – on several occasions. This work could be done during or after stages (1) or (2) or both.

2   The 'director or producer's' version. At this stage, camera angles may be introduced, and work may be done in rearranging and segmenting the script into sequences, scenes, and shots corresponding to the director's vision of how s/he intends to work on the script during production. Accordingly, the unit of segmentation in the director's version is ordinarily the numbered shot, whereas in the master-scene format the unit of segmentation is the scene. The distinction between this and the author's version is crucial, and helps to eliminate widespread confusion as to whether the writer should include such details as camera angles and musical cues into the script. In many earlier periods of studio production writers were routinely advised to include camera angles, which indeed appear in many surviving 'author's versions' from the classical and pre-classical eras. The argument against including them today is straightforward: they are the responsibility of the director or other departments, and not of the writer. Once again, this distribution of responsibility establishes a textual distinction between the work of a writer and

that of a writer-director. Nevertheless, more established writers may be trusted to include camera angles. David Mamet's script for *Hannibal*, for example, contains extremely detailed directions in this respect. On the other hand, this may be one of the reasons why his script was finally rejected and replaced with a wholly different version, by Steven Zaillian, in master-scene format.

3 Boyle's third category is what he terms the 'studio version', namely the script once it has been revised to meet the needs of stars, other talent, or commercial interests that the producer is trying to attract in order to complete the 'package'. There is no need to assume, however, that version (2) (the 'director or producer's version') will precede version (3) (the 'studio version'): (3) is just as likely to be an intermediate stage between (1) and (2), since the approval of members of the package is likely to be a requirement of the studio, regardless of whether or not a director has been engaged.

As either a 'director's' or a 'studio' version will represent the final stage before the film goes into production, it makes sense at this point to speak of the *shooting script*. This is a surprisingly confusing term, as one sometimes finds it used loosely to refer to the writer's final draft, or more appropriately to the version used by the director once scene numbers and camera angles have been worked out (version 2). It is safest to define the shooting script as '[t]he final version of the screenplay, used on the set or location by director and key members of the crew, and including not just the dialogue and general directions found in the screenplay presented by the writer, but details of the camera set-ups for each scene and other logistical information'.[18] The closest analogy is to the production 'Bible' from which theatre directors and stage crew often work in realising a play for stage performance, incorporating the full dialogue but with scene descriptions and directions rewritten or augmented to include movement, blocking, action, props, and sound and lighting cues. The amount of supplementary detail in the shooting script is a matter for the director and crew to determine.

4 A fourth version incorporates changes made during production. Boyle restricts his discussion here to what he terms the 'set' version, a retrospective record of any changes made during improvised scenes. One must add here all of those revisions made *during* production but before the shooting of the scene. Almost all films incorporate a large number of such changes, sometimes made by a writer retained on set for this reason. The material to be rewritten is excised from the manuscript and replaced by revision pages, colour-coded according to

the sequence in which changes are made. The first revision pages are printed on blue paper, the second on pink, third on yellow, fourth on green, and fifth on gold; at the sixth revision the paper reverts to white. There are established conventions by which the numbered sequence is maintained: for example, if the original page 2 is to be replaced by several pages, these will be numbered 2A, 2B, etc., with the same principle applying to scene numbers.[19]

5 A fifth version is what Boyle describes as the 'legal version'. This is more commonly known as the *release script* or the *cutting continuity* or the *dialogue cutting continuity*, or occasionally simply the 'continuity', although the latter term is best avoided as it is also commonly used to refer to the writer's script in the silent period. The cutting continuity is a technical, post-production document, a formal transcript of the release print 'containing shot and footage counts, dialogue, and extremely scant descriptions of the action' that provides 'a written transcription of the contents of the final edited version of a narrative film in the form in which it is intended for release to theatres. In general terms, it is an *alternative version of a film's text in a variant medium'.*[20]

The cutting continuity is prepared not by writers but by editorial assistants. Its function is to provide both a legal record of the final cut of the film that in the United States is deposited in the Library of Congress, and a transcript sufficiently accurate to function as a reference for both the studio and theatres to facilitate the replacement of damaged frames on a print, locate shots to be excerpted for promotional purposes, and enable the re-editing of the film in case cuts should be ordered after the release print has been made. Accordingly, it includes all dialogue and narration, but its description of the visual elements of the film is strictly for purposes of identification, including abbreviations for different kinds of long, medium, and close shots, for example, while being extremely staccato in its description of action and setting. It is ordinarily arranged in a series of columns running across the page from left to right, each containing a particular kind of information (reel number, length of shot, shot number, a highly elliptical description of the visual action, music and sound effects, and dialogue) that enables a given part of the film to be located easily on the film reels. A strictly technical record of the *film*, rather than of the script, the cutting continuity is for the exclusive use of industry professionals, and does not make comfortable reading for others. Nevertheless, for reasons considered in Chapter 6, cutting continuities have sometimes been used in preparing the copy text of a published screenplay.

6 In view of the number of changes through which the screenplay is likely to pass, regardless of the writer's original intentions or desires, it is hardly surprising that Boyle's sixth category, the published script, requires very careful scrutiny. Boyle's description, while now very out-of-date, indicates some of the problems: 'The redesign of the film's script [into stage play format] is done with little regard for the page-a-minute pacing. Ignoring the format of the author's version, they reach for the legal version and print a secretary's description of the action in their own format. This results in a distorted impression of a script'.[21] This is a fair description of many of the scripts published by 1980, when Boyle was writing, but screenplay publication has advanced and diversified, becoming infinitely more complicated, and in certain respects more reliable, in the process.

Before considering the problems of editing and selection surrounding the published screenplay in Chapter 6, we shall now consider in Chapter 5 a film whose script has not been published, yet which illustrates very well the range of texts generated by the development process. It also indicates both the strengths and limitations of conceiving of script development in the linear sequence outlined above.

5
The Birds

Detailed research into screenwriting naturally depends on the availability of substantial archival material. Scholars of the work of Alfred Hitchcock have been unusually fortunate in this respect, as the Hitchcock estate has donated a vast archive of materials to the Margaret Herrick Library (MHL) at the Academy of Motion Picture Arts and Sciences in Los Angeles. This has provided much of the primary material for several substantial, similarly-titled, and fairly recent studies of individual Hitchcock masterpieces, including Stephen Rebello's *Alfred Hitchcock and the Making of Psycho* (New York: Dembner, 1990), Dan Auiler's *Vertigo: The Making of a Hitchcock Classic* (London: Titan, 1998), and Tony Lee Moral's *Hitchcock and the Making of Marnie* (Manchester: Manchester University Press, 2002). Wider in scope but similar in vein are Bill Krohn's *Hitchcock at Work* (London: Phaidon, 2000), Steven DeRosa's *Working with Hitchcock: The Collaboration of Alfred Hitchcock and John Michael Hayes* (London: Faber, 2001), and Auiler's *Hitchcock's Notebooks: An Authorised and Illustrated Look Inside the Creative Mind of Alfred Hitchcock* (New York: Spike, 1999), published in the UK by Bloomsbury as *Hitchcock's Secret Notebooks*. This made a curious title even curiouser, since the material is neither from notebooks, nor secret, though it is previously unpublished. And as Thomas Leitch observes, the book is also 'copiously illustrated with pages of treatments and screenplay drafts that are not by Hitchcock'.[1]

Auiler's title does, however, capture the excitement of scholarly research that casts unexpected light on the familiar by disinterring previously unseen materials that are both connected to and detached from the known work. It also participates in the contemporary moment, when more and more films, CDs, and books are being republished, with archival 'extras' appended, to exploit advances in technological reproduction while attempting to preserve the authority of the artefact in an age of digital, and often illicit and royalty-free, reproduction. In this play of the known and the unknown, the new and the old, the tangible and the evanescent, *Hitchcock's Secret Notebooks* sounds like a visitation from the departed; it is the quintessential Hitchcock story, of which *Psycho* is but the most familiar telling, of the body that refuses to lie down and stay dead.

A certain murkiness has often been held to surround the authorship of Hitchcock's movies, at least at the writing stage. The director tended to spend a long period of time working with one writer on a co-authored treatment. Possibly the same writer would then be assigned the task of writing the dialogue and developing the characters, but Hitchcock would frequently call on the services of trusted collaborators to supply additional material or rewrites at later stages: partly, perhaps, because such confidantes would not publicly challenge his own status as auteur.[2] As Leitch argues, Hitchcock serves as a valuable case study for authorship, and indeed adaptation studies, since while no critic seriously challenges his authorial status, 'all Hitchcock's films are adaptations – if not of somebody else's novel or play, then of somebody else's original screenplay'.[3] There is a kind of repetition compulsion in Hitchcock's collaborations, with the same story recurring in the making of *Vertigo*, *Psycho*, and *Marnie*: 'All three show Hitchcock collaborating closely with a single writer, often meeting for daily story conferences over a period of weeks or months, until the writer runs into problems that leave Hitchcock discontented enough to dismiss the writer and find a successor.'[4]

Each project spawned a large range of texts of many different kinds, and the meticulous organisation of the MHL's Hitchcock files allows some estimation to be made of the nature and extent of each collaborator's contribution. Tony Lee Moral, for example, credits each of the writers on *Marnie* with developing a particular angle: Joseph Stefano, who had worked on *Psycho*, worked on a treatment that brought out sadomasochistic elements in the story; Evan Hunter, whose earlier collaboration on *The Birds* is detailed below, worked extensively in developing character and narrative in a full screenplay, but was so discomfited by the rape scene that it led to a terminal disagreement with the director; and the more amenable Jay Presson Allen, writing in ignorance of Hunter's screenplay, introduced major changes in characterisation, and was generally more compliant with Hitchcock's vision of the project.[5] Similarly, Auiler dedicates a chapter to the development of the screenplay versions of *Vertigo*, beginning with the source novel and explicating the various contributions of, successively, Maxwell Anderson, Angus MacPhail, Alec Coppel, and Samuel Taylor.[6]

There has been, to date, no comparable book-length study of *The Birds*, although several extensive articles and book chapters have critically surveyed the available materials, and Hunter wrote a short and somewhat bitter account of his work with the director. Not only do the MHL files enable a very detailed reconstruction of the writing process, they also help to identify the cause of Hitchcock and Hunter's falling-out as lying in antithetical views of what their story actually meant. These different interpretations were occasioned in part by Hunter's understanding of what kind of a writer he was, and how a writer should conceive of the film story. In the process, he completed three drafts, the last of which was then in effect taken over by Hitchcock and reworked into a shooting script from which he then diverged significantly both in the filming and in the editing.[7]

Pitch and synopsis

Each of these multifarious versions represents a different interpretation, adaptation, or telling of a story that had been worked out in advance even before Hunter began work on the first draft. Any direct indebtedness to the ostensible precursor text, however, was marginal. First published in 1952, Hitchcock only discovered Daphne du Maurier's long story (or short novella) 'The Birds' in the summer of 1961, ironically within the covers of one of the spin-off collections of stories published under his own name in the *Alfred Hitchcock Presents* series.[8] In an indication of the collaborative nature of the project, and the visual imagination that Hitchcock would bring to it, he solicited the views of art director Robert Boyle even before a screenplay had been written.[9] He also told Hunter, the writer who was eventually hired, to 'forget the story entirely' aside from 'the title and the notion of birds attacking human beings'.[10]

That this notion forms an exceptionally strong pitch is confirmed by the relationship between the completed film and Du Maurier's story. The single-page synopsis of the story in the MHL files contains a number of elements that survived the transition from Cornwall to California: the silent birds massing in dark weather before they strike, the barricading of the house, the attack on farmers, the radio broadcasts. Although it is quite possible that, consciously or otherwise, Hitchcock and/or Hunter drew on memories of the source text in constructing their own story, all of the transposed elements are very likely to arise in the mind of any imaginative writer presented with the pitch. There is no good reason to doubt, then, that Hitchcock and Hunter were 'starting from scratch and building an entirely new story'.[11]

Story conferences and story memo

For a period of about a month, beginning on 18 September 1961,[12] the two men would meet in Hitchcock's office at Paramount, where he would customarily begin by asking Hunter to tell him the story so far. The director would play devil's advocate with whatever the writer pitched to him, and in so doing 'edited the script before any of it was actually written'.[13] Hunter's memoirs preserve the only record of some of these story variants, which have otherwise vanished into the ether:

> In that first week ... Hitch shot down two ideas I'd brought out with me. The first of these was to add a murder mystery to the basic premise of birds attacking humans, an idea I still like. But Hitch felt this would muddy the waters and rob suspense from the real story we wanted to tell. The second was about a new schoolteacher who provokes the scorn of the locals when unexplained bird attacks start shortly after her arrival in town. In the eventual movie, the schoolteacher survived (but not for long) in the presence of Annie Hayworth.[14]

It was Hunter who finally came up with the idea of 'a screwball comedy that gradually turns into stark terror'.[15]

On 12 October 1961, the ideas that Hitchcock and Hunter had agreed upon to date were committed to paper in a 'story memo' apparently dictated by the director, which might alternatively be described as a synopsis or even a treatment, with additional, parenthetical questions and comments from Hitchcock for Hunter's attention. The names of the characters have not been finalised (for convenience, the synopsis below follows those used in the film), but otherwise the memo outlines the story in considerable detail. Much was to survive unchanged through to the released film, including the first meeting between Melanie Daniels and Mitch Brenner, the lovers-to-be, in a pet store. Having noted Mitch's car registration number outside the shop, Melanie visits her father at the *San Francisco Chronicle* office to ask if the owner's name can be traced. On the pretext of delivering a pair of lovebirds that Mitch had wanted to buy for his kid sister's birthday, Melanie follows the trail first to Mitch's hotel, and then to Bodega Bay. An indication of the detail in which the story has already been worked out can be seen in the description of the lovebirds trying to maintain their balance in Melanie's car, which would become a memorably comic image in the film.

On arrival in Bodega Bay, Melanie asks for directions to the house, inquires about Mitch's sister, and is told that she will receive better information at the house of the school teacher, Annie, from whom Melanie decides to rent a room for the night. She also hires a boat to make the secret visit to Mitch's house, but is struck by a gull; on seeing this, Mitch rescues her, subsequently inviting her to dinner and introducing her to his mother Lydia and sister Cathy. Melanie buys overnight things prior to the dinner engagement, at which it becomes embarrassingly clear that she knows nothing about pet shops. Later that evening, after Melanie returns to Annie's house, the two women discuss Mitch at length, and the following morning the major characters meet again at church, prior to the birthday party for Cathy at which the birds mount their first sustained assault. During a conversation at the sand dunes, Melanie reveals her identity to Mitch, but he confesses that he knew all along who she was. That evening, the birds attack again, swarming down the chimney. Next morning, while Lydia is away at Dan Fawcett's farm, Mitch and Melanie become intimate. Lydia returns in shock, having discovered Fawcett's corpse, and in an awkward exchange with Melanie insists 'you're not the type of girl for my son'. (In an aside, Hitchcock asks 'what the hell Evan Hunter is going to do with this', doubtless already sensing the conflicting demands of exploring the human relationships and maintaining the suspense surrounding the birds' behaviour.)

Mitch tries to convince the sceptical detectives who arrive to investigate Fawcett's death that it is no ordinary homicide. Tensions between Mitch and his mother concerning Melanie are rising, and Melanie prepares to leave. The schoolchildren's singing lesson is aborted as they try to flee the birds that also launch attacks on the restaurant and gas station in the town. After the assault subsides, the major characters return to the Brenner farm and, with Lydia being conspicuously more terrified than the others, begin to board it up. On hearing noises in the attic, Annie investigates, suffering a terrible attack. Again, this major difficulty in the story prompts a directorial aside: it is unresolved at this point whether Annie is to be killed, and Hitchcock raises it as a question for Hunter to answer. In the morning they attempt to escape in the car, finally gathering speed as the birds descend, tearing off the roof of the convertible as the car drives onwards – 'into what?'

The most significant differences between the plot as it appears in this story memo and the film as finally released concern the role of Annie. There is no suggestion in the memo that she has had any romantic involvement with Mitch, and she is not killed outside by the birds: instead it is she, and not Melanie, who is attacked by the birds in the attic.

First draft

Hunter now began writing the screenplay. The first of what would be three drafts, dated 13 November 1961, follows Hitchcock's story memo so accurately that it is essentially a realisation in screenplay form of the story as agreed between director and writer during their discussions, and dictated by Hitchcock on 12 October. Accordingly, it contains several minor characters that would later be excised, including Charlie Kamen, a gossip columnist, and Parker Daniels, Melanie's father and Charlie's employer, both of whom appear in a scene at the *Chronicle* office when Melanie, following her initial encounter with Mitch, decides to exploit her father's contacts to have Mitch traced. At Bodega Bay, the sequence of events prior to the dinner engagement at the Brenners' is rather convoluted: after first visiting Annie's house (to confirm the name of Mitch's kid sister), Melanie buys Cathy a card from the Brinkmeyer store, to which she returns, after the incident with the gull on the boat and Mitch's dinner invitation, to buy overnight things. She tries to find a room at the hotel, only to discover it is fully booked; instead she takes the room at Annie's, where she weighs up her appearance in the mirror before going to the Brenner house. Following an irritable conversation with Mitch, she drives back to Annie's, where the two women discuss at length Melanie's wealthy background, and Annie's opinions about Bodega Bay. Although Annie does not reveal her past relationship with Mitch – and Bill Krohn thinks that this draft (like the story memo) contains no implication that there ever was such a relationship[16] – she does mention that she left San Francisco because of a man who had a smooth line about drinking cappuccino.

The following morning Melanie encounters Mitch at church, eye contact establishing her irritation with him. Reverend Harris preaches on the dangers of wealth and vanity in the first of what would become a large number of apparent or actual explanations for the bird attacks that would be successively and ruthlessly excised. Mitch apologises for his behaviour at dinner, and invites her to Cathy's birthday party.

The birds strike, and afterwards, in a first and rather lengthy version of what in rewritten form would become an extremely controversial dialogue between the future lovers, Mitch betrays nothing when Melanie, apparently pursuing an idea planted by her conversation with Annie, mentions cappuccino. The moment is ambiguous: Melanie may well suspect he is the man from San Francisco referred to by Annie, and be testing him out. It is a fine example of the kind of indeterminacy in a screenplay that tends to be lost in filming, since any reaction shot of Mitch – and under Hitchcock's final direction, reaction shots in *The Birds* are remarkably revealing and/or extended to unnatural length – would confirm or dispel the suspicion.

Back at the house, Mitch fights off a bird attack via the chimney by lighting a fire, later attempting to explain the seriousness of the situation to the dim and sceptical policeman, Al Malone. In the first version of a scene that Hunter only recalled inserting in the second draft,[17] Mitch and Melanie attempt to both voice and conceal their fears by playfully improvising a deliberately fanciful explanation that the attacks are the sign of a bird revolution stirred up by one disgruntled sparrow: 'Birds of the world, unite! ... You have nothing to lose but your feathers.' Following this, in a moment anticipated in the story memo, '[t]hey kiss suddenly and fiercely'.

Following Lydia's discovery of Fawcett's body, one of the detectives mentions the Browne and Kennedy case in Britain, when killers shot out the eyes of the victim so as to erase the photographic image of the killers in them – an idea mentioned in correspondence between Hitchcock and Hunter on 28 October. After the next assault, on the schoolchildren, comes the first, lengthy anticipation of what would eventually become the celebrated 'end of the world' scene at the Tides Restaurant. In this first draft, Hunter dramatises a meeting of the town council that is strongly reminiscent of a comparable meeting in *High Noon* (Fred Zinneman, 1952). The protagonist willing to confront the crisis (Kane, in Zinneman's film; Mitch, here) is challenged by entrenched conservatism (represented by Henderson in Carl Foreman's script for *High Noon*, and by Sholes, the local businessman who would take a much less prominent position in the final version, in Hunter's draft), to the accompaniment of a chorus of local dignitaries, clergymen, and members of the general populace. Like Henderson, Sholes gives the appearance of decisiveness while actually having no plan should the birds mount a full-scale attack on the town. By contrast, Melanie says her father is sending someone from San Francisco to cover the story, while Mitch improvises at some length a plan to cover the town with smoke while setting up lights across the bay to confuse the birds. In Hitchcock's final edit, Mitch does make a similar suggestion, but it barely registers as attention suddenly shifts to the events at the gas station. In this first draft, as much of the town around the station goes up in flames, the attack reads as an ironic comment on the futility of Mitch's idea.

With Mitch's car succumbing to the flames, the lovers run for Melanie's car to rescue Cathy and Annie, after which they head for the farm and begin to board up the house. As they do so, the radio announcer briefly mentions the events at Bodega Bay, but most of the bulletin is a lengthy commentary on world events, such as the integration of the European Union and transportation segregation in the South. After the birds attack the house, now plunged into darkness due to the power cut, Mitch and Melanie fall asleep. Annie investigates noises in the attic, and is viciously assaulted as she tries to prevent the birds from breaking into the rest of the house, before finally being rescued by Mitch. They try to escape, coming across many dead bodies as they drive slowly through the town. As the birds attack and tear the roof from the car, they accelerate, finally escaping as Lydia comforts the almost insensible Annie.

Hitchcock's excellence as a script analyst and collaborator shines through in the five-page letter concerning this draft that he sent to Hunter on 30 November 1961, having conferred with several members of his technical staff. After outlining some general concerns – the script is too long and the principal characters are insufficiently realised – he identifies several examples of 'no scene' scenes, which may serve a narrative function but do not build to a climax and have no 'dramatic shape'. These include Melanie's visit to her father at the newspaper office, the convoluted sequence when Melanie buys clothes and visits a hotel on arriving at Bodega Bay, and the scene inside the church the following morning. Hitchcock credits production designer Robert Boyle with the idea that the birds should attack during the game of blind man's buff, and also feels that references to the birds should be introduced much earlier in the film, beginning with Melanie looking at all the birds in the sky during the opening sequence. Strikingly, Hitchcock also suggests that 'at the end of the night scene between Annie and Melanie there could be the sound of a thump on the front door. They open it to find a dead bird lying there and the scene could fade out on this'. All of these suggestions would be incorporated into Hunter's next draft, and survive into the film as released. Finally, Hitchcock is 'still wondering whether anything of a thematic nature should go into the script. I'm sure we are going to be asked again and again, especially by the morons, "Why are they doing it?"' This articulates a concern that would ultimately divide the director from his writer.

Second draft

For the time being, however, Hunter again seems to have been happy to follow Hitchcock's advice to the letter, submitting a second draft, with noticeably different emphases from the first, on December 14. The structure is tidied up by scene-cutting that also eliminates several minor characters. Melanie simply phones her father's newspaper office from the pet shop, instead of visiting it; the long-winded exposition of Melanie's early adventures in Bodega Bay is replaced by a series of elegant transitions that eliminate two scenes at the Brinkmeyer store, and one apiece at the hotel and the church; and the single character of Al Malone sufficiently represents the inept police force. The ominous behaviour of the birds becomes noticeable earlier, especially when Annie and Melanie discover the gull outside Annie's door. This version also introduces what proves to be the most effective mode of commentary on this behaviour, as Cathy asks the obvious question – 'Why are they trying to kill people?' – and Mitch is unable to answer: 'I wish I could say. But if I could answer that, I could also tell you why *people* are trying to kill people'.

The relationship between Mitch and Melanie, the role of Lydia as the greatest threat to its development, and the problematic character of Annie form an interconnected set of concerns that lie at the heart of this series of revisions. The possibility that the birds are in some way connected to Melanie is subliminally hinted at during her first meeting with Annie, who notices the lovebirds and immediately infers the reason for Melanie's visit. It is Annie herself who is the subject of the most substantial changes. First, she admits to Melanie that she loves Mitch, but that he does not form close attachments. As well as reinforcing the very Hitchcockian theme of the son whose sexual life is compromised by a dominant mother, Annie's self-effacing response to her romantic disappointment strengthens the character of Melanie, who appears much more assertive in consequence.

Leaving the field free for Melanie, while also suggesting that she may fail in her pursuit, casts Annie in the role of martyr, or self-destroyer, in a way that is intensified by a second crucial change: Annie is now discovered dead outside the house following the gas station attack. That this was a relatively late modification is suggested by the fact that Annie's name is still present in the December 14 script during the later scene in the attic, with the alteration being made by typing through her name and inserting Melanie's. In *Hitchcock at Work*, Krohn ekes out the almost subliminal implications: Annie sacrificed herself to save Cathy at the schoolhouse, and now Melanie is faced with exactly the same choice in the attic. According to Krohn, '[Melanie's] line, "Oh Mitch, get Cathy and Lydia out of here" was filmed, re-recorded by the actress during post-production to make it clearer, and then reduced during mixing until it is all but inaudible through the sounds of flapping wings'.[18]

Annie's death allows Melanie to emerge as the protagonist of the story, in a piece of unusually overt narration in the script that has not yet been fully translated into visual terms: 'It is Melanie who has the strongest reason for fearing the birds. It is Melanie, her fear growing, who makes the decision' that they should escape in the car, 'her fear growing as the scattered light beams [as the roof of the car is torn open] bring back the memory of the attic room and her flashlight battle with the owl', while 'Lydia, for the first time, recognizes Melanie's need and, again for the first time, truly accepts her'. These words would still be present in Hunter's final draft.

In notes from Hitchcock attached to the second draft, and dated 16 December 1961, he again asked for the elimination of several short scenes, realised that the gas station scene should be shown from Melanie's point of view, and suggested that just before they leave the house Mitch, instead of telling Lydia, 'I love you very much, and I want to stay alive', should instead say, 'I want to stay alive now – now I want to stay alive.' All of these suggestions would be incorporated within Hunter's third and last draft, as would the more extensive series of changes suggested in a letter dated 21 December 1961. While now happy with the scene at the bird shop, Hitchcock felt that Annie needed at least a veneer of sophistication (by making her a smoker, for example), so that she would not be entirely eclipsed by Melanie in their conversations together. While the second draft had eliminated the scene inside the church, the reunion of Mitch and Melanie had been effected outside it, creating another 'no scene' scene. Hitchcock was unhappy with the meeting of the townspeople, who all, he felt, spoke the same way. Finally, and crucially, Hitchcock asks, 'have we really related the whole of the bird invasion to our central characters? Maybe it's not necessary to do so, but you know we are going to run into all kinds of critiques from the high-brows', before noting in a postscript that '[p]eople are still asking "Why did the birds do it?"'

Third (final) draft

Hunter's final draft, incorporating changes made since 20 December, was sent to Hitchcock on 17 January 1962, and contained substantial alterations to entire scenes and many local, relatively minor variations. It apparently attempts to address a perceived difficulty, that Melanie's inner life is insufficiently developed to explain her actions, by having her recognise that her behaviour until recently has been 'silly and childish'. Moreover, the references to cappuccino, here and in Melanie's earlier conversation with Annie, have been removed. Such seemingly minor changes help to transform the relationship between Mitch and Melanie, in an apparent attempt to make the possibility of their romance more plausible, partly because the obstacles to it are more substantial.

The friendship between Melanie and Annie is sealed, as in the film, with Annie's revelation that her potential romance with Mitch failed due to the interference of the mother. The explanation for this is revealed following the penultimate bird attack on the house, when Lydia chides Mitch – 'If [only] your father were here' – to which he responds, '*Mother!* I'm trying my best!' The resolution of this family romance begins with the death of Annie and Melanie's shocking ordeal in the attic. Following this, Lydia helps to treat Melanie's wounds – in an attempt to apologise, she explains. As they attempt their escape in the car, Mitch asks Lydia: 'What do we have to know, Mother? We're all together, we all love each other, we all need each other. What else is there? Mother, I want us to stay alive!'

Other scenes reveal Hitchcock and Hunter's recurrent anxieties about whether the film should explicitly raise the question of why the birds are doing this. In what Krohn considers Hunter's 'best scene',[19] the choric meeting of the townspeople at the Tides restaurant is substantially condensed, compared to the parallel episode in the first draft, and the differentiation between the characters that Hitchcock had called for after the second draft is superbly achieved. Sholes is now portrayed as an ordinary man rather than a figure of influence, and Mitch enters much later in the scene. Accordingly, the echoes of *High Noon* have disappeared: the scene is no longer a confrontation between the self-interested indifference of authority and the courageous advocate of collective self-defence, but instead takes on the almost Shakespearean quality of the scene in the film, in which a range of minor, perhaps stereotypical, but vividly realised characters (including the amateur ornithologist Mrs Bundy and the drunken Irishman who keeps exclaiming 'it's the end of the world!') pithily express a range of opinions about the war of the birds.

Similarly, in place of the local and world news announcements of the first draft, here the radio announcer reads out parts of John F. Kennedy's first State of the Union address, including the assertion that 'it is the fate of this generation – of you in the Congress and of me as President – to live with a struggle we did not start, in a world we did not make'. In a kind of auditory equivalent of Hitchcock's much-loved Kuleshov effect, whereby the meaning of an image is conferred by its juxtaposition with those adjacent to it, the radio – and the President – appear to be intervening in Cathy and Mitch's inconclusive discussion (retained from the 14 November draft) about the bird attacks, and suggesting they are in some unspecified way occasioned, if not directly caused, by the United States itself.

In related vein, Hunter's final draft is also more explicit than the film, but less conclusive than a conventional thriller would be, in revealing what happens after the car pulls slowly away from the house – famously, the last image of the movie. Building on ideas for the ending that Hunter had developed in earlier drafts, the car drives through farmland, passing another dead body, before entering the town and passing through some of the story's landmark locations: Brinkmeyer's store, the Tides. The stores opposite have been smashed up, their contents strewn around the sidewalk. In a superbly grotesque touch that retains the ambiguity and uncertainty characteristic of much of the writing as well as the direction of *The Birds*, lying in the detritus and surrounded by birds is a dead man 'clutching a television set in his arms'. Perhaps he had innocently bought the set from the store and was killed by the birds as he left; but the description of the scene leaves open the possibility that they attacked as he was looting the store, suggesting once again a kind of moral retribution for the sins of humankind. As in all of the drafts, such images are ironically counterpointed by Cathy's need for reassurance that the lovebirds they have brought with them in the car will be all right.

Later rewrites

Nine pages of notes, suggesting many small changes to Hunter's final draft, especially to the first dialogue between Mitch and Melanie, were compiled on 20 January 1962. Much more significant – but unbeknownst to Hunter at the time – was that Hitchcock had already begun the process of rewriting the script without consulting his screenwriter.

Instead, he commissioned the opinion of Hume Cronyn, who had acted in, and helped with the scripts of, several previous Hitchcock films, and whose response had already been sent on 13 January 1962, prior to the arrival of Hunter's final draft. Cronyn suggested more humour for Mitch, and that the cappuccino speeches be cut – indicating that, to some extent at least, he was in agreement with the spirit of what Hunter was already doing. Cronyn considered that Melanie's character development would be assisted if she could be presented as moving from youthful silliness towards a mature sense of responsibility, saw in Lydia 'the strength of the cliché of possessive mommism', and indicated several places where he felt adjustments might be needed.

This was just the first of a series of rewrites that Hitchcock now commissioned or undertook. Between 26 January and 23 February 1962, he worked out a further revision, based on Hunter's final draft but incorporating more technical changes developed in consultation with '[matte specialist Albert] Whitlock, production designer Robert Boyle, cameraman Robert Burks and illustrator Harold Michelson'. Krohn thinks, quite logically, that Boyle was probably the major collaborator in the actual writing of this new version, in which Hitchcock 'began to develop, probably unconsciously, the theme of the "murderous gaze"'.[20] Like the preceding drafts, this rewrite uses the shot-numbering system akin to that of a shooting script, but it has clearly been constructed with the production more clearly in mind. There are many indications of matte shots, and the attack of crows on the schoolchildren includes indications of angle, the precise number of the crows in certain shots, the use of plates, and other technical details of this kind.

Intriguingly, the intricate shot sequences that so preoccupied Raymond Bellour and other theoreticians of the gaze – as Melanie takes the boat to and from Mitch's house to leave the lovebirds – have been worked out in detail in the script, now rewritten to present the sequence entirely from her point of view. The dialogue at the Tides Restaurant is less extensive than in previous drafts, but still contains much of the discussion, particularly revolving around Mitch's idea of confusing the birds by using smoke and lights in the bay, that would subsequently be eliminated. The high matte shot from the birds' point of view is present, as is the attack on Melanie in the phone booth – previously it had taken place against a wall – which now appears to anticipate the claustrophobic violence of the scene in the attic. On the other hand, several striking images from this version of the sequence do not appear in the film: a horse, attacked by crows, kicks its van to pieces, and Mitch enters a burning building to rescue a child and smashes a window to escape, before rescuing Melanie and dragging her to the Tides.

This version was preoccupied with the visual dimension of the film, but Hitchcock was still not satisfied with the verbal script, and commissioned the writer V. S. Pritchett to conduct what in Pritchett's words was a 'destructive criticism' of Hunter's final draft.[21] On 16 March 1962 Pritchett responded with several suggestions, which cohere around one crucial intervention – the idea that Melanie can be presented as 'someone who causes disasters because of her "wildness"'. On 9 April, Hitchcock asked Pritchett for something much more concrete: 'some reference to Melanie's mother having gone off with another man when she was twelve years of age'.

Pritchett responded three days later, with a rewrite of the sand dunes scene that was incorporated into what became the final pre-production script in the MHL files. As is conventional with screenplays produced by this kind of collaborative process (and as with the other drafts produced during work on *The Birds*), individual script pages on this draft preserve the date on which modifications were made. Evidently one draft of this script was prepared to incorporate the many changes, mostly minor, that were made until 30 April 1962. Pritchett's rewritten sand dunes scene, in which Melanie tells Mitch the story of her mother, who 'ditched us when I was eleven, went off with some hotel man in the East', was incorporated on 16 April and definitively changed the perception of Melanie's character. Substantial revisions were made to the problematic Tides Restaurant scene on 25 April.

The last changes were introduced on pages dated as late as May 22, including a breakdown of the 'progression of events' following Melanie's ordeal in the attic. At this time Hitchcock finally dropped the potentially sentimental dialogue between Mitch and Lydia about everybody loving one another; instead, Mitch outlines to Lydia his plans for the escape to San Francisco. A change of 30 April presents the scene outside the devastated farmhouse from Melanie's point of view: 'She does not have a normal perspective. She sees the birds in the foreground and then beyond on the barn, on the wires and in the bay, as though they are immediately behind one another: as though they are in layers, in seemingly undiminished size.' The car creeps out; then eventually roars out of sight. 'After a short while, the following small words appear, almost unobtrusively, at the bottom right-hand corner of the screen: *THE END*'.

Changes during production and post-production

Hitchcock 'was fond of saying that once the screenplay was finished, the actual making of [any] film bored him'.[22] As these changes show, however, the screenplay of *The Birds* never was finished to his satisfaction, and still further changes were introduced during filming. For example, there is no mention in any of the drafts of the unforgettable image of the broken teacups in the farmhouse just before Lydia discovers Fawcett's body. The climactic dialogue at the Tides Restaurant, in which Melanie dramatically rebuts the hysterical mother's charge that she is evil, appears to have been improvised. Conversely, as Krohn shows, some of the dialogue – especially Mitch's – that appears thematically important in the drafts was either cut during the shooting (including his remarks about everyone needing one another, and his exchange with Cathy about why the birds are killing people), or shot but eliminated at the editing stage, notably the 'bird revolution' dialogue, and also Kennedy's speech on the radio.

Conclusions

Case studies of this kind may reveal the logic behind each stage of the development from conception to post-production. An evolutionary or teleological narrative would show the screenplay progressively improving towards a final form which, if Hitchcock's statements on his film-making habits were to be believed, would allow the director simply to shoot the script as written. The second draft, for example, represents a clear advance on the first: minor characters and confusing narrative transitions have been eliminated, and it now seems unthinkable that Annie rather than Melanie could ever have been conceived as the victim of the bird attack in the attic. Beyond this draft, however, the successive changes seem less like improvements (with the undoubted exception of Hunter's final version of the Tides scene) than multiple, recurring interpretations or adaptations of a story that writer and director saw very differently.

Partly, this was for the obvious reason that Hunter thought of himself as 'a realistic novelist'.[23] He suspected that Hitchcock thought of him as 'the plot man',[24] and certainly it appears from both his drafts and his memoirs that he feels the need to explain, to narrate, and to give the material thematic and narrative coherence. This does not sit easily with the very contemporary and almost Beckettian premise of intensifying, inexplicable disaster. When Hunter explains in his memoir that '[i]n real life, birds *don't* attack people',[25] it is as if Beckett had paused to consider that Godot could have been held up in the traffic. At times Hunter shows a basic misunderstanding of material that he himself has written. He castigates himself for coming up with the brilliant narrative premise of a screwball comedy that turns into horror, which he subsequently but surely wrongly considered a mistake, yet suggests that prior to the scene in which Lydia departs for the Fawcett farm, 'we have no indication that [Melanie and Mitch] even like each other'.[26] The indication, of course, lies in the genre of screwball comedy itself, which prompts the lively interplay between characters who are destined from the beginning to come together.

The director, by contrast, was concerned to present the tale in visual terms, and the final shot, which stops the story rather than ends it, has the modernist, rather Brechtian effect of forcing the audience to recognise that it has been looking to narrative fiction's consolatory sense of an ending to resolve the disturbance in the natural order, which otherwise troublingly presents no mechanism by which it can be arrested. Hitchcock felt that in 'genre stories like *The Birds* ... the personal story [takes] second place. It's the event that takes over', so even though 'the personal story [surrounding Melanie] was weak' (and 'Hunter wasn't the ideal screenwriter'), nevertheless 'I didn't worry about it too much, because I had devised the basic shape of the film far in advance – making the birds gradually increase in number'.[27] Where Hunter was concerned with 'plot', then, Hitchcock was interested in 'shape'. This was the concern that had animated his critique of several scenes in the early drafts, and which contributed to the writer's accusation that director was trying to turn a slice of entertainment into a work of art, in an attempt to enhance his reputation as an *auteur*. Hunter cites Robert E. Kapsis's assessment of Hitchcock's intentions in making *The Birds*, which 'represents the first, the most ambitious, and certainly the most expensive project the filmmaker undertook for the purpose of reshaping his reputation among serious critics'.[28]

The archival evidence, however, suggests that Hitchcock was nonetheless very concerned about the 'personal story', and the role of Melanie in particular exercised him sufficiently to hire Pritchett to insert the additional explanatory dialogue at the sand dunes. This episode demonstrates that, contrary to reputation, the director was sometimes entirely indebted to the spoken (and written) word to carry essential information. It also shows that the recollections of both men about how the project developed were fallible. According to Kyle B. Counts, 'Hitchcock denied that another writer worked on the picture or that dialogue was ad-libbed', and he also quotes the director as stating that 'Hunter wrote the whole thing'.[29] Hunter himself vehemently denied Hitchcock's (accurate) recollection that in an earlier draft it was Annie, and not Melanie, who would be subjected to the torment in the attic: 'Never, I repeat, *never* was she to remain at the Brenner house throughout the film. Why, this would have necessitated a major rewrite after the first draft, and no such major overhaul ever took place.'[30]

One must trust the tale and not the teller, except that neither man seemed fully to trust the tale itself. Three recurrent anxieties are discernible in the revisions, and in Hitchcock's discussions with various collaborators: the explanation for the bird attacks, the character of Melanie, and if and how to connect the attacks to the actions of the humans. Krohn cogently summarises most of the explanations that were subsequently eliminated by what he terms 'Hitchcock's eraser': suggestions that the birds are a metaphor for Russia, Cuba, the Cold War, communism, or revolution; the idea that they are taking revenge for their mistreatment at the hands of humankind; the 'end of the world' motif, which had been prominent in the first draft's church scene, but which survives in the film only as a drunkard's catchphrase; or a kind of viral contagion whereby, beginning with a single bird, they either learn or contract aggression from each other.

While Hunter was not especially troubled by Melanie but felt the characters should discuss the birds, Hitchcock eliminated interpretation of the birds' actions but inserted dialogue to explain Melanie's behaviour. Hunter was never entirely happy with Melanie, but he was disinclined to probe too deeply the psychological motivations of characters he generally regarded primarily as instruments of the plot. Hitchcock, however, was exercised by the dramatic weight that Melanie (and, perhaps, the novice actor Tippi Hedren) was being made to bear. He, Hunter, and Pritchett were all aware that the movement from romantic comedy to horror film demanded that Melanie be transformed from the lightweight free spirit of the opening sequences to a character ready to sacrifice herself to protect Cathy, once the decision had been taken after the first draft that Annie must die outside the schoolhouse. One solution was to articulate the change verbally, and both Hunter and Pritchett rewrote Melanie's dialogue accordingly.

Yet Hitchcock was also working on a visual approach to this and another problem surrounding Melanie: the question of what, if any, connection should be traced between the bird attacks and the behaviour of the humans. Hitchcock had pressed Hunter on this, and the writer felt that his final draft successfully revealed how the characters change partly through their 'reactions' to the attacks.[31] In a brilliant analysis of the revisions made by Hitchcock and Boyle, and of the relevant sequences in the film, Krohn argues that Hitchcock (and, later and independently, Pritchett) gave an alternative answer: 'the developing relationships among the characters might be the cause of the attacks rather than the effect'. In yet another exceptionally detailed analysis of scenes that have long fascinated film theoreticians, Krohn argues that, with the exception of the sequence in which Melanie crosses Bodega Bay, 'the avian aggressors always erupt in a particular character's field of vision, as if the character's look had summoned them'.[32] In other words, 'Hitchcock and his [latest] collaborators [were] tracing in the film's visual structure a cause that will never be spoken of in the dialogue'.[33]

Since Melanie is also a surrogate for an audience who have been attracted to the cinema by the very idea of watching 'birds attacking humans', perhaps we – and she – have summoned them. The idea of Melanie's responsibility is voiced in the film, but only by the mother at the Tides Restaurant who, in a fit of hysteria, accuses her of being the evil cause of events. Krohn believes this moment was improvised on set; in any case, 'no written trace survives'.[34] He argues that the idea that Melanie is somehow guilty is decisively erased when she slaps the woman into silence, but that the mother's look into the camera still suggests that we, the spectators, may be to blame. Yet this episode may be interpreted in quite the opposite way: once spoken, the notion that Melanie may be responsible cannot be taken back (and the mother herself does not retract it); it continues to circulate as one more possible reading of a series of events that defies explanation.

The Birds may not provide answers, but it does offer suggestions. The improvised scene is merely the latest in a series of versions stretching back to du Maurier's source tale. Each version is an adaptation of something that came before it, and every adaptation is always also an interpretation. Hunter recognised this very clearly. 'By extending the screenplay [in the ending he had written but Hitchcock had not shot] to show havoc wreaked in town, we dismiss any possibility of this having been a personal bird vendetta against a small group of people.' If this narrows the spectrum of interpretive possibility, however, Hunter felt that Hitchcock's ending does so also: 'By ending the film on a shot of the birds after the car has moved away from them, it seems clear that they are being left *behind*', producing an ending that is not 'ambiguous' but instead 'simply puzzling'.[35] And yet, despite Hunter's feeling that '[t]his was not the original intention', in this respect it is not so very different from the writer's own, preferred ending, in which the birds succeed in penetrating the convertible's roof and yet the car finally pulls away towards an unknown future.

In either case, the suddenness of the ending means that whatever answer the audience proffers to the obvious question of what happens next becomes the answer to another, still more troubling question: what is happening now? As the two words that conclude Hitchcock's first major story memo – 'into what?' – demonstrate very clearly, that car is no more heading for San Francisco than Beckett's tramps are. It is heading for wherever, and whenever, we are when we see it. The drafts anticipate that the audience will find the meaning of the film in its contemporary situation, but removing the references to the Cold War and Kennedy's State of the Union address does not close down interpretation: it opens it up. The world didn't end in 1962 – though it was a close thing – but the intimations of looming environmental catastrophe sound much more insistently today than when the film was made. One cannot but be struck by the sudden changes in animal and human behaviour, their possible cause in viral transmission, the image of a petrol station going up in flames, the gloomy pall over the town, and the sight of Melanie burning fuel so quickly that the only reason the lovebirds don't fall over as she careers around a corner is that they were manufactured in a studio and glued onto their perch. And because the narrative arc, over which various writers expended so much effort, traces Melanie's transition from carefree recklessness to adult responsibility, *The Birds* asks, even if it does not articulate, another question: are we responsible? Are we responsible for what is happening now?

Another of Hitchcock's late, radical decisions impacts directly on our experience of both the film and the drafts. Instead of a conventional musical score, which always has the effect of narration because it directs the audience's emotions, Hitchcock used electronic sounds developed by Remi Gassmann and Oskar Sala. These approximated the sounds of birds, but with an alienating, grating effect. Just as Hitchcock's revisions to the screenplay eliminated commentary and maintained the enigma, so the soundtrack excises narration and replaces it with noise. The decision puts the spectator in a similar position to the screenplay reader, in that s/he experiences events largely without the affective direction and commentary of non-diegetic music. Yet the electronic noise, like the matte shots, also closes the gap between humans and birds: the disaster is not a natural event but instead is an effect of human activity, because the attacks have quite literally been made by people.

It's an interpretation, just as Hunter had his, and Hitchcock had several, some of which are seen in each of the adaptations he made to the material. That the changes to the ending were so extensive, so late, and continued throughout the filming, indicates both the degree of uncertainty Hitchcock continued to feel about aspects of the film, and the multiple interpretive possibilities the story provokes. The screenplay drafts show that these uncertainties were present from the beginning and were partly due to the differences between written and cinematic texts, and that a reading of any one of the drafts will introduce a wealth of interpretive possibilities that the film almost, but not quite, manages to suppress.

6
Editing and Publication

The multiplicity of textual variants produced by a single film like *The Birds* gives some indication of the scale of the difficulty confronting attempts to establish the screenplay as a viable genre for textual analysis. While there is currently a paucity of critical studies, when it comes to primary material the problem is quite the opposite. Not only have Hollywood studio record-keeping practices and the studios' ownership of scripts ensured that script materials are extant in abundance, but the frequent absence of an authorially agreed final version creates profound editorial problems concerning which text to publish, and how it should be edited. Moreover, the documentary record in publicly accessible archives remains patchy, and in most cases copyright resides with the studios, presenting potentially unique hazards for researchers and prospective publishers alike.

Nevertheless, the proportion of studio script materials being donated, filed, and made accessible to scholars has increased to the point at which there is a superabundance of material that defies convenient classification, beyond recognising that, unsurprisingly, Los Angeles remains the unchallenged centre for screenplay research. By the 1970s, the increasingly influential film schools at several institutions in that city, possibly aided by the presence of the Writers Guild of America – West (and its library), were developing significant archival holdings. For example, the April 1971 *Checklist of Motion Picture Screenplays* held at the Theater Arts Library at the University of California at Los Angeles catalogues approximately one thousand unpublished scripts held in the Theater Arts Division of the Department of Special Collections; by the time of the February 1973 supplement, a further 600 or so had been added to the collection. The 21st January 1977, *Checklist of Screenplay Holdings in the Charles K. Feldman Library* at the American Film Institute mentions holdings of over two thousand screenplays. As of 2008, the centrally compiled *Motion Picture Scripts: A Union List*, held at the Margaret Herrick Library, catalogues close to twenty-five thousand screenplays held by various institutions in and around Los Angeles. Other significant collections are held at the University of Madison-Wisconsin, and in the New York Public Library, while individual screenwriters have made their personal collections available for viewing at diverse institutions.

Although only a tiny proportion of screenplays are published, the number is increasing: the British Film Institute's database in October 2009 contains a list of two thousand five hundred and eighty-seven published scripts. Screenplay publication in the last twenty years has advanced and diversified, becoming infinitely more complicated in the process.[1] Yet the nature of screenplay writing makes it peculiarly difficult to accommodate within the conventions of publishing. A publishing house ordinarily deals with an author or authors who have vested interests, both commercial and artistic, in securing publication of their preferred version of the text; and with a few exceptions, the publishing house itself will wish to be satisfied that there is a sufficiently large market to merit publication.

The screenplay appears to fall at every hurdle. In many, but by no means all, cases, the writer of the material is not the owner of the work; instead, ownership and copyright belong to the studio, which may have no particular interest in publication, or even in permitting the material to be used for academic purposes. An exception that proves the rule is the agreement between Warner Brothers and the University of Wisconsin Press to publish a series of shooting scripts for major Warner Brothers films made between 1930 and 1950. This was only possible because Warners donated the material. Because these screenplays were developed within the industrial context of the Warners studio organisation, their explicitly defined readership was initially restricted to industry professionals; that they were then published, much later, by an academic press implies that the perceived market beyond the confines of the studio is largely restricted to film historians and other specialised readerships.

A relatively recent development that better illustrates the priorities of the studios is the commercial exploitation of a screenplay by including it within the package of 'extras' bundled, in whole (for example, *Sunrise*) or in part (*Sunset Boulevard*) – the latter almost invariably to demonstrate the existence, in textual or other form, of 'deleted' scenes – in a DVD release.[2] Both of these examples suggest that commercial studios perceive little benefit in publishing screenplays other than as a minor element within a series of features designed to differentiate the DVD product as an artefact from the film as a viewing experience in the cinema or on television.

Even when a publisher is satisfied that there is a viable market, a greater problem emerges in deciding which 'version' to publish. For different reasons any one of a first draft, a final draft, a shooting script, a cutting continuity, a critical edition, a description of a film in screenplay form, or an editorial construct may be considered the most appropriate. Until relatively recently, it was very common for a published screenplay either to contain little or no apparatus, commentary, or introduction that would enable the reader to establish the provenance of the text, or to contain a limited amount of such material but without any particular consistency or rationale concerning the status of the copy text.

A case in point is the range of screenplays published in London by Lorrimer, in two different but related series: Classic Film Scripts, between 1968 and 1986, and Modern Film Scripts, between 1969 and 1975. The dates of publication, and the screenplays selected, imply that the target readership was academics, film historians, and others who were more interested in auteur movies or 'classic films' than in commercial blockbusters, and who used the text as a mnemonic device in the days prior to the advent of home video. The Lorrimer scripts were generally prefaced by a short introduction which gave some indication of the status of the script; some also contained critical essays on the film or screenplay.

The difficulty arises with the almost complete absence of the kinds of critical apparatus that are routinely supplied in scholarly editions of 'literary' texts. There is no substantial commentary concerning the translation of foreign-language works into English, or any consistency or evident rationale in the selection and preparation of the copy text. A few examples, selected at random but listed here in order of film release, will sufficiently indicate the riotous confusion surrounding the Lorrimer screenplays, as well as the light many of them cast on the problems confronting screenplay publication in general:

1 *The Cabinet of Dr. Caligari* (Robert Wiene, 1919). This edition contains excellent supplementary materials in the form of previously published scholarly essays that discuss how and why the screenplay came to be written, the nature of the collaboration between writers Hans Janowitz and Carl Mayer, and the history of the production, which is of particular importance in this film due to the complete reversal in the meaning of the film brought about by the addition of the frame

story. Alarmingly, however, the title page credits 'English translation and description of action by R. V. Adkinson'. As in the case of most of Lorrimer's editions of foreign-language screenplays, there is no commentary on any problems presented by the translation; but much more troubling is the failure to explain the source of the 'description' Adkinson has supplied. Consequently it becomes impossible to know from this edition what material is in any original script Adkinson may have seen, and what is not. As with Lorrimer's edition of *Pierrot le Fou*, its *Caligari* is essentially an alternative to novelisation, presented in a kind of bastardised dramatic form instead of prose.[3]

2 *Pandora's Box (Lulu)* (G. W. Pabst, 1929). This takes a much more scholarly approach, establishing the provenance of the script (it is based on G. W. Pabst's shooting script), and indicating clearly the few places where the finished film diverges from the screenplay.[4]

3 *Eisenstein: Two Films [October and Alexander Nevsky]* (Sergei Eisenstein, 1927 and 1938). Although the text of *October* uses the scene-numbering method, it is not a shooting script but is instead 'the latest version ... and the one which most closely resembles the film ... [A] full version of the shooting script never in fact existed – scenes were constantly re-worked during shooting'.[5] This could have provided the opportunity for a critical analysis and presentation of the text that would enable the reader to see as closely as possible how and why such 're-working' took place. At the very least, it would have cast a critical perspective on the problems created by an attempt to establish a critical edition of a screenplay. Such concerns, however, lie beyond the remit of the series.

4 *The Rules of the Game* (Jean Renoir, 1939). The script had been published in French in 1965 by l'Avant-Scène du Cinéma; the acknowledgements in Lorrimer's edition credit 'Nicholas Fry and Joel Finler for some of the supplementary material which has been added to the text'.[6] It is unclear precisely which additions they are responsible for, but the English edition comments, for instance, on modifications made in a 1959 'reconstituted' French version, and includes precise records of the number of frames in each shot, and where each reel ends. Despite such commendably clear statistical evidence, which is presumably derived from a cutting continuity, the reader again has no clear idea either of the relationship between the 1959 and 1939 versions of the film, or of the role and extent of the 'supplementary material'.

5 *Stagecoach* (John Ford, 1939). This is 'based on Dudley Nichols's original screenplay for the film'. However, it 'has been carefully checked ...

with the final version of the film now available for viewing, in order to make it as accurate a rendering as possible of the film which the English or American spectator will see on the screen'.[7] Surprisingly, then, where there is a difference between the screenplay and what is visible or audible in the film, it is the editorial description of the film that takes priority, with the screenplay variants relegated to a set of endnotes, rather than the other way around. Moreover, the editing has been done in such a fashion that it is impossible fully to reconstruct the screenplay. Still more remarkably, a 'revised edition' published in 1984 substitutes an afterword by Andrew Sinclair in place of these variants, although a note at the beginning informing the reader of their presence is reprinted from the previous edition. Since they are no longer mentioned in the table of contents, however, it must be assumed that the intention was indeed to eradicate them. Either way, it is a fitting index to the series' chaotic editorial practices.

6 *Singin' in the Rain* (Stanley Donen and Gene Kelly, 1952). This is 'an account of what is in the film itself prepared by the authors of the script, Betty Comden and Adolph Green', including '*post facto* descriptions of the musical numbers and montages'.[8] This might helpfully be compared to the University of Wisconsin Press's edition of *42nd Street*, discussed later in this chapter, which preserves a 'final' draft in which such descriptions have not been supplied. The Lorrimer *Singin' in the Rain*, like most of its titles, assumes that the reader is primarily interested not in the screenplay as a form but in a memorial reconstruction of the film, using the screenplay as a base material to be moulded as necessary.

7 *Wild Strawberries* (Ingmar Bergman, 1957). This is derived from a translation of Bergman's shooting script, omitting only shot numbers and sequences that do not appear in Bergman's final cut, but appending a cutting continuity. Once again, these editorial decisions confirm the priority of 'help[ing] the reader to visualise the action' rather than allowing the 'sheer literary quality' of the script to stand by itself.[9] Nevertheless, this edition goes some way towards preserving the qualities of the screenplay while retaining the essentially reconstructive function of the series.

Theories of textual editing

Clearly, what is lacking in the Lorrimer series is any consistently applied theory of editing. In recent decades this field of literary studies has undergone something approaching a revolution, and the concepts behind these radical changes indicate both the ways in which the screenplay could function as a model that exemplifies some of the central issues, and some of the obstacles to critical editing of the screenplay text.

Very broadly, four theories can be discerned in recent bibliographical work.[10] The first is the view that the copy text should be based on that which most closely approximates the author's final intentions. Prior to the critique of this approach in the work of the 'New Bibliographers' W. W. Greg, Fredson Bowers, and G. Thomas Tanselle, editorial practice since the nineteenth century had been to use as a copy text the final version of a text published during the author's lifetime, the assumption being that through successive revisions the author would refine the work until it approximated his or her final (or simply last) intentions. The flaws in this thinking lie in the hope that authors would have either the inclination or the power to exert such influence, that they indeed had a 'final intention' towards which earlier versions groped, and that successive editions did not merely add layers of corruption the further they were removed from the first edition, like the progressive deterioration produced by successive generations of an analogue tape.

Recognising the lack of sophistication in unquestioning fidelity to the latest edition, a number of scholars, beginning with W. W. Greg in 1949, developed a second approach that came to be known as the 'New Bibliography'. This school held that the earliest version should be adopted as the copy text, for the reasons indicated above. Whether this should be the first edition or the author's own manuscript remained a matter of controversy, since it could be argued either that the published text was liable to introduce errors or even censorship, or that in seeing the text through to publication the author was able to revise the manuscript so that it more accurately reflected his or her final intentions. Moreover, especially in cases where the author consciously created more than one version of a work (as in the earlier and later versions of Wordsworth's *Prelude*, for instance), it becomes even more problematic than usual to determine what the author's final intentions really were.

Neither first nor final intentions, however, seem suitable criteria in the case of the screenplay, in which, as argued in Chapter 3, it may be inappropriate even to speak of 'intentions' at all. In many cases, the screenwriter – as opposed, perhaps, to the writer-director – is less concerned with personal expression and more with providing what might be described as a working hypothesis to be tested by others. Even in the case of the Romantic poet, however, it is doubtful whether 'intentions' should have the priority that earlier generations of editors attached to them. The 'conversation' poems of Coleridge, or the odes of Keats, repeatedly express the difficulty of capturing a fleeting emotion or insight in textual form. Such poems comment on their self-dissatisfaction and provisionality, and it is partly this self-reflexivity that accounts for the widespread phenomena in Romantic literature of the constantly revised poem and the unfinished poetic fragment.

Meanwhile, the recognition that much of the literary canon owes its existence to more extensive collaboration than was hitherto recognised has led to a reconsideration of the viability of thinking in terms of singular authorial intention. As Stillinger observes, '[u]ntil fairly recently, all editorial theories without exception were based on a concept of single authorship and the ideal of "realizing" – approximating, recovering, (re)constructing – the author's intentions in a critical edition'.[11] A different view, which began to gain ground in the 1970s, holds that all such approaches distort the historical record by substituting, in place of the multiplicity of versions actually created by the author(s), a single, often hybrid text that is in fact the creation of the editor. It should not be assumed that authors have a single, final version in mind; instead the work is a process, something to which the writer may return frequently, reworking to generate new, different versions, rather than one authoritative form. This 'new Germanist' approach granted no priority to any one version, but instead sought to preserve these multiple versions, unlike other theories that perversely erase the author's work in the name of seeking to recuperate it.

Largely inextricable from this 'theory of versions' is a fourth approach which rethinks the question of collaboration. Most prominent here is the work of McGann, who aims to reveal that 'the signifying processes of the work become increasingly collaborative and socialized' due to the effect on textual production of authors, editors, publishers, the expectations of readers and audiences, the nature of the markets into which the work is released, and so on. Authors themselves do not have 'single identities; any author is a plural identity'.[12] Crucial in this respect is his distinction between the 'linguistic' code – the language content of a literary text – and the 'bibliographical' code that takes account of the materiality of production, including 'paratextual' materials such as prefaces, footnotes, and the like, but also the socialised aspects of literary production. There are 'hidden ideological histories ... imbedded in the documentary forms of transmitted texts', which can be revealed through the processes of 'labelling', whereby 'the documentary features of writing' evoke 'a "context" for the text's linguistic system (its erstwhile "content")'.[13]

What is perhaps most striking in the present context is that, once again, the screenplay looks as if it could serve as the paradigm for what are ostensibly radical new approaches in literary studies. The combination of multiple, often unauthorised versions and the socialised text are precisely what has bedevilled the screenplay from the beginning. Literary studies is now embracing these concepts as a general condition informing all texts, and in the process, it is demystifying many of the concealed practices that have aided it in defining itself in opposition to the non-literary. In contrast to the literally marginal place of socialisation in the literary work, teased out by McGann in the bibliographical code, the overt labelling *within* the linguistic code of the screenplay text formally separates its 'contextual' labels – slug lines and so forth – from its 'content', calling into question the very possibility of fictive illusion. The critical work that McGann would have readers perform involves a process of defamiliarisation, recognising the contextual, material fields, the 'hidden ideological histories', within which the content secretly operates. The screenplay reader almost has to do the opposite: the contextual field is so insistently foregrounded by the industrial format that it can require an effort of will to suspend disbelief and enter what Brecht would call the 'dramatic' fictional world.

All of these things suggest that the screenplay is becoming conceivable as an object of literary study. This is not to say that writers like McGann necessarily propose to do away with the field of literature, or to admit the screenplay within its ranks. On the contrary, literature is in part defined by a quality of 'thick description', in which 'excess and redundancy flourish', which he opposes to communication theory, in which these literary virtues would be regarded as mere 'noise'.[14] As we shall see in Chapter 7, the screenplay contains few of the qualities of thick description. Indeed, it is frequently conceived as a straightforward act of communication; in the words of a 1998 screenwriting manual, 'a screenplay is *nothing more than a set of notes to a production crew*'.[15]

In other respects, however, the screenplay could contribute valuably to the theory of editorial practice in literary studies. For example, the theory of versions has to answer two challenging questions. The first concerns the simple practicability of this concept in the field of editorial practice. If we are to do away with both editorial construction and the desire for evaluation, we will be left in many cases with an unfeasibly large number of versions. How are these to be presented, if not by either producing an 'eclectic text' synthesised by the editor from various sources, or selecting a privileged copy-text with variants reduced to footnotes? Neither McGann's 'series of versions' nor the 'continuous production text', which aims 'to display the work's evolution from its earliest to its latest productive phases in the author's lifetime', can in the case of longer works have much practical value for all but the most specialised readerships. The remaining possibility, namely the 'genetic text', which aims 'to produce a continuous compositional text – a portrait of the authorial process of creation',[16] suddenly looks remarkably like the method that the Arbitration Committee in Hollywood has been using for decades to settle disputes about authorship. The difference is that literary studies has neither the materials nor, perhaps, the inclination to subject its authors to a process of credit arbitration. Unlike the commercially produced screenplay, the writing of literary texts is a largely covert affair in which documentary evidence of who supplied which ideas and when is almost invariably lacking. And this in turn is precisely because the context of writing in Hollywood is acknowledged to be radically different from that of literary creation.

There is a second problem: what constitutes a version? Does any textual change produce a new version? This conceals a further difficulty: while appearing to eliminate notions of editorial evaluation, in fact the editor produces a vast number of versions, each of which is presumed to have its own integrity. Each 'version' is both a text, and a variant upon some predetermined structure that allows a given text to be recognised as a version of it. Screenwriting complicates this picture. One writer may be rewriting another; the first writer is highly likely to suspect that his work will be rewritten; writers may even be working on the same aspects of the same project simultaneously, or different writers working on different parts. There may quite literally be no intention towards which they are working – they may not even know how the script is *supposed* to turn out.

As the example of *The Birds* reveals, even under the aegis of a powerful director a screenplay, regardless of the number of 'versions' it generates, is often less an integrated whole than what we might term a modular text: an aggregation of component parts, any one of which may be changed at any time in the process, without necessarily raising fears of compromising the integrity of the whole—since this integrity may itself be an illusion.

Publication

Which 'version' of a text will or should be published depends not only on how one conceives of the text, but on whose priorities are given precedence.

(1) Authorial intentions: writers' drafts

The vagaries of the production process mean that the film as released will almost certainly differ substantially from the writer's final version, as well as from his or her 'preferred' version, should this be different. This is especially likely to happen if the writer is not also the director. Among the best-known examples of films where the director departed significantly from a script by a well-known writer are *Natural Born Killers* (director Oliver Stone, writer Quentin Tarantino) and *Chinatown* (director Roman Polanski, writer Robert Towne). Dissatisfaction with the result sometimes leads a writer to arrange for publication of his or her preferred version, but this is not the only motive. The book of *The Usual Suspects* presents Christopher McQuarrie's final draft, which was the document used for selling the project to potential backers; it differs significantly from the shooting script.

(2) Shooting scripts

The 'Wisconsin/Warner Bros. Screenplay Series', published by the University of Wisconsin Press between 1979 and 1984, was made possible by United Artists' donation in 1969 of many of its film collections to the Wisconsin Center for Film and Theater Research. Among these collections was the Warner Film Library, which UA had acquired in 1957, and which contained screenplays for most of the Warner Brothers films made between 1930 and 1950, a period which saw both the introduction of sound and increasing generic specialisation within the studios. Not surprisingly, then, the screenplays selected for publication by the University of Wisconsin Press are of especial interest to historians of gangster movies and musicals. The first volume made available the screenplay of the prototypical part-talkie, part-musical, part-silent *The Jazz Singer*, and most of the others are for canonical films such as *Little Caesar*, *The Public Enemy*, *42nd Street*, and *Gold Diggers of 1933*. All of these were made prior to 1934, after which the Production Code was more strictly enforced. Therefore, although censorship was certainly an issue, sound scripts between 1930 and 1934 allowed writers greater leeway with dialogue and character than was possible for many years afterwards.

Although the series is therefore of considerable interest to film historians in many different fields, its aim, as explained by General Editor Tino Balio, is 'the explication of the art of screenwriting during the thirties and forties, the so-called Golden Age of Hollywood'. Individual editors were asked to include in their introductions an account of 'the development of each screenplay from its source to the final shooting script, [and also]

differences between the final shooting script', which was the text chosen for annotation and publication in each volume, 'and the release
print'.[17] In editorial terms, then, the shooting script became the equivalent of taking 'final authorial intentions' as the basis of the copy-text, if
by this we mean corporate studio intentions as distinct from the wishes
of any given script writer.

Despite the series' aim of demonstrating 'the art of screenwriting', it
would be more accurate to say that it exposes aspects of the craft of film-
making by taking the screenplay as a starting point. For example, Rocco
Fumento, the editor of the series' volume on one of Warners' finest
musicals, believes that 'the screenwriters seem to have contributed the
least to the success of *42nd Street*', and more generally that 'it is the rare
screenplay that can stand on its own merits'.[18] Instead, this particular
shooting script is of interest for revealing starkly the notably provisional
relationship of written text to release print in the case of a musical. The
script reproduced by Fumento is the 'final' version prepared by Rian
James and James Seymour, James having been hired late in the day to
sharpen the versions delivered by Seymour and the ultimately uncredited Whitney Bolton. Although this 'final' script is undated, it post-
dates a Bolton-Seymour 'temporary' dated 16 September 1932; shooting
began in 'late September'.[19] In keeping with the usual conventions of
'final' or 'shooting' scripts of this period, the James-Seymour script
breaks the action down into numbered shots. Fumento details many
differences between this 'final' version and the release print, many of
which must have required written changes by one or more persons
unknown. He argues that Warners would not have kept the screenwriters on salary during filming, and speculates that producer Darryl
F. Zanuck or director Lloyd Bacon may have been involved.[20] As usual,
then, the 'final shooting script' is something of a chimera.

Of more particular interest are the ways in which the script anticipates the input of other members of the production team. None of the
song lyrics is reproduced, and indeed the only musical song or number
mentioned by name in the script is '42nd Street' itself. Otherwise, the
screenplay merely gives cues: at shot 333, an orchestra leader 'taps
baton on music stand and orchestra starts introduction', and at shot
343 the 'orchestra leader starts Billy's number'. In the film, these are
'Shuffle off to Buffalo' and 'Young and Healthy', respectively.[21] In this
respect the script is a good deal more provisional than, say, the screenplay by Sarah Y. Mason and Victor Heerman for MGM's *Meet Me in
St. Louis* (1944), which does include lyrics.[22] Still more revealing are shots
355–7, which are simply marked as 'ALLOWED FOR TRICK SHOTS',

with a few suggestions as to what these might be. The script thereby defers to the professional role of choreographer Busby Berkeley. This is confirmed by some later script materials preserved in the Warner Brothers collection at the University of Southern California. In the cutter's copy of the final script, these shots form part of a sequence boxed in blue ink and marked 'Berkeley' in the margin; in this collection's copy of the 'final – master' (dated 22 September 1932), the sequence is marked in pink as 'Buzz'.[23]

The Wisconsin/Warner Bros. Screenplay Series is a landmark both in the publication history of the screenplay, and in the understanding of the relation of the shooting script to the release print. However, this very 'authenticity' presents a problem for the non-professional film scholar, since the version of the script it presents is likely to correspond neither to any given author's 'final intentions', whatever they may be, nor to the release version of the film, nor to the needs of readers seeking a visualisation or reconstruction of the film experience.

A slightly different approach to 'authenticity' is taken in the University of California Press's facsimile editions of the final drafts of several films directed by Billy Wilder. This is an especially useful format because it directly reproduces one form of studio-generated script, while certain local details in the Wilder screenplays are particularly valuable to the film scholar. For example, the facsimile of a 25 September 1943 script for *Double Indemnity*, by Wilder and Raymond Chandler, preserves both the text of a final scene that Wilder shot but cut in the editing, which has subsequently been lost, and a handwritten change which indicates that Walter Neff's superb description of the Dietrichson house – 'It was one of those Californian Spanish houses everyone was nuts about 10 or 15 years ago. This one must have cost somebody about 30,000 bucks – that is, if he ever finished paying for it' – was a late addition.[24] The Wilder scripts are equally valuable for preserving a number of Hollywood conventions that had passed into near-disuse even by Wilder's time, and are rarely seen in the commonly reproduced master-scene format: the division into sequences (lettered A to E in *Double Indemnity*, E being the concluding scene deleted from the film, in which Neff's friend and adversary Keyes looks on as Neff is executed in the gas chamber); the separation of certain scenes into two columns, one for the visual and one for the voice-over, which is more common in the documentary script; and several passages of description that are not broken up into brief paragraphs corresponding to individual shots, but read instead as continuous prose. These editions are also distinguished by the short scholarly introductions that establish the provenance of the script.

(3) Mnemonic screenplays: textual constructions derived from release prints

Many published 'screenplays' are far removed from the master-scene or shooting script, and instead are editorial constructions compiled specifically for publication, aiming to provide a detailed record of the released film, complete with stills and other production information. This results in published texts that differ radically from any text generated during the development of the film.

Although not screenplays in any accepted sense of the term, it is worth mentioning the range and prevalence of these texts as a reminder of the function played by textual materials as mnemonic devices prior to the advent of home video in the late 1970s. In general, the greater the amount of visual material reproduced in the published text, the less the need for linguistic matter other than dialogue transcribed from the film. An extreme example is Richard J. Anobile's edition of *The Maltese Falcon* (John Huston, 1941), the inaugural publication of the 'Film Classics Library' in 1974. This contains hundreds of stills, blown up from frames taken directly from a print of the film; where dialogue is present in the movie, this is transcribed below the relevant frame, along with the speaker's name. The effect is similar to watching a commercially produced DVD with subtitles turned on. Neither of these options, however, reproduces the dialogue of the screenplay: the book transcribes the words spoken by the actors, which may differ in innumerable small ways from the words on the page, while DVD subtitling ordinarily condenses dialogue at many points to enable the viewer to read them while following the film in real time.

Of course, Anobile does not pretend to reproduce Huston's screenplay. Instead, 'every scene and camera setup, as well as every word of dialogue, is recreated to give as permanent and complete a record of the film as it is possible in book form': partly for entertainment, but more importantly to enable the reader 'to closely examine the work of one of our finest directors'.[25] It is Huston the director, and not Huston the screenwriter, who is really the object of this act of homage. Even this is questionable, however, since the frames are not directly copied but frequently cropped, generating a variety of different aspect ratios on the page. Anobile's edition indicates very clearly the kinds of compromises required of editors attempting to provide 'a record of [a] film ... in book form'.

The stills-plus-dialogue approach represents an extreme textual parataxis: it preserves the fragmented nature of screenplay dialogue, without providing any supporting textual matter, which instead is supplied by visual images. The opposite, hypotactic extreme is provided by the 'novelisation'. Aside from the book cover, such texts need contain no visual images. They may attempt to reproduce the dialogue with a greater or lesser degree of accuracy and completeness, but otherwise will replace the usually minimalist connective textual matter of the screenplay with the devices of continuous prose narrative. These will include scene and action descriptions, use of the past tense, and – depending on the extent to which it attempts to reproduce the experience of reading a novel as opposed to seeing a film – other devices of prose narration such as free indirect speech and other means of accessing the consciousness of the characters. In most cases, however, as with Anobile's *Maltese Falcon*, such texts function more or less explicitly as substitutes for the viewing experience, although a book like Anobile's has some scholarly potential, while novelisations are more obviously 'tie-ins'. One of the first and most notable of these early examples of 'synergy' was *Love Story*, a novel by Erich Segal derived from his original screenplay for Arthur Hiller's film of 1970.

(4) Critical editions and eclectic texts

A much more recent publication similarly oscillates between recording both the writer's final intentions in the screenplay and reconstructing the final cut of the film. The text published by editors John Schultheiss and Mark Schaubert in *Force of Evil: The Critical Edition*, published in California State University's ambitiously titled 'Film as Literature' series, conflates material from Abraham Polonsky's master-scene shooting script and the cutting continuity. In addition, '[t]he dialogue printed is, of course, a verbatim transcription of the words spoken in the film.... When content in the film has no counterpart in the shooting script, the editor provides simple descriptions of the action ... in order to complete a stenographic continuity record'.[26]

It is difficult to see why these decisions should proceed as a matter 'of course'. On the contrary, there would be a logical editorial method behind the decision either to publish Polonsky's shooting script, or to produce a transcription of the dialogue and record of the accompanying action, although as noted there is little need any longer for the latter kind of text. Privileging this over the screenplay gives greater weight to the film than the screenplay (hence, perhaps, the 'film as literature' tag), but dilutes the effect of Polonsky's own writing. It would be more accurate to describe this book as a 'conflated' or 'eclectic' text than a 'critical edition', although it does benefit from the inclusion of materials and essays in addition to the editorial version of the script. Like the other kinds of post-production texts we have so far examined in this chapter, this edition of *Force of Evil* takes the screenplay as the copytext while adding material as necessary to assist the reader to approximate the viewing experience, for which the text acts as a substitute. It is an eclectic text not simply in conflating the shooting script with additional textual material supplied by an editor, but in creating a text that combines material from two sources: the screenplay and the film.

This dual-sourcing of material has on occasion led to the publication of a cutting continuity alongside a screenplay. For example, Lorrimer's edition of Ingmar Bergman's screenplay for *Wild Strawberries* appends a continuity of sorts, although (in Lorrimer's edition, at least) it differs from standard continuities in omitting many of the elements described above, most notably the dialogue. Instead, it merely describes in a continuous series of 582 entries each of the shots into which the film is segmented. For example, the continuity description of shot 2 is: 'MCU [medium close-up] of Isak's head and shoulders, back view; he moves back and pan to reveal his profile in CU [close-up]. He lights a cigar. Voice over.' As with Lorrimer's Classic Film Scripts in general, the purpose here is to assist the reader in translating the screenplay into an approximation of the viewing experience.

(5) Cutting continuities

The post-production cutting continuity constitutes the studio's definitive textual record of the released film. It has nothing to do with the screenwriter, but instead is compiled by office staff working directly from the release print. Its formal arrangement, and the crude and abrupt descriptions of the action, make it a particularly alienating document for all bar its intended users (see Chapter 4). This is because it is derived directly from a film that is materially present (either as it is screened or as the frames on the print itself are examined), and is compiled quite separately from the screenplay. Under ordinary circumstances, then, there are few good reasons for publishing a cutting continuity. In compiling his 'reconstruction' of Orson Welles's *The Magnificent Ambersons*, the ill-fated successor to *Citizen Kane*, Robert L. Carringer was not working under ordinary circumstances. After disastrous previews, the film was notoriously hacked by the studio into a severely truncated and in places incoherent film, some scenes of which were shot by other directors, especially Robert Wise. In the process, some of the footage that was eliminated or replaced has been lost.

Carringer supplies extensive narrative and critical material in the course of advancing a hypothesis about Welles's culpability in contributing to the disaster. His second aim, of greater relevance to the present study, is 'to bring the reader into as close touch as possible, from such materials as survive, with the masterwork that might have been'.[27] In other words, Carringer is constructing an *edition*, not so much of the screenplay (in which case he would not have resorted to the very unreaderly cutting continuity), but of the *film*. For the best scholarly reasons, then, he draws primarily, although by no means exclusively, on the surviving cutting continuity that was made of the preview version of the film, before the studio ordered the cuts.

'The first necessity in preparing the reconstruction was to convert a purely functional document of this sort into a readerly one. This involved such matters as rearranging the format, correcting errors, making the text internally consistent, and rewriting for clarity and, sometimes, for accuracy' (p. 2). This results in a most unusual text. Unlike selling screenplays, which aim to be suggestive rather than definitive, or many published screenplays, the reader of which has often seen the film and can allow the text to function as a mnemonic device, Carringer's *Magnificent Ambersons* is a very particular kind of halfway house: referring back to the release print, in an attempt to construct in the reader's mind as precise a visual approximation as possible of what the remaining material must have looked like.

Only a brief indication of the nature of this material need be given here. It includes scenes that were cut in their entirety, and others that fell victim to brutal truncation. Most prominent among these is the 'ballroom sequence', edited to remove certain conversations that do not significantly advance the plot, especially as it emerges in Wise's re-editing. Carringer notes that these cuts destroyed the rhythm and spatial integrity of Welles's conception of 'a series of backward-moving camera shots that traversed the third floor of the Amberson mansion, where the ballroom was located, along a circular course, twice' (p. 77, n. 19). The sequence contained '[p]erhaps the most lamented of all the lost footage: most of a four-minute, single-take, horseshoe-shaped tracking shot', of which only a concluding fragment survives (p. 97, n. 28).

Wise's re-editing focuses on plot, omitting many aspects of the commentary – by characters on one another's foibles, by the town gossips, and by the narrator. In other words, he has acted in accordance with the convention that narrative coherence is paramount, and that aspects of the story that can be conveyed by visual means or at least by dramatic interaction should take priority over verbal commentary and interpretation. Ironically, as in the ballroom sequence, prioritising these aspects has actually destroyed the visual conception as developed by Welles and his cinematographer, Stanley Cortez.

As Carringer notes (p. 133, n. 36), the release version consistently omits passages that detail the ongoing transition from an agrarian to an urban society. The release version therefore focuses on the domestic and love drama at the expense of the wider context of American industrialisation. This detracts from what the cutting continuity reveals to have been a powerful, almost Chekhovian drama, in which the Ambersons fail because they cannot adapt to social and economic change, and make the wrong choices in trying to come to terms with it. The release version omits both a well-developed story strand that shows the Major desperately building houses on the mansion's land for their rental income, only to realise too late that he should have built apartments; and Jack and Fanny investing in a failed headlight invention that is alluded to only briefly in the released version in what consequently seems a very perfunctory explanation for their own ruin.

Much like the film, the text of Carringer's version becomes increasingly complicated and hard to follow in the final third, following Isabel's death, where the most drastic alterations were made. There were huge cuts; entire scenes were reshot in truncated and rewritten form by Wise and the assistant director, Freddie Fleck; and the continuity of the narrative was ruined by the decision to take several of the later scenes out of sequence and insert them as a series 'without apparent logic' (p. 242), in Carringer's words, after the moment when George says goodbye to Uncle Jack at the train station. Carringer's reproduction of the cutting continuity rediscovers the logic of Welles's version, and provides a forensically detailed dissection of the changes made for the release version. These aims do not combine easily as far as a reading text is concerned, however, since the extensive editorial matter demanded by the analysis of the re-editing intrudes upon the remarkably smooth coherence of Welles's conception. Each time Carringer edits a sequence directed by Welles that was re-edited or reshot, he first reproduces the Wellesian version from the cutting continuity, and then gives a transcription of the material as it appears in the release version. Thus a scene from the cutting continuity will be followed by the scene as it appears in the release version before the cutting continuity is picked up again.

A possible solution would have been to provide a parallel text edition that reproduced the cutting continuity and the release version on facing pages. This would certainly have resulted in a more pleasurable reading experience, but might also have served as a model for how critical editions of screenplays could be developed in future, whether for the purposes of comparing a version of the screenplay with the release print or simply of showing the script at two different draft stages. Such editorial methods would emphasise for the reader the provisional and unstable nature of all screenplays.

7
The Scene Text

Format

One of the arguments frequently advanced against the screenplay as a literary form is that it is obliged to follow rigidly defined rules of format that reveal its function as an industrial blueprint. The problem with the blueprint metaphor has been addressed in Chapter 3, but it is undoubtedly the case that, to a far great extent than with the superficially comparable stage play, it is required to demonstrate the mechanisms by which it may be realised within its target medium in terms prescribed within the conventions of a more or less standard format. Some of its conventions are rather arbitrary (a screenplay usually begins with the words 'FADE IN', whether the writer actually envisages a fade or not), and much of the language is purely functional, as in the form of the slug line (see below). Margins, layout, and lineation are subject to established convention, which are all specified in any competent screenwriting manual. The purpose of this aspect of format is partly to enable individual members of the cast and crew (actors, location managers, lighting technicians, and so forth) rapidly to locate those places in the script that call for their individual input. Nevertheless, within the 'master-scene' format reproduced here, this is less important initially than ease of reading for the target reader of either the selling or the published script.

The present book follows Claudia Sternberg's separation of the screenplay into the 'scene text', considered in this chapter, and the 'dialogue text' in the next. Essentially, the scene text is everything bar the dialogue text, the latter of which includes not just the words spoken by the characters but also indications of whether the speech is voiceover (V.O.), offscreen (O.S.), or continued (CONT.) after interruption by either a page break or an element in the scene text. Parenthetical direction concerning the delivery of the line is widely discouraged on the grounds that it is the job of the actor or director, but not the writer, to determine how it should be delivered. Screenplays vary widely in the degree to which they conform to this and other prescriptions of this kind; if such a direction is indicated, it will be centred below the speaker's name.

The scene heading, unattractively but generally termed the 'slug line', contains three elements: an indication of whether the scene is interior or exterior, the location, and time of day. This is frequently merely a statement of whether it is day or night, but for local reasons, a more specific indication of time will sometimes be given. The elements in the slug line contain information that assists location managers, lighting crew, camera operatives, and so on. The slug line also, of course, indicates scene divisions. Most screenplays and films consist of a large number of short scenes, and it is usually argued that in classical narrative films these scenes are linked together into coherent sequences of cause and effect. Just as in cinematic montage the meaning of the individual shot is only revealed in the succession of images, so the meaning of the individual scene is determined by its position in a sequence of scenes.

Although screenplays take this form for collaborative industrial reasons, the result is a form that incessantly and inescapably refers to its own construction: this is the most self-reflexive of textual genres. Not only does it continually identify itself as a fictional construct, as does the lineation of poetry, for example; it also constantly reminds the reader of the industrial process that is its *raison d'être*. Unlike poetry, then, the conventional communication between implied author and implied reader is broken, and the non-professional reader is forced to recognise that the implied reader appears to be someone other than himself or herself. Once this is recognised, however, and once the conventions of the format have become sufficiently familiar, there is no intrinsic reason why reading screenplays should be any more alienating an experience than reading any other kind of text. Moreover, many aspects of this format tend to be used quite flexibly by the most accomplished screen-writers; arguably, the better (or at least more successful or prestigious) writers have greater scope for experimenting with the form without jeopardising the commercial prospects of the script.

Modes

Aside from the dialogue, the most prominent aspect of the screenplay text is the prose narrative. As with theatre plays, this is written in the present tense, for the same reason: the script is a direction to a reader who is imaginatively present at the performance. Sternberg helpfully distinguishes between three 'modes' in the prose narrative: description, comment, and report (she adds a fourth – speech – but as this is simply the dialogue text she considers it separately). To illustrate these, Sternberg discusses the Prologue sequence from the Third Revised Final Script of *Citizen Kane* (dated 16 July 1940 and incorporating revisions from 19 July). This is the script published alongside Pauline Kael's essay 'Raising Kane' in *The Citizen Kane Book*.

'The *mode of description* is composed of detailed sections about production design in addition to economical slug-line reductions'. Description generally combines two qualities to create a unique hybrid. The first is the 'frozenness' of prose description: a prose writer who pauses on an object in order to describe it in detail generally renders it inactive, and freezes the narrative action in so doing. The second, unique to the screenplay, is the frequent indication of camera movement.[1]

'The *report mode* is typified by events and their temporal sequence and generally centers on the actions of human beings' (p. 72). This focus on human activity, combined with the movement of the camera in the description mode, gives the screenplay its characteristic quality of dynamic movement in time.

The remaining mode, that of 'comment', which 'explain[s], interpret[s] or add[s] to the clearly visible and audible elements' (p. 73), is on the face of it the most problematic. As Sternberg notes, screenwriting manuals tend to insist that a screenplay should omit comment, because it cannot be translated into visual terms. We may add that the convention that one page equals a minute of screen time means that excessive comment will interfere with this temporal equivalence. While all screenplays are written substantially in the report, action, and dialogue modes, there is considerable variation between scripts concerning the comment mode. Sternberg suggests that 'screenwriters rarely miss the opportunity to use the mode of comment. It is in this mode of presentation that ever new forms and designs of screenwriting shall be revealed' (p. 74). This is certainly the case with the Prologue of *Citizen Kane*, which is replete with comment, such as information about the past history of the location, or the screenplay description of Kane's Xanadu as 'literally incredible', which by definition cannot be filmed. The Prologue is extraordinarily evocative, largely because of such comment. The mythical associations of ancient, dead kingdoms summoned up by 'Xanadu' are amplified by the 'exaggerated tropical lushness, hanging limp and despairing – Moss, moss, moss. Angkor Wat, the night the last king died'.[2]

Citizen Kane is undoubtedly a remarkably rich text, offering a wholly different kind of experience either from other screenplays or from watching the film, and it repays careful analysis. Precisely because it offers perhaps the most extreme example in all of screenwriting of a very literary use of the comment mode, however, it does not well illustrate how that mode functions in screenplays more generally. The textual qualities of a given screenplay are inseparable from the anticipated production context. Welles was co-authoring a screenplay that he knew he was to direct, and therefore was at liberty to develop a style that was appropriate for him as his own reader. The scripts of some other directors (such as David Mamet) are exceptionally minimalistic when it comes to the scene text, but arguably for the same reason: he either knows how he wants to film it, or he knows he will be relying on the contributions of others (notably the cinematographer) to help him realise it. In general, the scene text in a screenplay is skeletal, precisely to make it amenable to multiple realisations.

Sternberg considers the 'modes' separately from the rest of the scene text, it seems, because they can be considered aspects of *style* rather than of industrial *form*. This division, which has a certain logic, suggests a distinction between what might be termed literary and industrial aspects of the screenplay. Partly in consequence, she tends to give less emphasis to the former, in keeping with the overall methodology, which is that of a linguist and film scholar rather than that of a literary critic. Nevertheless, this rigorous approach can prove restrictive. The elements of the scene text combine clearly definable formal and semantic elements that can be pointed to within the script (specifications of light or setting, for example) with more dynamic, less concrete aspects of screenwriting, such as narration and characterisation. These are detectable less as a series of separate semantic elements than as effects of the dynamic structure of the screenplay as a whole. Moreover, the distinctions between the three modes are not as clear as they first seem. For example, action that is reported is also action that is described. The frequent absence of modifiers in screenplays is not an absence of description; it is a style of description, and one that could be regarded as commenting on, as well as describing, a reported action. In effect, Sternberg offers a version of 'close reading', but unlike the close reading of poetry, hers reveals a text that must constantly refer outside itself (to the film) and, in a kind of reflexive recoil, bring the film back into the verbal text as a reminder of that text's inadequacies.

Clearly, most screenplays suggest that the material can be realised on the screen; this is its *raison d'etre*. Equally, however, the majority of screenplays do not make substantial reference to many of the 'elements' Sternberg identifies, including colour, lighting, sound, and music, which are ordinarily regarded as the responsibility of other specialists working on the film. The same is true to some extent of camera, montage, and mise-en-scène. This indicates not the proximity between screenplays and films, but their difference. Reading a screenplay, even of a film one has seen, provides a very different experience from watching a movie.

Constructions such as 'we see', or 'the camera moves' (rather than 'pans' or 'tracks', for instance), allow the screenplay to give an indication of what an image may look like on the screen without specifying how it is to be shot. Importantly, Sternberg finds that most of the scripts she studied 'occupy a middle position' between the master scene script, in which 'only changes of time and location directly designate cuts', and a shooting or numbered script 'in which each cut is predefined'. In these middling scripts, '[e]diting markers may sometimes be hidden in the report and description modes in the form of paratechnical "shadows"', such as indications of type of shot (pp. 209–10). Spatio-temporal change is easily indicated without specifying the precise technical means of transition (cuts or dissolves, for example), by the simple juxtaposition of images or scenes to create stylistic, narrational, or functional effects.

The relationship between screenplay and film is perhaps most persuasively discussed by Pier Paolo Pasolini, in an essay entitled 'The Screenplay as a "Structure that Wants to Be Another Structure"'. Here, Pasolini is concerned not with the screenplay as merely a stage in a creative process. Instead, he investigates 'the moment in which it can be considered an autonomous "technique", a work complete and finished in itself'.[3] He gives the example of a script that is neither an adaptation of another work nor has been filmed itself, although it could be argued that in theory one should be able to consider any screenplay according to these criteria, since one can always encounter a screenplay of a film one has never seen.

Pasolini argues that the methodology of what he calls 'stylistic criticism' is inappropriate to the analysis of the screenplay. First, the screenplay is distinguished not so much by the nuances of textual detail we might expect to analyse in a poem or a piece of prose fiction, but instead by 'an element that is not there, that is a "desire for form"' (p. 54). Second, the screenplay demonstrates 'the *continuous allusion to a developing cinematographic work*' (p. 53), and this compels the reader, whom Pasolini regards as a kind of collaborator with the screenwriter, '*to think in images, reconstructing in his own head the film to which the screenplay alludes as a potential work'* (p. 59). Once again we see a doubling, since 'the word of the screenplay *is thus, contemporaneously, the sign of two different structures*, inasmuch as the meaning that it denotes is double: *and it belongs to two languages characterized by different structures'* (p. 59). What connects these two things is an idea of a dynamic process moving between two different kinds of 'stylistic structure' or 'linguistic system' (p. 60). Pasolini thereby implies the necessity of both a macro-system of analysis, in which meaning is supplied by a post-facto recognition of form or structure, and a micro-level that attends to the specific ways in which the screenplay negotiates between, or simultaneously keeps in play, its verbal and visual sign-systems.

Radically different, less precise, but perhaps still more suggestive is a short essay by Sergei Eisenstein, which explores from a director's perspective the consequences of working with these two distinct sign-systems. The difference between a written text and a film cannot simply be erased. Eisenstein gives the example of a phrase uttered by one of the survivors of the *Potemkin* mutiny, which became the source of one of the director's most celebrated films. The veteran said that 'A deathly silence hung in the air'. Eisenstein saw no difficulty with a writer incorporating these words in the script, which

> sets out the emotional requirements. The director provides his visual resolution. And the scriptwriter is right to present it in his own language.... Let the scriptwriter and the director expound this in their different languages. The scriptwriter puts: "deathly silence". The director uses: still close-ups; the dark and silent pitching of the battleship's bows; the unfurling of the St. Andrew's ensign; perhaps a dolphin's leap; and the low flight of seagulls.[4]

Equally, of course, the emphases may be reversed: the script may describe a setting or character in literary terms that apparently exceed or cannot be resolved into the language of film, but the verbal language may prompt the director's imagination into providing a correlative image, mood, or texture.

Time

The screenplay is written in the present tense, because it specifies what the spectator is to imagine is happening on the screen at that moment. The use of the past tense in almost all prose fiction tends to draw attention to narration, because the discourse demonstrably comments retrospectively on story elements that have occurred prior to the moment in which they are narrated. The use of the present tense in the screenplay obscures this gap between story and discourse, as does its construction as a series of more or less brief episodes, each of which purports to describe a short scene within the film. In other words, unlike the retrospection of conventional prose fiction, the screenplay hovers between present-tense narration and shadowy anticipation of a future realisation in a different medium.

The stage play similarly unfolds in the present tense, yet there is a significant difference between theatre and screenwriting on the one hand, and cinema on the other, because the image on the screen is at best an approximate record of an event that can only have happened at some point in the past. On the cinema screen, it is *never* now. The screenplay reads in the present, but it is the past of the film. Two of Woody Allen's films make great comic play with exposing this mechanism. In *The Purple Rose of Cairo* (1985), a character within a film steps out from the screen and enters the auditorium to join one of the spectators who has fallen in love with his screen image. The joke lies not just in the erasure of the distinction between the fictional world of the film and the 'real' world of the spectator, but in removing the distinction between the past-ness of the film world and the present of the spectator. A similar conceit is seen in *Deconstructing Harry* (1997), in which an actor who is out of focus when filmed remains so in the 'real' world. In each case the conceit plays upon the powerful illusion of present-ness in a medium that is inescapably a record of the past.

Convention holds that one script page represents one minute of screen time, and that the writer will ordinarily construct the script in accordance with the rhythmic demands of this equation. This has important consequences: lengthy enumerations of the items in a room, for example, are precluded, and only the significant detail can be recorded. This means that the screenplay can never have the wealth of detail often found in the realistic novel; it is more akin to poetry, the short story, or the Chaucerian *fabliau*.

James F. Boyle goes a little further in positing a 'reading time' that is considerably shorter than the projection time:

A script page	= Reading time	= Projection time	= Fictional time[5]
eleven inches	approx 25 sec.	1 minute	variable

This is, of course, merely a hypothesis, a guess; different readers will read at different speeds, and some screenplays are harder to read than others. Nevertheless, empirical observation of one's own reading habits tends to support this assumption, which is not surprising in view of the dialogue-intensive nature of many screenplays, the economy of their descriptive modes, and the generous margins and line spacing demanded by studio conventions. The experience of reading a screenplay, then, should correspond rhythmically to the viewing of a film, but at an accelerated speed: accepting Boyle's approximation, the hundred and twenty-page script for a two-hour film should take something under one hour to read.

Boyle's 'fictional time' is what most film theorists would describe as 'story time': that is, the duration of events as they 'really' happened. This is to be distinguished from 'discourse' or 'plot' time, which is the temporal frame within which the story events are narrated, and which, in the classical narrative theory of Gérard Genette and others, can distort story time in three basic ways.[6] The discourse may rearrange the order, by the use of flashbacks (analepsis) or flash forwards (prolepsis); it may alter the duration (much easier to quantify in cinema, by the use of slow motion for example, than in prose fiction); and it may change the frequency, as in *Rashomon* (Akira Kurosawa, 1950), in which the same event is shown on multiple occasions. The technological constraints on the earliest films, such as the Lumières' *Sortie d'Usine* (1895), meant that there was no distinction between story and discourse time. A rare example of a later film that supposedly unfolds in 'real time' is *High Noon* (Fred Zinneman, 1952), in which the discourse time purports to be exactly equivalent to that of the story time, with many shots of clocks to tell the spectator exactly how long they will have to wait before the climactic arrival of the train at noon. As such, it is an illustration of pure Hitchcockian suspense.

In fact, there are some slight distortions in this equivalence in *High Noon*, but it remains highly unusual, since almost all films condense story time in the discourse through the use of cuts and other transitional devices such as fades and dissolves. A much more radical experiment is *Last Year at Marienbad* (Alain Resnais, 1961). Its writer, Alain Robbe-Grillet, 'saw Resnais's work as an attempt to construct a purely mental space and time – those of dreams, perhaps, or of memory, those of any effective life – without excessive insistence on the traditional relations of cause and effect, nor on an absolute time-sequence in narrative'. As an avant-garde novelist, Robbe-Grillet was interested in questioning out of existence the whole basis of narratology, which depends on the assumption that there is a story in the past that can be recovered in the present discourse. Instead, 'our three characters ... had no names, no past, no links among themselves save those they created by their own gestures and voices, their own presence, their own imagination'.[7] Robbe-Grillet was so fascinated by the potential for fiction of Resnais's radical approach to time in cinema that he described his own script for the film as a 'ciné-novel'.

Narration

Narration has long posed a difficult problem for film theory, one with its roots in the Aristotelian distinction between 'showing' and 'telling'. The early *actualités* of waves breaking on a beach, trains entering a station, or leaves blowing in the wind had the appeal of apparently unmediated realism: for the first time, a technological apparatus could record the movement of natural forces that could not be captured in a theatre. The camera therefore appeared to be 'showing' incident, rather than 'telling' or narrating it.

A screenplay composed solely of Sternberg's modes of dialogue, description, and report, and lacking the mode of 'comment', is possibly the textual medium that comes closest to realising the ideal of 'showing' without narration. With the dialogue and report modes being simply a record of what is said or seen, the screenplay lacks either the first-person or third-person narrator of prose fiction. This is undoubtedly part of what is really an ideological argument against the use of voice-over that one frequently encounters in the same manuals that counsel against the comment mode.

The difficulty with this argument is that it presents screenplay and film in impossible terms: as media that evade mediation. This lies at the heart of the problem of cinematic narration, which needs to be differentiated from narration in the screenplay. A comparison to the beginning of a short story by Ernest Hemingway, who has a very 'cinematic' style in the sense that it is often rigorously confined to the report mode, the description mode, and dialogue, establishes this well:

> The door of Henry's lunch-room opened and two men came in. They sat down at the counter.
> 'What's yours?' George asked them.
> 'I don't know', one of the men said. 'What do you want to eat, Al?'
> 'I don't know', said Al. 'I don't know what I want to eat.'
> Outside it was getting dark. The street-light came on outside the window. The two men at the counter read the menu. From the other

end of the counter Nick Adams watched them. He had been talking to George when they came in.

'I'll have a roast pork tenderloin with apple sauce and mashed potatoes', the first man said.

'It isn't ready yet.'

'What the hell do you put it on the card for?'

'That's the dinner', George explained. 'You can get that at six o'clock.'

George looked at the clock on the wall behind the counter.

'It's five o'clock.'

'The clock says twenty minutes past five', the second man said.

'It's twenty minutes fast.'

'Oh, to hell with the clock', the first man said. 'What have you got to eat?'

'I can give you any kind of sandwiches,' George said. 'You can have ham and eggs, bacon and eggs, liver and bacon, or a steak.'

'Give me chicken croquettes with green peas and cream sauce and mashed potatoes.'

'That's the dinner.'

'Everything we want's the dinner, eh? That's the way you work it.'[8]

Superficially, such a style has the effect of minimising or even eliminating narration. It simply records a series of events as they happened, and invites the reader to supply the connections that would integrate them within a coherent story.

'The Killers' is a very well-known text, but even on first encounter the style is likely to seem very contemporary to a reader today, partly because the set-up of the two voluble hit-men has undoubtedly influenced, directly or indirectly, such well-known works as Harold Pinter's stage play *The Dumb Waiter* (1960), Quentin Tarantino's Academy Award-winning *Pulp Fiction* (1994), and Martin McDonagh's *In Bruges* (2008), nominated for an Oscar in the original screenplay category. It is not coincidental that Pinter and McDonagh were acclaimed dramatists before turning to film, or that in Tarantino's screenplays there is such a preponderance of dialogue that, in this respect, on the page they often bear a closer resemblance to stage plays. In all of these works the dialogue is both exceptionally prolix and remarkably vivid.

We shall consider a comparable sequence of dialogue in *Pulp Fiction* in the next chapter, but it is clear that part of the effect of the dialogue in 'The Killers' comes from its juxtaposition with the style of the prose description. The latter is syntactically simple and eschews modifiers, enumeration, and metaphor. The same is largely true of the dialogue, except that the two men are extremely particular in detailing the items they want from the menu. This could be read in a number of ways (a psychopathic need to order the world by naming things with precision, as in the obsession with brand names in Bret Easton Ellis's *American Psycho*, or indeed Tarantino's dialogue; an attempt to intimidate George by establishing linguistic mastery), but it clearly emerges as a distinctive idiolect, a style.

The description is also, on closer examination, heavily stylised in ways that bear comparison with the modes of report and description in the screenplay. Compare the first scene of a random example, William Peter Blatty's *The Exorcist* (William Friedkin, 1973):

> An Old Man in khakis works at section of mound with excavating pick. (In background there may be two Kurdish Assistants carefully packing the day's finds.) The Old Man now makes a find. He extracts it gingerly from the mound, begins to dust it off, then reacts with dismay upon recognizing a green stone amulet in the figure of the demon Pazuzu.
>
> Close shot. Perspiration pouring down Old Man's brow.
>
> Close shot. Old Man's hands. Trembling, they reach across a rude wooden table and cup themselves around a steaming glass of hot tea, as if for warmth.[9]

The series of shots specified or implied in this passage (and almost any screenplay would have worked as well or better to illustrate the point) resembles the prose of 'The Killers' in privileging the report mode: actions are described simply and in sequence. Most important is the use, in each case, of parataxis: events are described without being connected by the use of conjunctions. This seemingly eliminates narrational commentary and plainly records events as they happen.

Hemingway's use of parataxis, however, contributes to what is in fact a highly distinctive style that creates his masculine, existentialist world view. 'Character' is action, as Aristotle – a ubiquitous authority in screenwriting manuals – observes. In 'The Killers', all of the characters decide to perform or not to perform certain actions (to give the men what they want or not, to contradict them or not), and this sequence of actions builds towards what will turn out to be the story's major event: the decision of Ole Anderson, the man the killers are seeking, *not* to act on the knowledge that they have arrived in town. He does not explain this; it is decision, revealed in action, that defines the situation and the character. A similar effect is produced by the succession of actions in a screenplay. Because this sequence implicitly or explicitly anticipates its realisation in cinematic editing, it is usually presented, as in the example from *The Exorcist*, as a series of events without conjunction or comment. Yet this does not at all mean that there is no narration here. On the contrary, narration is supplied in at least two ways. First, the style is metonymic: it is a *selection* of events or objects consciously chosen from within the implied story world. We are directed to look at the amulet, the perspiration, the hands, and the glass of tea. Realist prose fiction sometimes attempts to conceal this process of selection by providing excessive, redundant detail. By contrast, other forms, such as the medieval *fabliau*, depend for their effect on the conventions of metonymic selection. In Chaucer's 'Miller's Tale', for example, every element that is introduced in the first part of the story will contribute to the humiliations visited on the characters in its comic climax. Most screenplays therefore have something of the structure of a joke. Because of the compressed nature of the form, any object to which it directs attention is liable to be shown to be a set-up, to have a particular significance that will only be revealed later on: the child's red coat in *Don't Look Now*, the snowshaker in *Citizen Kane*, the amulet in *The Exorcist*.

The narration implied by the process of selection is then confirmed by a second, corollary process: the selected shots are arranged into a sequence, again in anticipation of film editing. Although this combination of shots is paractactic (there will ordinarily be no comment to explain exactly why the images follow in this particular sequence), the reader will ordinarily have no difficulty in inferring the explanation for it. Parataxis in the screenplay therefore appears to have the opposite effect to parataxis in prose fiction: in the former, knowledge of the conventions of montage causes the reader to detect a directorial or narrational presence, yet in fiction, parataxis attempts to suppress the effect of narration altogether.

The resulting problem in film theory has involved the question of who or what is doing the narrating. As Christian Metz observes, 'The spectator perceives images which have obviously been selected (they could have been other images) and arranged (their order could have been different). In a sense, he is leafing through an album of predetermined pictures, and it is not he who is turning the pages but some "master of ceremonies", some "grand image-maker".'[10] As the scare quotes suggest, the question of how to describe the presence and activities of this image-maker remains problematic, because in Edward Branigan's words 'the "person" whose voice is "heard" in a [film] text may be a much more complex (invisible and inaudible) entity than a voice-over narrator or someone being interviewed'.[11]

These complexities have been discussed at length in at least two major studies, by Edward Branigan and David Bordwell, and the specifically filmic aspects of narration are not necessarily relevant to narration in the screenplay. What is remarkable about the analysis of cinematic narration in the present context, however, is that the screenplay is almost never mentioned as its possible source. For example, Bordwell notes that in Eisenstein's films 'there is the sense that the text before us, the play or the film, is the performance of a "prior" story', and is narrated by 'an invisible master of ceremonies who has staged this action, chosen these camera positions, and edited the images in just this way', so that there is 'a continual awareness of the director's shaping hand'.[12] This captures very well the ontological status of the film in relation to its 'prior' sources, and as noted in Chapter 3, the relationship between film and screenplay is of major importance in this respect. The difficulty in film theory appears to be prompted in part by the desire to construct a single narrator (hence perhaps the status of the director as *auteur*), even though Bordwell dismisses the 'implied author' of a film as 'an anthropomorphic fiction'.[13] Bazin's paradoxical 'genius of the system' appropriately suggests that the sense of a single centre of consciousness may in fact be the result of extensive collaboration.

Within the screenplay, as opposed to the film, Sternberg distinguishes between an impersonal narrative 'voice', which 'shows' by indications of editing, mise-en-scene, and overt or covert 'perspectivemes' (indications of perspective); and the personal narrative voice, which 'speaks' in voice-over, on-screen narration, or a written text (pp. 133–41). Yet it is difficult to concur that in the screenplay '*telling* by a narrative agent does *not* take place despite its high degree of prose. The text only anticipates a narrative perspective in the target medium of film' (p. 157). This sits uneasily with Sternberg's conclusion, in which she suggests that the 'scene text' tends to 'narratize' for the blueprint reader, and '[t]he screenwriter therefore becomes a *hidden director*' (p. 231).

Character

Superficially, character is a much more straightforward concept than narration; we all know what we mean by the characters in a film. Even so, much of what we think of as a film character is supplied by the actor, and this must be differentiated from a character in the written text. Screenplays are often vague when using the descriptive mode to portray a character, partly because it is not the writer who will cast the actor. The comment mode is also widely regarded as an inappropriate means of presenting character, as these comments cannot be filmed. As in the description of action, it appears that one is left with only the resources of dialogue and action, which consequently tend to construct the protagonist in particular as a more or less existential being. Moreover, because 'it is general screenplay practice to introduce and describe characters when they first appear',[14] the text usually lacks the resources available to the novelist of the accumulation, modification, and even contradiction of detail during the course of the narrative. Accordingly, characterisation in the screenplay, in this sense at least, is skeletal.

Before simply accepting this as fate, however, it is worth pausing to consider the enormous number of highly acclaimed screenplays that pay no heed to these strictures, and describe the characters in some-times highly novelistic ways. At the beginning of *Taxi Driver* (Martin Scorsese, 1976; written by Paul Schrader), before any slug line or action comes a detailed physical description of Travis Bickle, interspersed with a crisp, vivid dissection of his blasted past and inner life:

> [O]ne can see the ominous strains caused by a life of private fear, emp-tiness and loneliness. He seems to have wandered in from a land where it is always cold, a country where the inhabitants seldom speak. [...] He has the smell of sex about him: sick sex, repressed sex, lonely sex, but sex none the less. He is a raw male force, driving forward; towards what, one cannot tell. Then one looks closer and sees the inevitable. The clock spring cannot be wound continually tighter. As the earth moves towards the sun, TRAVIS BICKLE moves towards violence.[15]

The objections that could be made to this passage in its entirety require no elaboration: you can't film smell, you can't film the inevitable. Yet it would be difficult to deny that Schrader has captured the essence of the character as most spectators experience it; or, more accurately, that Scorsese and Robert De Niro have managed to film the 'unfilmable' elements of the script, and that this is done in the manner suggested by Eisenstein: the writer has one sign-system, the director another, and while it may be the job of the writer to think in the visual terms of the director, it is equally the director's job to find correlatives for the verbal text within the cinematic system. The issue returns to Steven Maras's previously considered question of whether the film should be regarded as merely the execution of a prior conception detailed in the screenplay. In any case, even if the script contains material that cannot be filmed, it can still be read.

Some screenplays go still further, and preface the script with descriptions of the characters in a list of the most significant dramatis personae. In the 18 October 1950 'final' draft for Hitchcock's *Strangers on a Train* (credited to Raymond Chandler and Czenzi Ormonde), two pages are devoted to paragraph-long descriptions of eight characters. The longest, of course, are for Bruno Anthony and Guy Haines, with Bruno's portrait being particularly novelistic:

> About twenty-five. He wears his expensive clothes with the tweedy nonchalance of a young man who has always had the best. He has the friendly eye of a stray puppy who wants to be liked, and the same wistful appeal for forgiveness when his impudence lands him in the doghouse. In the moments when his candor becomes shrewd calculation, it is all the more frightening because of his disarming charm and cultured exterior. It is as if a beautifully finished door, carved of the finest wood, were warping unnoticeably, and through the tiny cracks one could only glimpse the crumbling chaos hidden inside – and even then, not believe it.
>
> (p. 1)

After the opening description of the shoes, our first view of Bruno repeats the description from the first two sentences above; the same pattern is repeated with Guy, introduced at the same moment (p. 2).

Such descriptions can be viewed in several ways. They may, of course, be dismissed as merely the novelistic character sketches of a prose writer who has failed to realise the script in visual terms. Alternatively, the writer may be doing the very opposite: rather than continually interrupting the narrative to indicate aspects of character, providing a figurative insight into the character may enable the director and the actor to draw on this conception in the course of the film. The metaphor that describes Bruno has a temporal dimension: the door is 'warping unnoticeably'. The challenge to the director (and actor, and designer) is to translate this unfilmmable conceit into a cinematic equivalent, just as a similar challenge routinely confronts a screenwriter adapting a source novel.

The same script furnishes one of the most memorable introductions to a pair of characters in all of cinema: the feet – or, more precisely, the shoes – that serve to characterise Bruno and Guy. Chandler and Hitchcock rapidly fell out, and it has been widely accepted that Hitchcock simply abandoned Chandler's work and substituted Ormonde, an inexperienced and compliant writer, after which Chandler tried unsuccessfully to have his name removed from the credits.[16] However, Bill Krohn reports that, after previously submitting a short treatment on 18 July 1950, Chandler then wrote a second that anticipates the film's memorable opening:

> [Chandler's] next treatment, written between 29 and 12 August, begins with the image of the feet walking, although here and in all subsequent versions of the screenplay there are three tracking shots of the feet before they touch, rather than an alternating montage as in the film.... It is possible that Chandler ... misunderstood the idea of the feet, if it was in fact Hitchcock's, or else came up with it himself, but in a less 'cutty' form which Hitchcock simply never took time to change in the script.

Aside from one crucial scene 'where it looks as if Guy is going to kill Bruno's father, which Chandler [ironically] found absurd', 'all Hitchcock kept from [Chandler's] draft were the feet at the beginning.'[17]

It may be that this is all of Chandler that survives, but if so, there are other moments in the screenplay that follow a similar method. Towards the end, Bruno scratches around frantically for the incriminating cigarette lighter, which has fallen into a drain. Warners put out a press release to the effect that Hitchcock 'spent the afternoon directing Robert Walker's hand. At the end of the day the actor was exhausted, but Hitchcock was satisfied with his "performance"'.[18] The emphasis on the hand is anticipated in the script.

These are but two examples of a method of characterization that is peculiar to the screenplay among textual forms. As Sternberg points out, '[i]n contrast to the theatre, which must present the performer on stage as physically "whole", film is able to fragment space and objects as well as the human body' (p. 115). Samuel Beckett is radically different from almost all other playwrights in the frequency with which he *does* present the onstage body in a state of fragmentation: Nell and Nagg confined to dustbins with only their heads occasionally visible in *Endgame*, Winnie buried up to her neck in *Happy Days*, the isolated Mouth in *Not I*. As we shall see, there is also a cinematic quality to the use of voice-over in *Rockaby* and *Footfalls*. But Beckett is very much the exception that proves the rule.

In contrast to the excess of descriptive information in the realist novel, most screenplays indicate character with minimal recourse to modifiers. For example, *The Usual Suspects* (Bryan Singer, 1996, screenplay by Christopher McQuarrie), introduces two of its characters as 'Todd Hockney, a dark, portly man in his thirties', and 'Fred Fenster, a tall, thin man in his thirties'.[19] McQuarrie's screenplay is deservedly regarded as a masterpiece, but the characterization in this particular respect is pure Agatha Christie. The obvious alternative for a writer aiming to write 'cinematically' is to make a virtue of visual fragmentation by selecting a salient metonymic feature to indicate character. A part of the body stands for the whole body, or is selected as a particularly memorable feature, so that it simultaneously signifies something of the inner self while introducing a kind of shorthand method of reference to the individual.

There is a superficial resemblance to what E. M. Forster described as 'flat' characters in a novel, those who possess a single repeated quality that is not in contradiction with others. Some of Dickens's characters are represented by a dominant physical characteristic, such as the proto-detective Mr. Bucket in *Bleak House*:

> Mr. Bucket and his fat forefinger are much in consultation together under existing circumstances. When Mr. Bucket has a matter of this pressing interest under his consideration, the fat forefinger seems to rise, to the dignity of a familiar demon. He puts it to his ears, and it whispers information; he puts it to his lips, and it enjoins him to secrecy; he rubs it over his nose, and it sharpens his scent; he shakes it before a guilty man, and it charms him to his destruction. The Augurs of the Detective Temple invariably predict that when Mr. Bucket and that finger are in much conference, a terrible avenger will be heard of before long.
>
> Otherwise mildly studious in his observation of human nature, on the whole a benignant philosopher not disposed to be severe upon the follies of mankind, Mr. Bucket pervades a vast number of houses and strolls about an infinity of streets, to outward appearance rather languishing for want of an object. He is in the friendliest condition towards his species and will drink with most of them. He is free with his money, affable in his manners, innocent in his conversation – but through the placid stream of his life there glides an under-current of forefinger.[20]

What is noticeable, however, is how unnatural and *un*cinematic this seems: one cannot film 'an undercurrent of forefinger'. Dickens's method is more complex than at first appears, since the forefinger has become de-naturalised, and used to signify qualities that cannot easily be reconciled to the signifier itself. Another reason why it appears stranger than the seemingly comparable method of the screenplay, however, is simply because in the latter, bodily fragmentation is so ubiquitous as to have become naturalised, whereas in prose fiction it represents a conscious and seemingly perverse choice on the part of the author.

A concentration on the eyes is a staple of film theory and criticism: from the commonplace observation that the eyes are 'the windows of the soul', and therefore especially revealing of character, to the development of the 'eyeline match' and the need to avoid the direct look into the camera as principles of continuity editing, to more theoretical elaborations of the ways in which the 'eye' of the camera dramatises or destabilises the interaction of spectator and screen. Hitchcock's films have offered particularly fruitful illustrations: one thinks, for example, of the extraordinary crane shot that closes in on the eyes of the killer in *Young and Innocent* (1937), the dead eye of Marion Crane on the shower floor in *Psycho* (1960), or Norman Bates's unnerving stare into the camera at the end of the same film.

While the eyes may have a privileged status, the fragmentation of the body in general became almost a necessary condition of cinema once technological advances and innovations in editing in the early 1900s had allowed directors to dispense with the theatrical framing of the body in long-shot as the usual means of shooting character. Today, entire genres – the horror film, pornography, any post-watershed cop show with a wisecracking pathologist – exist partly to display the body in pieces. These are particular illustrations of the general ontology of film. Movies are almost compelled to cut up the body via close-ups and editing, although some will do so more self-consciously than others, and some will use the body part as a persistent signifier of character or motivation: the hands in *Pickpocket* (Robert Bresson, 1959), the nose in *Chinatown* (Roman Polanski, 1974).

In exploring the relationship of the fragment to the whole, this screenwriting method recalls the technical and psychoanalytical analysis of 'suture' – the stitching together of disparate shots in the continuity system to create an ideological effect of seamlessness – which has long been a staple of post-structuralist and Lacanian film theory. From this perspective, the film text can be deconstructed into its constituent elements to show that cinema, while offering an illusion of wholeness, never entirely succeeds in repressing its scandalous revelation that the human subject is not individual, indivisible, complete, but instead decentred, incomplete, lacking. Cinema, then, may be a representation of the 'mirror stage', that moment when a mother holds a baby before a mirror and pronounces its name. For the child, this is a profoundly ambivalent event: the previously involuntary motor functions of hands and feet now appear to be the movements of a complete, individual self, its identity confirmed by its possession of a name; yet that self is revealed to be separate from the mother who confers the name, and the figure in the mirror is itself illusory, a representation of the self that perceives it. And this is, perhaps, what 'character' and 'identification' mean in the cinema: the spectator temporarily loses the sense of self-possession, and becomes caught up – or 'stitched up', via the effects of suture – in the world of a protagonist who problematically represents the viewer without being identical to him or her.

This process is unique to the experience of cinema spectatorship, and has no direct analogy in the screenplay, which nevertheless seems to prefigure it through the process of bodily fragmentation. Instead of gaining an illusion of wholeness, the reader oscillates between experiencing the visible character as an accumulation of body parts and as a rough sketch of a figure containing minimal signifying detail. This sense of fragmentation need not be confined to the visible. The multiply authored screenplay, depending on its stage of development, will often include contributions from writers brought in to change or add to an individual role, perhaps to accommodate the wishes or requirements of a particular actor. For this reason or otherwise, it is not difficult to think of roles that have been supplied with what might be termed 'personality' rather than 'character'. 'Personality' confers a sense of individuality by means of non-essential attributes (Nicolas Cage's Beatles obsession in *The Rock* [Michael Bay, 1996], for example), instead of subordinating the character to its structural functions within the plot.[21]

It is with character that creative writing classes and screenwriting manuals on the one hand, and literary criticism on the other, diverge most sharply. The former tend to promote 'naïve' thinking: that is, for practical purposes they encourage the reader and writer to think of the characters and the story world as 'real'. This has been outmoded in literary criticism at least since the 1920s, and some of the most important screenwriters (such as Mamet) and screenwriting gurus (Robert McKee) have explicitly rejected it in favour of seeing character as both a textual construct, and a concept that is meaningful only when the individual character is seen in relation to the structure of the screenplay as a whole. It is what enables Mamet to argue that '[t]here *is* no character. There are only lines upon a page'.[22] Whatever the creative advantages of naïve thinking, then, the analysis of screenplays as texts should insist on the critical distinction between writing a screenplay and reading it.

Mamet describes the task of the writer as beginning with the creation of a 'logical structure', after which 'the ego of the structuralist hands the outline to the id, who will write the dialogue'.[23] From this point of view, to speak of a 'character' as an individual would be misleading, because in a properly structuralist analysis the character has no essence – no 'positive' terms – but gains its meaning only from how it is positioned within a set of relationships. A less purist approach might see a creative contradiction in screenplays such as *Taxi Driver* that make a heavy investment in individuality. On the one hand, the character is to be seen as an autonomous person with the capacity for choice: life is goal-oriented, and redemption is available. On the other hand, he is a function of the structure of the screenplay, which maps out his life for him.

However we view this question, character is inseparable from the structuring role that is generally argued to be the screenplay's primary function. More broadly, then, and to borrow Rick Altman's terms in his analysis of film genres, we may see Sternberg's 'elements' as local, semantic properties of the screenplay text, but to understand fully how screenplays operate we have to understand their syntactic organisation.[24]

Structure and structuralism

In *The Art of the Moving Picture* (1915, rev. 1922), and *The Photoplay: A Psychological Study* (1916), Vachel Lindsay and Hugo Munsterberg, respectively, argued in different ways that film was a visual medium, whereas literature and drama are linguistic. Therefore, language should play no part in the ideal film, and a scenario must be 'entirely imperfect and becomes a complete work of art only through the actions of the [director]'.[25] Such arguments imply that the literary writer is concerned solely with the aesthetic effects of words in combination, and that drama is merely dialogue. This overlooks the structuring force both of the dramatic text, and of the scenario in silent film in particular, and in cinema in general. More perceptive in this regard is Victor O. Freeburg's *The Art of Photoplay Making* (1918), which explores film as a synaesthetic medium and recognises the effects of time, fluidity, and arrangement, all of which imply the writer's structuring role. Freeburg thereby anticipates some of the discoveries of Soviet montage, and it is perhaps significant that both Vsevolod Pudovkin (in *The Film Scenario and Its Theory* [1928]) and Sergei Eisenstein were to write trenchantly on this function of the scenario. Eisenstein puts it simply: 'the basic and chief task of the shooting-script is in forming that compositional spine along which must move the development of the action, the composition of the episodes and the arrangement of their elements'.[26]

While this is arguably the major function of the screenplay, it provides one more explanation for its critical marginalisation, since it favours story structure over enunciation (the particular qualities and choice of words that are privileged in literary texts). Moreover, a reader cannot simply point to structure but, instead, has to infer it or construct it, usually retrospectively, since it is often only at the end of a screenplay that its shape becomes entirely clear. In this way the screenplay exemplifies at a purely structural level the temporal dynamics of anticipation, re-evaluation, and retrospection emphasised in literary reader-response theory.

Structuralism has always been most effective when used to analyse a large corpus of texts, especially those which are 'unliterary'. Literary criticism, by contrast, tends to privilege the individual, the different, the unique; indeed, it is arguably precisely these qualities, often combined with ideas of stylistic complexity and self-reflexivity, that constitutes literature itself. It is no accident that one of the most influential structuralist analyses, Roland Barthes' 'Introduction to the Structural Analysis of Narrative', used the James Bond novels to illustrate a structuralist methodology.[27] Barthes's predecessors include Vladimir Propp's *Morphology of the Folktale* (1928) and Joseph Campbell's *The Hero with a Thousand Faces* (1949), studies that seek to uncover the pattern – the 'monomyth', in Campbell's revealing word – connecting an enormous range of fairy tales and myths, respectively.

It is not implausible to regard the story departments of the major Hollywood studios as possessing an acutely structuralist sensibility long before even Propp's investigations. From the beginning, Hollywood was developing a story-gathering organisation and analysing the results generically, and soon began the systematic combing of the world story market. America was producing two thousand five hundred films a year by 1910, six thousand five hundred by 1915, and with the Western European powers crippled by war, 'by 1917 the American industry was making nearly all the world's motion pictures'.[28] The producer Dore Schary reported that in the 1940s the readers at Loew's offices in New York, Paris and London would, between them, provide synopses of almost 25,000 items per year; of these, just thirty to fifty would go into production.[29] From all those synopses the producers were looking for just a few things:

> First of all a story must be 'for us': it must fit our program, permit practical casting, and generally be ready to go. But it must always have wide appeal to all kinds of people, it must be adaptable to visual telling, contain fresh pictorial elements to satisfy the audience eye, must be built around strong and intriguing characters (preferably with a good part for one of our contract stars), permit telling on the screen in not much more than ninety minutes, be non-topical enough not to 'date' before we get our investment back. And it must sparkle with enough of that intangible showmanship.[30]

Hollywood also shows parallels with structuralist thinking in its approach to story development. Michael Hauge's popular screenwriting manual argues that a 'story idea ... can be expressed in a single sentence: It is a story about a ————— [character] who ————— [action]'.[31] One reason for this is crisply explained by one of the Hollywood producers in Mamet's stage satire *Speed-the-Plow*: 'You can't tell it to me in one sentence, they can't put it in *TV Guide*'.[32] Yet the idea that a text, or body of texts, is structured like a language is classically structuralist. Hauge's sentence has both a linear (in structuralist terms, syntagmatic) axis, and a vertical (paradigmatic) axis. The linear axis provides the story development; the vertical axis allows for the substitution of different characters and actions. Such a model can very rapidly generate enormous numbers of 'different' stories.

In his analysis of the recurrent structural forms of the folk tale, Propp does not speak of character in the ways that a traditional, humanist literary critic would; instead he speaks of a common structure to the tales, each of which consists of a selection of thirty-one possible 'functions', performed in an invariable sequence by the dramatis personae, who occupy seven 'spheres of action' (villain, donor, helper, princess, dispatcher, hero, and false hero). In an early example of the practical application of this model to a cinematic genre, Will Wright offered a 'liberalized version' of Propp's methodology. He incorporated 'attributes' as well as 'functions' into his analysis of the Western, noted the distinction between simple and collectively retold folk tales and the complex individual film text, and found 'unnecessarily restricting' Propp's insistence on an unvarying sequence of actions.[33]

The structuralist model has certain advantages as an analytical tool in the present context. It is very clear; applicable to both adapted and original screenplays; helps to account for the recurrence of narrative paradigms across different periods, cultures, and media; suggests that even most art-house films operate according to more codified generic demands than is the case with "literary" fiction; and shows how the individual screenplay is intertextually related to a large number of others. Sensitively applied, it can provide a particularly convincing demonstration of the internal structuring mechanisms of the individual screenplay. And it also helps to differentiate the screenplay from the film text: it is the latter that challenges the system of the screenplay by inescapably introducing the structurally redundant signifiers of the actor's appearance and performance, for example, and the general serendipity of production. The primary theoretical weakness of classical structuralism is that it has an unwarranted confidence in the stability of the system, as if stories were chess games that may have infinite number but that all obey the rules of a game confined to sixty-four squares. As an analytical tool, it is universally applicable – any narrative film can be expressed within Hauge's sentence or Campbell's monomyth – yet for this reason, lacks discriminatory power.

Most important from the present perspective, however, is that examining the screenplay as a self-reflexive structure problematises analysis that breaks it down into its constituent elements. The meaning of each aspect of the text is bound up with other, answering signs: 'Rosebud' changes its meaning, the action and report mode becomes a commentary on the nature of the character, an individual scene acquires its meaning through its position within larger sequences, and so on. Consequently the screenplay should make its own sense within its own structure, even though this verbal text will also be read in relation to an external, cinematic sign-system, so that its fragmentation into discrete elements suitable for reading by individual professionals in no way prohibits the reading of it as a text like any other.

8
The Dialogue Text

Dialogue in film has received very little attention in comparison to the technical and theoretical sophistication of image-based studies of cinema. Those attempting to establish the credentials of film as an art form have tended to emphasise its medium-specific qualities: in particular, the expressive possibilities unleashed by the editorial juxtaposition of moving images in a linear sequence. From this perspective, the introduction of sound in the late 1920s represents a retrograde step because it arrested the camera's freedom of movement and compromised the integrity of the medium, although Busby Berkeley's work for Warner Brothers amply demonstrates that the technical difficulties of marrying sound to the moving camera had largely been eliminated by 1933. Moreover, 'silent' movies had almost always had some form of aural accompaniment, from the commentary of early exhibitors to the near-ubiquitous use of a musical score, improvised or otherwise.

As Mary Deveraux observes, '[t]he first sound film, *The Jazz Singer*, brought not sound but a new kind of sound ... [t]he real change brought about by synchronization was speech'.[1] It is dialogue specifically, rather than sound in general, that preoccupied much subsequent analysis of the medium. Devereaux surveys a range of theoreticians and practitioners, from Alexander Dovzhenko to René Clair to Charlie Chaplin, to show that there was a 'split conception of sound' in which the ideal was 'a wordless cinema, not a soundless one'.[2] For example, the theoreticians of Soviet montage, including Eisenstein and Pudovkin, were excited by the possibilities of counterpointing sound and image; but the problem with the voice specifically, as far as Eisenstein was concerned, was that it presented a kind of rhythmic tautology, since (in Devereaux's summation) 'the sound of human speech exactly correspond[ed] to a shot of a man talking'.[3]

The theoretical foundations of this position are perhaps most influentially expressed in Rudolf Arnheim's *Film as Art*, first published in German in 1933, significantly just after sound had eliminated silent film production. Devereaux shows that Arnheim's objections to dialogue derive from an aesthetic and philosophical essentialism, which holds that artistic value is inextricable from the materials peculiar to each medium. He is therefore obliged to enforce the boundaries that separate film from other arts, one consequence being that the sound film, which utilises a form of speech with theatrical antecedents, must be dismissed as (in Devereaux's word) a 'mongrel'.[4] Hence Arnheim's insistence that pantomime of the Chaplin variety was preferable to speech as a medium of human communication in cinema. In the slightly more liberal and equally influential view of Siegfried Kracauer, '[a]ll the successful attempts at an integration of the spoken word have one characteristic in common: they play down dialogue with a view to reinstating the visuals'.[5]

Although this hierarchical conception of film is still dominant in many areas of film study, Devereaux's conclusion that Arnheim 'refus[es] to see film as a continually evolving art form' and 'elevates the practices of a particular moment in film history to the principles of film art'[6] expresses an increasingly widespread view. As Noël Carroll observes, to object to sound films on the basis that they are theatrical is illogical: the specificity thesis itself shows that they are distinct. On the other hand, if one believes that the one can contaminate the other, then neither can in fact be unique and self-contained, and the specificity thesis falls. The plain conclusion is that art forms tend to be both more hybrid and more varied in their applicability than the 'specificity thesis' can concede.[7] The only result to be expected from creating a hierarchy of channels of communication within a medium as synaesthetic as cinema is a canon in which certain films will be excluded purely because they fail to meet a narrowly restrictive set of criteria. As Devereaux, Claudia Sternberg, and Sarah Kozloff all point out, certain genres are almost unthinkable without dialogue, while many others possess distinctively genre-specific modes of speech, as the second half of Kozloff's *Overhearing Film Dialogue* demonstrates in its analysis of westerns, screwball comedies, gangster films, and melodramas.

Although the prominence of the specificity thesis in film studies helps to explain the scant critical attention to screenwriting dialogue, even those scholars who have attempted to establish the screenplay as a serious form of writing have tended either to accord dialogue a relatively marginal status, or to have distinguished it insufficiently from stage dialogue, everyday conversation, or the film actor's vocal delivery. Kevin Boon's chapter on 'dialogue as action' in *Script Culture and the American Screenplay*, for example, is inexplicably devoted to a scene from *Glengarry Glen Ross*, which David Mamet's screenplay reproduces almost verbatim from the same writer's original play for the stage. Consequently, Boon's analysis of the screenplay dialogue might with equal effect be applied to Mamet's published play text, and Boon discusses it in terms similar to those adopted by the theatre critics he cites.[8] Sternberg's chapter on the dialogue text occupies just fifteen pages, and although her account is much more critically rigorous than Boon's, it is noticeably sketchier than her analysis of the scene text, which at 121 pages takes up around half of her book.

Screenwriting manuals, too, routinely ignore dialogue almost completely. Robert McKee's discussion of dialogue in *Story* begins on page 388, occupies six pages, and concludes by counselling that '[t]he best advice for writing film dialogue is *don't*'.[9] In *Screenplay*, Syd Field simply tells the aspiring screenwriter not to worry about dialogue (it 'can always be cleaned up'), to remember that 'the more you do [it] the easier it gets', and to wait for the characters to 'start talking to you'.[10] Lew Hunter's *Screenwriting* devotes seven pages to dialogue, Michael Hauge's *Writing Screenplays that Sell* twelve, and so on.[11] The ostensible reason for this is that as far as the screenwriter's job is concerned, story or structure are assumed, no doubt rightly, to take priority over dialogue. This view is often accompanied by some variant of the specificity thesis: '[n]ever write a line of dialogue when you can create a visual expression', as McKee puts it.[12] Even granted that the structuring role of the screenplay is paramount, however, Kozloff demonstrates that the recommendations regarding dialogue itself that are routinely prescribed in screenwriting manuals '*have never been followed by American cinema*'.[13]

In short, the screenplay's dominant element proportionally is also, apparently, the least important critically. Devereaux puts it succinctly: 'Film dialogue is presumed to lack literary value or to possess it and lack cinematic value'.[14] Such constructions obscure the particular qualities of screenplay dialogue by substituting an artificial criterion of value for a critical set of discriminations. Three major distinctions need to be made in attempting to identify any unique qualities of screenplay dialogue: what distinguishes film and stage dialogue from everyday conversation is the implied or actual presence of an auditor in the cinema or theatre; what distinguishes film from stage dialogue is the relative fluidity of space and time in cinema; and what distinguishes screenplay dialogue from film dialogue is that the former is written and the latter is spoken.

Sternberg argues that the screenplay offers an effect of more 'natural conversation' than that of the stage play, and that 'deviations from natural conversation' within the screenplay are due less to any quality of the language itself than to the technical devices – voice-over, split-screen, and direct address to the camera – by which it is mediated.[15] Such arguments are in a long tradition of film theory that seeks to ensure that dialogue does not compete for prominence with the visual. As Kracauer puts it, '[p]ractically all responsible critics agree that it heightens cinematic interest to reduce the weight and volume of the spoken word so that dialogue after the manner of the stage yields to natural, life-like speech'.[16] It is hard to agree. Kozloff proposes that 'a proportion of dialogue in every film serves primarily as a representation of ordinary conversational activities',[17] but it has to be stressed that it is only a proportion, and only a representation. 'Natural conversation' and 'ordinary conversational activities' are inherently problematic terms, but they serve very well if regarded not as categories within film dialogue, but as necessarily distinct from it. Unlike 'natural conversation', film and theatrical dialogue has not one but two addressees (at least): the character(s) to whom the words are spoken within the story world, and the spectator in the auditorium. It is not just the actor but the *character* who is speaking dialogue that has been written with this dual communicational model in mind. Kozloff quotes the words of drama critic Jean Chothia:

> The actor must seem to speak what in reality he recites ... it is not the hearing of the words by the interlocutor that completes the exchange, as it is in everyday speech, but the witnessing and inter-preting of both the utterance and the response by the audience. Much of the particular effect of drama derives from the gap between two ways of hearing, that of the interlocutor on the stage and that of the audience, and from the audience's consciousness of the gap ... dialogue, however natural it may appear, must be most *un*naturally resonant with meaning and implication.[18]

Both screenwriting and the writing of stage dialogue consciously or otherwise take this dual audience into consideration.

This is not to minimise the differences between the two media. More so than with theatre, perhaps, 'films disguise the extent to which the words are truly meant for the off-screen listener',[19] although the film-specific modes of address, such as voice-over, that Sternberg identifies are but the most obvious 'deviations from natural conversation'. Drawing on Manfred Pfister's *The Theory and Analysis of Drama* for purposes of comparison and contrast, and perhaps finding many parallels as a result, Sternberg lists may of the 'auxiliary' kinds of stage dialogue that are rarely found in cinema. These include 'the messenger's report, teichoscopy, word-scenery or expository narrative'.[20] The primary explanation for this is that a film can combine several techniques in order to make speeches and dialogues shorter and to create a more fluid presentation of space and time. Such devices involve various ways of directing the audience's attention as to whether image or dialogue is more important, the use of radio and telephone conversations, a greater number of speakers in small roles, and other visual techniques, such as montage. In practice, however, the relative fluidity of space and time in cinema means that cinematic dialogue is radically different from stage dialogue, as we shall see in the discussion below of the particular functions of both.

Not surprisingly, the critics who have fought a rearguard action against the marginalisation of dialogue are almost invariably scholars of the general film text rather than of the written word specifically. Devereaux is 'concerned not with words as written but as spoken', and with 'the particular juxtaposition of aural and visual elements', so that '[i]nstead of proposing that we approach film dialogue as a literary text, I recommend we approach it as part of the cinematic text'.[21] Similarly, Kozloff seeks 'to understand how spoken words create meaning in *film*'.[22] Yet it does not follow that the performance of the dialogue will invariably be preferable to a silent reading. As Richard Corliss observes, a director 'can do one of three things [with a screenplay]: ruin it, shoot it, or improve it',[23] and the same may be said of an actor with the words on the page. In any case, directors and actors will always, by definition, produce something that is *different* from the written text. As film historian and commentator David Thomson remarks, 'I don't know that there is any reliable correlation between scripts and films. I'm not even sure that there should be in a medium so open to the vagaries of performance, accident, shifts in the light, or improvisational brainstorms'.[24]

Philip Brophy observes that '[w]hen the written becomes spoken, a whole range of potential clashes arise between the act of enunciation, the role of recitation and the effect of utterance, in that, for example, one can vocally "italicize" an earnest statement, just as one can compassionately "underline" a self-deprecating quip'. This captures well the slipperiness of cinematic speech in general, which is routinely complicated and de-naturalised by the recognition that it is at once a recitation of a written text and an address delivered to multiple audiences simultaneously.[25] In practice, it is almost impossible for the film actor to disguise the act of recitation in the delivery of the dialogue – an ultra-realistic experiment such as *Nil by Mouth* (Gary Oldman, 1997) may be an exception – even should s/he want to. This is largely because dialogue in the screenplay text is written with certain structures and effects in mind that differ from those of everyday conversation. Moreover, a silent reading will be different from a vocal performance: any performance of any text will inflect it in various ways, while an unvocalised reading of the text will often cause the dialogue to be experienced relatively free of affect; hence the common phenomenon of dialogue in prose fiction that reads well on the page but fails utterly when spoken aloud. Still more generally, the meaning of any statement in any film is produced not simply by the soundtrack but by the interaction of word and image.

While it is important to bear these distinctions in mind, the studies of film dialogue by Brophy, Devereaux, and Kozloff clearly have a value to any study of the written screenplay text. In particular, Kozloff's chapter on nine 'functions of dialogue in narrative film' works very well as a provisional study of screenplay dialogue – even more so, perhaps, than the discussion of six 'structural and stylistic variables' that follows it, and which explicitly 'concentrate[s] on the dialogue as a verbal text'.[26] Six of the nine 'functions' concern narrative communication: exposition, narrative causality, speech acts, revelation of character, effects of realism, and attempts to direct the emotions of the spectator. The remaining three functions are more eclectic: 'aesthetic effect', which concerns 'exploitation of the resources of language'; 'ideological persuasion' ('thematic messages/authorial commentary/allegory and interpretation'); and the commercially driven exploitation of 'opportunities for "star turns"' for particular actors.[27] Of course, Kozloff concedes that these categories do not exhaust the possibilities: philosophical digression, for example, is rare in American film, but Quentin Tarantino's *Reservoir Dogs* (1992) and *Pulp Fiction* (1994) both contain significant, if deeply ironic, examples. The six 'variables', meanwhile, concern the amount of dialogue within scenes, the number of speaking and non-speaking participants, the nature of their conversational interaction, the language peculiar to individual speakers, the use of foreign languages, dialects, and jargon, and the patterns of dialogue within individual films.

The critical distinctions outlined above offer a range of possible approaches to the analysis of screenplay dialogue. We shall now turn to concrete examples, beginning with two kinds of dialogue commonly analysed in theatre plays.

Deixis and offstage space

One of the most important functions of stage dialogue is deixis. This is the set of signs that indicates relationships between speakers and between the speaker and the surrounding, on-stage space. It includes personal pronouns such as 'I' and 'you', adverbs of place and time such as 'here' and 'now', and demonstrative pronouns such as 'this' and 'that'. By implication, too, the definition of the spatial limitations of the onstage space helps to define its own relationship to the offstage world. Because deixis is almost unavoidable in the playwright's task of establishing relationships of space and time in the theatre, it is arguably 'the most significant linguistic feature – both statistically and functionally – in the drama'. It has been argued, for instance, that even in such a highly poetic and conceptual play as *Hamlet*, more than 5,000 out of 29,000 words are deictic.[28]

As well as establishing these on-stage relationships, dramatic dialogue ordinarily does far more work than film dialogue in creating an imaginative link between the scene that is presented to the spectator, and offstage or off-screen space. To cite only the most obvious example, the theatre audience of a play by Harold Pinter is wholly reliant on the characters for information about the world beyond the room. As Pfister remarks, '[t]his sort of semantic interpretation of the contrast between interior and exterior space is particularly common in modern dramas written under the intellectual auspices of existentialism'.[29] There is an insistent pressure on the Pinter character to justify his or her existence in the dramatic here and now; appeals to whatever may be happening or may have happened outside the room, in the past, are to be treated with suspicion. When Pinter adapted *The Caretaker* for the 1963 film version directed by Clive Donner, he created several new exterior scenes that, in cinematic fashion, 'opened out' the action. While largely wordless, these exterior scenes significantly alter the ontological status of the interior episodes. Combined with a number of cuts to the lengthier monologues, and some additional new writing, they make the screenplay of *The Caretaker* a substantially different text to the stage version.[30]

It was argued early in the history of film criticism that the restrictions of time and place confronting the dramatist make writing for the theatre a more exacting discipline than writing for the screen.[31] This is possibly another contributory factor in the general evaluation of the two forms, since the essentially functional and expository demands of deictic dialogue are significantly reduced in film. Indications of camera movement, close-ups, establishing shots, and easy cutting between locations separate in space and time – for example in the now clichéd use of the expository montage sequence – are merely some of the most obvious illustrations of the screenplay's capacity to provide alternatives to deixis and verbal presentation of off-screen space. Moreover, the comparative brevity of scenes enables the writer and director to return at will to situations that in drama must be developed continuously and at greater length.

The differences between screenplays, films, and stage plays in their treatment of deixis and space, and the potential for confusion between them, are well illustrated by a consideration of the screenplays for two different versions of Shakespeare's *Henry V*. In the introduction to the published screenplay of the 1944 version, Laurence Olivier described his *Henry V* as 'perhaps, the first serious attempt to make a truly Shakespearian film'. In this, Olivier felt that he was simply exploiting a notable quality of the plays themselves. 'Shakespeare, in a way, "wrote for the films"' by 'splitting up ... the action into a multitude of small scenes', while 'more than one of his plays seems to chafe against the cramping restrictions of the stage'.[32]

Certainly, in *Henry V* Olivier exploits the space-time fluidity of film. He at first attempts a reproduction of Shakespearean staging, by having the Chorus speak within the confines of the Globe theatre. Then, beginning with the Prologue to Act II, the camera dissolves the stage walls by moving from the Globe to an obviously theatrical-looking ship that nevertheless is not contained within the confines of the stage, before moving to scenes that are clearly not to be regarded as being played in front of the theatre audience seen at the beginning. Yet it is not quite accurate to say with Olivier that '[f]rom the very beginning the play suggests a film'.[33] On the contrary, the play is unique in the Shakespearean canon in the degree to which it insists from the beginning that this is a play and nothing but a play, as the Prologue explicates with exceptional richness the deictic problem of using stage space to represent scenes that are imaginatively present yet physically absent.

Kenneth Branagh also saw the play as 'tremendously "filmic"', but his version was in part constructed in conscious opposition to Olivier's 'nationalistic and militaristic' wartime production. Instead, Branagh was excited by the prospect of using 'close-ups and low-level dialogue to draw the audience deep into the human side of this distant medieval world'. His original intention was to have the Chorus begin to speak in a disused theatre before 'throwing open scenery doors to allow the camera to travel outside and into the "real" world of our film'.[34] Early in the writing process, however, the decision was taken to situate the Chorus 'in a deserted film studio' with 'a semi-constructed set'.[35] Possibly to accentuate the cinematic effect Branagh cut lines 19–27, in which the Chorus, conceding the necessary limitations of stage representation, asks the audience to 'Piece out our imperfections with your thoughts' by imagining that the 'monarchies' of England and France are contained 'within the girdle of these walls'. Like Olivier, Branagh felt that the Prologue 'can be interpreted as alluding to the mystery and imagination employed in the medium of film'.[36]

Yet however impressive the respective films are in accommodating the Shakespearean text to the demands of cinema, they nevertheless remain bound by the essentially theatrical deixis. Russell Jackson has recently noted, in a discussion of Shakespeare on film, that Elizabethan plays may resemble cinematic adaptations of theatrical texts in the ways in which they 'open out' the action; yet 'changes of place and time' are generally indicated simply by 'statements in the dialogue'.[37] *Henry V* compels both Branagh and Olivier to find a space – a theatre or a film set – equivalent to that in which the Chorus speaks, and to preserve, with only very minor cuts, the rousing words that establish a spatial as well as temporal connection between the Chorus and the audience. This in turn is provoked by a desire to preserve a kind of authenticity (for all the radical cutting of the text later in the screenplay, Branagh wanted the film to remain 'Shakespearean in spirit'[38]) doubly prompted by traditional notions of adaptation and by the pre-eminent place of Shakespeare within the literary canon. A much more radical approach, difficult to visualise in film but perhaps attempted by Peter Greenaway in *Prospero's Books* (1991), might have been an attempt to realise in cinematic terms the insight of director Peter Brook, who once declared that 'the power of a Shakespeare play on stage stems from the fact that it happens "nowhere"'.[39]

Speech acts

Devereaux and Kozloff reject any assumption that speech stands opposed to action; speech itself is action. Drawing on the work of Seymour Chatman and other theorists of literary narrative, Kozloff notes that dialogue itself can itself often be a key story event, as in the disclosure of a secret or a declaration of love. She also enumerates several different kinds of conversational interaction, noting that in each case the effect depends on the dramatic context, and the degree to which the speaker is successful in securing the understanding of the on-screen listener and the off-screen audience. For example, elliptical dialogue may signal to the audience that the characters are intimate, and part of our interactive engagement with the film will lie in trying to penetrate or decode a private language. Alternatively, the characters may misunderstand one another, leading to 'dialogues of the deaf'. The progress or interruption of dialogue can also reveal or change the nature of a relationship, as in overlapping dialogue, the deployment of 'tag questions', or the silencing of a character, including by the use of 'toppers' (killer lines that attempt to shut down a conversation and often conclude a scene).

Studying dialogue in this way naturally leads both Kozloff and Devereaux to mention speech-act theory, a philosophy of language developed by J. L. Austin. Austin began by proposing a distinction between 'constative' (proposition-bearing) utterances, and 'performative' utterances in which 'the issuing of the utterance is the performing of an action'. He eventually concluded that the opposition was false, since 'stating is performing an act ... It is essential to realize that "true" and "false", like "free" and "unfree", do not stand for anything simple at all; but only for a general dimension of being a right or proper thing to say as opposed to a wrong thing, in these circumstances, to this audience, for these purposes and with these intentions'.[40]

It is easy to see why speech-act theory has proved to be a productive method of analysing drama. As Andrew K. Kennedy observes, 'the very names given by Austin and other philosophers to "the speech act" and to "performative" utterances points to their relevance to both conversation and to dramatic/theatrical performance'.[41] Austin E. Quigley, for example, brilliantly clarifies the dialogue of Pinter's plays by recognising that apparent contradictions and uncertainties about facts, and about the past, are really the result of the characters' attempts 'to negotiate a mutual reality'. This challenges the referential theory of meaning as regards not only facts but also 'personality', which is not individual (or indivisible), but instead 'is a function of a compromise negotiated in a particular relationship'.[42]

Although speech-act theory can be relevant to the discussion of film dialogue, its range of application is much more restricted. It does not adequately serve the various kinds of dialogue detailed later in this chapter, principally because dialogic exchanges in cinema tend to be much shorter than in theatre. It is revealing that Boon, in a chapter designed to elucidate the quality of film dialogue, selects a scene from *Glengarry Glen Ross*, a stage play transposed to the screen by the same writer, David Mamet. In the scene in question, one of the real estate salesmen, Moss, persuades his colleague, Aaronow, to participate in a robbery:

> AARONOW: I mean are you actually *talking* about this, or are we just ...
> MOSS: No, we're just ...
> AARONOW: We're just *'talking'* about it.
> MOSS: We're just *speaking* about it.[43]

Each character is self-consciously aware of using language to create relationships, in the literal sense of being particularly interested in defining precisely what words like 'talking', 'speaking', and 'saying' mean. This is part of a verbal negotiation of a contract by which they attempt to establish precisely the rules according to which the discussion is to be conducted. In the conversation above it appears that Moss has established a fine linguistic distinction, in which 'talking' is serious business while 'speaking' is merely idle or hypothetical banter. But this turns out not to be so at all: Moss almost immediately reassures Aaronow that 'We're just *talking*', thereby setting up an opposition not between 'talking' and 'speaking' but between 'talking' and *'talking'*. It soon transpires that even this remodelled distinction is of no use to Aaronow, who is startled to discover that 'we sat down to eat *dinner*, and here I'm a *criminal* ...', even though 'I thought that we were only talking'.[44]

Aaronow has been duped not just by the rule-governed nature of dialogue, but by what the Russian linguist Roman Jakobson called the 'phatic' or 'contact' function of verbal communication. These are 'messages serving primarily to establish, to prolong, or to discontinue communication, to check whether the channel works', and which 'may be displayed by a profuse exchange of ritualized formulas, by entire dialogues with the mere purport of prolonging communication'.[45] Aaronow repeatedly checks with Moss to confirm that the channel is working, and that the rules are clear, but Moss in fact has effectively severed the channel and made up the rules to suit himself.

The possibility of theatrical simulation challenges the very idea of "successful" performatives, which depend for their effect on a distinction between the genuine and the counterfeit. In fact, Austin's observation of 'infelicities' acknowledges the possibility of a mimetic, insincere replication of a speech act; and 'infelicity is an ill to which *all* acts are heir which have the general character of a ritual or ceremonial, all *conventional* acts'.[46] The danger is that the conventional procedures which constitute the successful performance of an illocutionary act by themselves eliminate the possibility of establishing the sincerity of the person who performs them, and Kennedy is certainly right to argue that '"Sincerity" can seldom be taken for granted in dramatic dialogue'.[47] The same is true of film dialogues, but since they are ordinarily briefer than those of stage plays, the opportunities for tracing the establishment, maintenance, and dismantling of a speech-act relationship are relatively limited. Even Mamet's screenplay adaptation of *Glengarry Glen Ross* follows the familiar cinematic method of breaking up some of the lengthier duologues by repeatedly intercutting between two scenes, each of which is self-contained in the stage play version.

Polyfunctionality

Of course, neither dramatic nor film dialogue is restricted to the establishment of personal and spatial relationships. Pfister observes that dramatic language is 'polyfunctional', and distinguishes six kinds: 'referential' (as when a character gives a report of events that happened off-stage, in the past); 'expressive' (the character reveals information about his or her thoughts or emotions, either to another character or, in the case of soliloquies, to the self and the audience); 'appellative' (as when a character addresses another in an attempt to influence or persuade – essentially, this is a speech-act function); phatic; 'metalingual' (a variant of the phatic in which the code itself becomes the object of discussion: the dialogue about 'talking' and 'speaking' in *Glengarry Glen Ross* provides an excellent illustration); and 'poetic', which refers to an 'external communication system and not to the communication processes taking place between the various figures'. An example is Shakespearean blank verse, which must be addressing the external but not the internal communication system, since 'if the opposite were true, the figures would presumably express their astonishment at this "unnatural" manner of speaking'.[48]

A given utterance may possess more than one of these functions, and all of them may be used in film as well as in stage dialogue. The difference lies in the proportion of speech that belongs to each function. These proportions vary according to genre: a highly realistic film drama such as *Nil by Mouth* will display a preponderance of appellative and phatic speech as the characters struggle to maintain their personal relationships, while a Marx Brothers comedy will make great play with the metalingual and phatic functions. As Kozloff observes, however, film dialogue generally minimises the phatic function.[49] Post-Pinter, and for reasons discussed more fully below, the expressive function has come to be treated with great suspicion by many writers for both stage and film. The expressive and referential functions are instead staples of television soap operas, operating as a kind of short-hand for character development and action respectively, in a genre in which significant quantities of drama have to be written and filmed on a daily basis.

While all of these linguistic functions are equally available to stage and screenwriters, the greater visual flexibility of cinema means that dialogue tends to be more compressed in the screenplay. The resources of editing and camera enable the film director 'to select, emphasize, undercut, distract, reveal, or deform the filmgoer's interpretation', while 'the phenomenological absence of actors from the filmgoers' space and reality ... allows the spectators' cathexis with the characters more free play'.[50] This also impacts on the proportional distribution of the functions. Broadly speaking, film writing tends to take advantage of the increased opportunities for visual representation to minimise certain kinds of dialogue. Scenic representation substitutes for the referential function; a good screenplay is likely to be deeply suspicious of relying on the expressive function to exhibit much truth-value in character interaction; and character relationships may be developed by means of metonymic visual representation and scenic juxtaposition, with a consequently lesser proportion of appellative and phatic dialogue than is commonly found in theatre.

Certain gangster movies, however, especially those of the post-Pinter era, have made great play of the sense of threat that can be generated by the phatic function, as in the unforgettable conversation about hamburgers in *Pulp Fiction*:

JULES:	Looks like me and Vincent caught you boys at breakfast. Sorry 'bout that. What'cha eatin'?
BRETT:	Hamburgers.
JULES:	Hamburgers. The cornerstone of any nutritious breakfast. What kinda hamburgers?
BRETT:	Cheeseburgers.
JULES:	No, no, no, no, no. I mean where did you get 'em? McDonald's, Wendy's, Jack-in-the-Box, where?
BRETT:	Big Kahuna Burger.

JULES: Big Kahuna Burger. That's that Hawaiian burger joint.
              I heard they got some tasty burgers.[51]

The dialogue appears disproportionate in three different ways: the prolonged examination of trivial topics (Tarantino announced himself to the world in the conversation about Madonna at the beginning of *Reservoir Dogs* [1992]), the imbalance between this verbal frivolity and the dramatic situation in which the reader or spectator infers that murder is imminent, and the quantity of such dialogue in a medium that is routinely presumed to emphasise the visual.

The dialogue about hamburgers creates a sense of threat, not only because we have already seen Jules and his partner Vincent preparing themselves for violence against Brett and his associates, but because of an effect comparable to that of the extended shot in cinema. The theory of suture argues that the reverse shot in classical Hollywood editing exists partly to quell a potential unease. A single shot implicitly poses questions: who is looking at this, and why? The reverse shot reassuringly fills in the empty space that might be occupied by this hypothetical voyeur (and is in fact occupied by the camera), revealing that nothing is there that shouldn't be present in the diegetic world of the film. This creates the illusion that there is no narration; the events just exist, and they are not being shown to us by a mediating agent.

The above dialogue in *Pulp Fiction* creates an effect similar to that of an unanswered shot. After a while – the discussion about fast food continues for two pages – the reader is likely either to wonder why so much time is being expended on this particular dialogue (in effect, the narrator becomes present as a figure of whom such questions may be asked), or will begin to consider the dialogue as an object worthy of attention in itself (fulfilling the 'poetic' function). A conversation that would ordinarily be regarded as phatic – idle chit-chat as a means of keeping the communicational channels open – is therefore both poetic and performative, since in context it constitutes a form of aggression.

Pinter can be credited with first developing the theatrical possibilities of such dialogic forms in what have been termed his 'comedies of menace', but it is arguable that the screenplay routinely places greater emphasis than theatre plays on the poetic function. Because the realistic stage play relies on dialogue to develop character relationships, a certain suspension of disbelief is required on the part of the audience. Monologues and dialogues are liable to be lengthier and more syntactically articulate within the internal communication system than is to be expected in 'real life', and constant references to the metalinguistic and poetic functions would break this illusion by making the audience aware of its own status within the external communication system. Because the screenplay can more flexibly develop such relationships by means of visual representation, dialogue more frequently has the effect of addressing the external audience as well as, or even instead of, the internal audience. Such cinema-specific verbal phenomena as the one-liner and the voice-over consequently tend to call attention to themselves as constructs, as something *written*; and in this lies much of the textual specificity and pleasure of the screenplay.

Pfister's poetic function has much in common with the eclectic range of possibilities that Kozloff groups under the function of 'aesthetic effect'. As well as carefully patterned dialogue, she includes in this category jokes, irony, and internal storytelling. As the example of *Pulp Fiction* shows, however, any element of screenplay dialogue can take on a poetic function simply by virtue of being expressed within such a tightly controlled form.

Duologues

Abraham Polonsky's script for *Force of Evil* provides another frequently cited example of a script in which the dialogue attains a poetic quality, largely because of its rhythmic cadence. Film noir in general, indeed, tends to be marked by dialogue that draws attention to its own construction. Partly this is derived from some of the source novels, and the fact that 'hard-boiled' writers frequently gravitated towards Hollywood themselves. More importantly, it is because the world view of these films is of a ruthless existential masculinity that affirms itself in what Hemingway called 'grace under pressure'. This is frequently shown not in physical action but in the ability to respond to situations of extreme emotional intensity with verbal toughness and sangfroid, which is so mannered that it seems not to issue from within the situation itself, but instead to be a comment upon it by a character possessing an almost psychopathic detachment from events.

For example, in *Double Indemnity* (Billy Wilder, 1944), Walter Neff calls at the home of a client, Dietrichson, to sell him a renewal on his car insurance. Finding that he is out, Neff immediately becomes captivated by Dietrichson's wife, Phyllis, and starts flirting with her:

PHYLLIS: There's a speed limit in this state, Mr. Neff. Forty-five miles an hour.
NEFF: How fast was I going, officer?

PHYLLIS:	I'd say about ninety.
NEFF:	Suppose you get down off your motorcycle and give me a ticket.
PHYLLIS:	Suppose I let you off with a warning this time.
NEFF:	Suppose it doesn't take.
PHYLLIS:	Suppose I have to whack you over the knuckles.
NEFF:	Suppose I bust out crying and put my head on your shoulder.
PHYLLIS:	Suppose you try putting it on my husband's shoulder.
NEFF:	That tears it.[52]

The impossibly smooth patterning of the dialogue takes place in Pfister's 'external communication system', but internally shows the characters playing a kind of verbal poker in which they must keep raising the stakes on the same root phrase. This strategy, by which erotic or violent tension is both contained and intensified by excessively mannered and articulate language, has been anticipated in the preceding scene, to which we shall return later, in which Neff's voice-over hints not only at the nature of his relationship with Phyllis, but also at the plot that they will hatch against her husband. The above exchange between Neff and Phyllis is a flashback inside the frame of Neff's voice-over, and both his monologue and the characters' dialogue function as commentaries upon the scene, even though the internal communication system unfolds in the here and now. This has the overall strategic effect of constructing the characters as possessing a sufficiently extreme degree of emotional detachment to make their almost whimsical decision to kill Dietrichson appear at least aesthetically credible.

The one-liner

In 2005 the American Film Institute published as part of its centenary celebrations its list of the top 100 quotations in the history of American movies.[53] Almost without exception, these were short, pithy one-liners of the kind that frequently acquire a resonance beyond the film in which they are first uttered. One-liners often furnish the most prominent signifier of a film or a star, being recycled as a movie's 'tag line' or in the 'Eastwood/Stallone/Schwarzenegger model of exploitation production[, which] has consistently centred not only on the self-defined iconic status of their personae, but also on the trailer whose climactic point is the delivery of a one-liner'.[54] And many lines from cinema have crossed the boundary into broader areas of cultural and political life, as when an anti-trespass law passed in several American states in 1985 became popularly known as the 'make my day law', after the three words uttered in *Sudden Impact* (Clint Eastwood, 1983) that most comprehensively define the character of Harry Callaghan (Eastwood) in the 'Dirty Harry' movies.

In 2003 the Writers Guild of America made prominent use of famous lines from the movies in a campaign to highlight the importance of screenwriters. In one sense, this gave writers their due as the providers of one of the most pleasurable qualities of films, as any number of anthologies of film quotations attests. Yet the Guild's own arbitration procedures for screen credit give a much higher priority to structure than to dialogue.[55] The Writers Guild itself, then, tends to de-emphasise the one quality of screenwriting that might most clearly establish a writer's individual style, and that most successfully translates from the written text into the cinema.

One reason for this is simply that the nature of much Hollywood rewriting in fact effaces authorial identity, with the spoken dialogue becoming an agglomeration of lines from many disparate sources. But another is a consequence of the reduced importance of deixis and speech acts in comparison to theatrical dialogue. The one-liner frequently offers a sardonic or ironic comment upon a scene, rather than contributing to its dramatic development; the use of such lines to close a scene is ubiquitous in the James Bond movies, for example. As Brophy observes in 'Read My Lips: Notes on the Writing and Speaking of Film Dialogue', the one-liner always has the effect of being recited, and therefore *written*, rather than of simply being spoken. 'In all the important scenes in a Bond movie, [Sean] Connery throws a heavily-scripted line of dialogue that is either the dry coda or wet cadence to some absurd act of espionage violence. Timing is crucial not in the sense of dramatic rhythm but in the structural placement of narrative cues. ... [I]n a Bond movie words speak louder than actions because words *announce* action.'[56]

Although such lines may be deployed for many different reasons in various kinds of film, Brophy's analysis indicates that they are predominantly genre-specific. They belong within the category of what Kozloff terms 'toppers' – they are, literally in the case of many horror films, killer lines that terminate the dialogue, the scene, and often the verbal opponent. Bond is like the heroes of many detective, action-hero, and science-fiction movies, such as Dr. Who, or Sam Spade in Humphrey Bogart's incarnation, who 'surrender themselves to the power of the written by evaporating themselves on-stage and in place manifesting on-screen the presence of the script, of the structural organizer of the narrative, of the written word'.[57] In *Superman* (Richard Donner, 1978), Christopher Reeve 'looked *graphic* while speaking *literally*, as though you could almost see the speech balloons emanating from his mouth'.[58] In *The Terminator* (James Cameron, 1984), the eponymous robotic antihero has to search his memory bank to find the most appropriate verbal response to a given situation. The database functions as a kind of searchable screenplay, moving the character (and arguably Arnold Schwarzenegger) a step further from realism, since the terminator 'doesn't quote dialogue – he quotes the act of delivering dialogue'.[59] The horror film furnishes further striking examples of characters who are largely defined in terms of their mode of delivering what is transparently scripted speech. In *The Shining* (Stanley Kubrick, 1980), Jack Torrance (Jack Nicholson) 'is literally possessed by literal quotations', and 'appears to delight in ironic quotation', while in *A Nightmare on Elm Street* (Wes Craven, 1984), 'Freddy is a *blank page*: a cypher [sic] of scripted one-liners, almost to the extent that he is only killing innocent children so that he can crack a joke about their demise'.[60]

Monologue and internal storytelling

Part of the appeal of the one-liner is that it has the effect of pure style. Typically delivered deadpan at the climax of a scene of violent emotion or action, it makes the speaker seem unutterably 'cool'. Conversely, 'expressive' speech, in which the character seemingly provides a moment of verbal self-revelation, is apt to sound weak and suspect. The problem with the expressive function of dialogue is bound up with both speech acts and the ontological status of the screen or stage event as something that always occurs in the dramatic present. Any statement a speaker may make about himself or herself will always be perceived as an attempt to secure something from an addressee present within the scene. If the speech is not doing this, it can only be addressed to the external audience in a clumsy act of authorial exposition.

This recognition is perhaps most strongly associated in the theatre, again, with Pinter. As he famously remarked early in his career, '[t]he desire for verification ... is understandable but cannot always be satisfied. ... A character on the stage who can present no convincing argument or information as to his past experience, his present behaviour or his aspirations, nor give a comprehensive analysis of his motives is as legitimate and as worthy of attention as one who, alarmingly, can do all these things'.[61] Holding to this principle demands eliminating exposition, including any speeches that reveal in earlier experiences a formative incident that would provide a psychological explanation for the character's behaviour. For Mamet, similarly, any such speech is simply a technical flaw in the writing, because it needlessly interrupts the action in order to display feeling or emotion in what he memorably dismisses as the 'death of my kitten' speech,[62] or what one of his mentors, Sidney Lumet, ridicules as 'the "rubber-ducky" school of drama: "Someone once took his rubber ducky away from him, and that's why he's a deranged killer"'.[63]

There is one major exception to Mamet's otherwise rigorous adherence to this rule when Bobby Gold, the secular Jewish detective who is the protagonist of *Homicide* (1991), reveals to Chava, a female member of a Jewish resistance group, his own self-loathing: 'They said I was a pussy, because I was a Jew. Onna' cops, they'd say, send a Jew, mizewell send a *broad* on the job, send a *broad* through the door ... All my goddamned life, and I listened to it ... uh-huh ...? I was the donkey ... I was the "clown" ....'[64] It is a noticeably unconvincing speech, however, and perhaps deliberately so. Gold appears weak at this moment – it is he, and not Mamet, who is trying to generate an affective response by resorting to a rubber-ducky monologue – and he is about to discover that Chava will betray him, leading to the climax in which he is brutally disabused of the notion that any of his fellow Jews, let alone one who is also a woman, will be moved to sympathy by his account of being made to feel like a 'pussy'. This is an excruciating 'death of my kitten' speech *par excellence*, and Gold is duly punished for it.

Screenplay dialogue need not either describe character, place, or relationship (deixis), or advance, change, or constitute either plot or relationship (speech acts). Instead, for the same reasons as indicated in the discussion of one-liners, what Kozloff terms 'internal storytelling' need not be expressive, but can instead offer a poetic or thematic commentary on the story. Some of the most striking examples are the stories or digressions delivered by Orson Welles in a number of different films. The story about the sharks in *The Lady from Shanghai* (Welles, 1947) is one; another is the unforgettable parting speech of Harry Lime to Holly Martins in *The Third Man* (Carol Reed, 1949):

> When you make up your mind, send me a message – I'll meet you any place, any time, and when we do meet, old man, it's you I want to see, not the police ... and don't be so gloomy ... After all, it's not

that awful – you know what the fellow said ... In Italy for thirty years under the Borgias they had warfare, terror, murder, bloodshed – they produced Michaelangelo, Leonardo da Vinci and the Renaissance. In Switzerland they had brotherly love, five hundred years of democracy and peace and what did that produce ...? The cuckoo clock. So long, Holly.[65]

It is in the nature of screenplay texts that this, one of the most famous speeches in all of cinema, exists in published form only as a footnote. The text printed first by Lorrimer and reprinted by Faber was derived from the shooting script; material deleted in the film is indicated in square brackets, and interpolations are recorded as footnotes. Accordingly, the cuckoo clock speech, which was improvised by Welles himself during the filming, quite properly appears only as a note at the foot of the page, and is presumably transcribed from a viewing of the film rather than from any textual material supplied by Welles.

To think of the speech as a footnote is also peculiarly appropriate, since it is a marginal comment both within and about the film. It does not further the story; nor does it develop the relationship between Lime and Martins, but instead terminates it in the manner of a classic 'topper'. As such, it comments on the moral world of the story and of Lime himself. Because it is spoken (and written) by Welles, however, it has the distinct feeling of being uttered by two different speakers to two different audiences: by Lime to Martins, within the diegetic frame, but also by Welles to the audience outside it, for it is absolutely in keeping with the beautifully crafted anecdotes and stories associated with the Welles persona both on- and off-screen. The speech has become so well-known that, despite its tangential nature, it is now difficult to think of *The Third Man* – or, unfortunately, Switzerland – without bringing it to mind. It is thereby representative of film dialogue in general: marginal, and therefore essential.

Voice-over

For very similar reasons, Welles is also among the most prominent examples of film-makers who obsessively return to the voice-over. Kozloff notes that voice-over narration appears most commonly in films made by writer-directors; prominent among these are figures like Billy Wilder and Woody Allen, and it is significant that as well as writing and directing, both Allen and Welles usually deliver their own off-screen narration. Welles had come to cinema not only from theatre but also from radio; 'two-thirds of Welles's finished feature films use voice-over', and both in his own films and as a narrator in films directed by others, 'we see clearly the imprint that radio narration made on Welles, and the influence that his delight in narration has had on the history of American cinema'. As he remarked, 'I know that in theory the word is secondary in cinema but the secret of my work is that everything is based on the word. I do not make silent films. I must begin with what the characters say'.[66]

Film criticism has long regarded voice-over with suspicion, for reasons (or 'prejudices') that Kozloff helpfully summarises. Many are again variations on the specificity thesis, but the assumption that underlies most of them is that the presentation of images is somehow less manipulative than the often overtly narrational function of language or soundtrack. This distinction, as Kozloff demonstrates, is false. Just as 'showing' is always just another way of 'telling', so 'all [voice-over narration] does is superimpose another type of narration on top of a mode that is already at least partly narrative'. Moreover, far from being merely a clumsy expositional device, or simply redundant, 'all complementary pairings of narration and images provide more information than would have been available from either alone', the result often being an ironic interplay between the two.[67]

Partly to rebut the common charge that voice-over narration is a 'literary' device that calls attention to writing, Kozloff compares it instead to the onstage narrators sometimes found in theatrical works, on the grounds that the narration is both spoken and intermittent. The differences, however, are far more significant. In plays such as Tennessee Williams's *The Glass Menagerie* (1944) and Arthur Miller's *A View from the Bridge* (1956), the narrator is a visible presence. The voice-over narrator by definition is not, since such narration consists in 'oral statements, conveying any portion of a narrative, spoken by an *unseen* speaker situated in a space and time other than that being simultaneously presented by the images on the screen'.[68] The physical presence of the stage narrator is one reason why, from Plautus onwards, s/he is generally the focus of the audience's attention while speaking. By definition, s/he addresses the audience; whatever else is visible on the stage behind or beside her is of lesser importance during the narration. The cinematic equivalent is the character who speaks to the camera directly, as in *Alfie* (Lewis Gilbert, 1966). In voice-over narration, by contrast, the speaker is absent, and audience attention is divided between soundtrack and visual image.

The only theatrical analogy that springs readily to mind is the 'Voice' heard in some of the shorter plays of Samuel Beckett. In *Footfalls* (1976) the sole figure on the stage, a woman called May ('M'), paces to and fro while the voice of another woman ('V'), apparently that of her mother, speaks 'from dark upstage'; in *Rockaby* (1980), similarly, a woman identified simply as 'W' sits in a chair, rocking to the rhythmic accompaniment of her own 'recorded voice'.[69] The combination of precisely calculated movement and the amplified voice of an unseen speaker is highly cinematic, and the versions arranged specially for videotaping, starring Billie Whitelaw, are extraordinarily powerful. Yet the Voices differ from voice-over narration because they are, however mysteriously, part of the diegetic world inhabited by M and W, who interact with them, responding to what they say and even commanding them to speak. Beckett is most unusual in experimenting with the severance of words from action on stage, but the separation of diegetic and non-diegetic worlds is never as absolute as in voice-over narration. The Beckettian Voice is an interlocutor, rather than a narrator, and its function illustrates the centrality to Beckett's vision of the 'narrator/narrated', with the protagonist's actions seemingly prompted by a voice that appears to issue simultaneously from within and outside the self.

Dramatising this perception constitutes the entire action of *Film*, written in 1963 and the only one of Beckett's works intended directly for its eponymous medium. Rarely described as a screenplay – but that is what it is – the five-page 'outline' of the action is equalled in length by the prefatory material and notes, which describe the proposed method for realising cinematically the ontological drama, in which 'the protagonist is sundered into object (O) and eye (E), the former in flight, the latter in pursuit'. Numerous diagrams show the precise spatial relationships between O and E, essential to a film that depends on the conceit that O will experience the 'anguish of perceivedness' if E, following behind O, breaks the 'angle of immunity', which Beckett sets at 45°.[70] This breaks the illusionistic frame of cinema: the camera becomes the gaze to be avoided.

Film looks like no other screenplay before or since. Although a script for a film that is to be silent save for a single 'sssh!', it is typical of screenplays in its struggle with the inadequacy of the word to find an appropriate textual form in which to represent a complex relationship between the object perceived and a perceiving or narrating agent. Similarly, *Rockaby* is prefaced by a diagrammatic representation of the pacing of the feet, and *Footfalls* by extensive directions orchestrating the lighting, which just as much as the Voice appears both to prompt and to be prompted by W. In all three cases, the framing of the visible action by extensive textual matter represents an attempt to resolve the difficulties of approximating the duration of the action as the spectator is to perceive it, while also indicating for the reader the nature of the relationship between visible action and the offstage or off-screen voice. This relationship is expressed quite differently in the screenplay as compared to the film, and to contrary effect. An audience watching a film experiences the soundtrack and the image simultaneously, including of course in the case of a scene accompanied by a voice-over. Disconcertingly, however, voice-over in the dialogue text of a screenplay cannot comfortably approximate this. Instead it must do one of two things: either the description may precede the voice-over (or vice versa), or the scene text must be presented in one column and the dialogue text in another. In either case, the scene text insists that the events described are unfolding in the present tense, while simultaneously – or *nearly* simultaneously – the voice-over casts them into the past and installs its own moment of narration as the present. We are in the realm of the uncanny, of déjà vu.

The difference between this and on-screen narration is well illustrated by the screenplay for *Double Indemnity*. In the source novel by James M. Cain, Neff writes his confession as a memoir. Wilder and Chandler – prompted, perhaps, by the recognition that voice-over creates a presumption of direct oral transmission[71] – instead came up with the brilliant idea that he would speak his confession into a dictaphone. His narration begins after he struggles, wounded, into his office at the insurance company in dead of night:

> He presses the button switch on the horn. The sound stops, the record revolves on the cylinder. He begins to speak:

> NEFF: Office memorandum, Walter Neff to Barton Keyes, Claims Manager. Los Angeles, July 16th, 1938. Dear Keyes: I suppose you'll call this a confession when you hear it. I don't like the word confession. [...]

The confession continues for a whole page, interrupted only by two brief descriptions of Neff looking at his wounded shoulder and taking a drag on a cigarette. The layout then changes:

DIETRICHSON HOME – LOS FELIZ DISTRICT

NEFF'S VOICE

Palm trees line the street, middle-class houses, mostly in Spanish style. Some kids throwing a baseball back and forth across a couple of front lawns. An ice cream wagon dawdles along the block. Neff's coupe meets and passes the ice cream wagon and stops before one of the Spanish houses. Neff gets out. He carries a briefcase, his hat is a little on the back of his head. His movements are easy and full of ginger. He inspects the house, checks the number, goes up on the front porch and rings the bell.

It was mid-afternoon, and it's

funny, I can still remember the

smell of honeysuckle all along

that block. I felt like a million.

There was no way in all this

world I could have known that

murder sometimes can smell like

honeysuckle...

The double-spacing in the second column indicates an effort to synchronise the delivery of the lines with the visuals in the first; elsewhere in the screenplay both columns are single-spaced, again providing an approximate indication of timing.[72] The screenplay reader, however, is presented with not an image and a soundtrack, but with two forms of writing. The necessity of doing this exposes voice-over as a particularly cinematic device, but it also creates a highly unusual, and in a certain sense impossible, textual form within the screenplay itself: it is as if the eyes were being asked to scan a column each and then report back.

The difference in register between the two columns emphasises the differences between prose description and oral narration. More specifically, Neff's voice gives not a statement of the action but an interpretation of it. Objections to voice-over tend to state or imply that it introduces a subjective, literary form of narration, whereas the camera simply records what is put in front of it. If this were so, however, the left-hand column would present us with an irresolvable contradiction. On the one hand, it states without inflection the succession of images that are to appear in the film. On the other hand, it is every bit as bound up with literary, verbal narration as is the material in the second column; it possesses the characteristically metonymic, paratactic style of the scene text as discussed in Chapter 7.

Style that doesn't draw attention to itself is the most manipulative style of all. Neff's narration, being a confession, has a kind of honesty: he has already told us he is a murderer, and here he elaborates on the emotions that will lead him to become one. The depersonalised description in the left-hand column, by contrast, insidiously sketches out an ideology. The houses, the children, the baseball, and the ice cream van metonymically represent a clean-cut, all-American life, healthily balanced between home and sports, with the nuclear family at its centre. These are the images to be presented on the screen, while the voice-over leads us towards the homewrecker, the femme fatale, the killer. The opposition could not be clearer, but it is not an opposition between visual truth and narrative fiction. It is between narration that takes the form of a sequence of images chosen to create one effect – perhaps a reality effect, to borrow Barthes's term, but still an effect – and an oral narration designed to draw us into complicity with the speaker.

For Neff is a sympathetic character, while even the plastic, psychotic object of his attraction, Phyllis Dietrichson, possesses a ghoulish fascination. At least they are not boring, and perhaps that is why theorists influenced by the specificity thesis have a problem with voice-over: if it is well written it becomes intrinsically interesting, effectively challenging the hierarchical dominance of the visual. How dull the images in the left-hand column are, how relatively drab the language that creates them, and how stiflingly conformist the world they represent. That, at least, is part of the meaning of *Double Indemnity*, just as it is part of the meaning of *film noir* in general. You can have the American Dream, it seems to be saying, but once inside that antiseptic domestic nirvana you'll want to commit bloody murder to get yourself out.

Action as speech

The verbal sign-system of screenplays, combined with the convention that a page of text equals a minute of screen time, means that reading a dialogue-intensive scene will be very different from seeing the same scene in a film, irrespective of how the text attempts to visualise it, because the reader's attention will focus on the language rather than the action. In *The Usual Suspects* (Bryan Singer, 1995; screenplay by Christopher McQuarrie), Verbal Kint watches as his lawyer and the prosecutor engage in pre-trial negotiations about which charges are to be brought against him.[73] The scene text reports simply that 'Verbal's eyes follow the voices back and forth', and the dialogue text scrupulously repeats before each of the lawyers' speeches that it is delivered off-screen. The scene will therefore be visualised as a close-up on Verbal's face, or possibly just his eyes, in keeping with the convention that the expressive potential of eyes receives priority in classical cinema. Such a shot will keep the spectator's attention focused on Verbal, and a director has the option of mixing the lawyers' voices either high or low on the soundtrack to signal to the viewer whether or not the words themselves are significant; it may be that we simply need to register that Verbal is peculiarly attentive to what is happening to him, with the precise topic under discussion being of little importance. In such cases a screenplay may simply report that a discussion is taking place, without providing the dialogue itself, in which case it will be improvised and mixed in the film to indicate its low priority. For example, towards the end of the lawyers' exchanges, their voices 'mumble off-screen. Verbal fidgets in his chair', and the written dialogue resumes with the information that Verbal is to be charged only with 'Misdemeanor one'.

Up to this point in the scene, McQuarrie's screenplay records all of the lawyers' dialogue, without interruption from the scene text. It occupies two full pages, topped by the one-line report about Verbal's eyes, and tailed equally laconically with the report that 'Verbal lets out a long-held sigh of relief'. When reading those pages, rather than see-ing the film, the visualisation of the image is likely to be subordinate to the dialogue, in which Verbal's lawyer ruthlessly negotiates immunity from prosecution in return for his testimony. The dialogue lays bare some of the intrigues within, and jealous competition between, the political networks in New York and Los Angeles, a theme that emerges more prominently in the script than in the film. Regardless of thematic considerations, however, reading and viewing the scene will be two markedly different experiences.

On second reading, moreover, other interpretive possibilities become apparent. The lawyer scene is experientially different from many in *The Usual Suspects*, a script in which Verbal's voice-over forms the principal mode of narration. At a crucial point, towards the end, Verbal tells a story of how Keyser Söze came to acquire his terrifying reputation – a story which, he tells us, may or may not be true, though he himself believes it. Söze had returned one day to find his wife and children violated by a Hungarian mob, with whom he was engaged in a turf war. Rather than let his family live with the humiliation, Söze kills both them and the gang, aside from one that he allows to flee to begin circu-lating the story of Söze's terrible vengeance. The events are described in Verbal's voice-over as well as in a series of images in the scene text:

He kills their kids, he kills their wives, he kills their parents and their parents' friends.

We see glimpses of Keyser Söze's rampage. Bodies upon bodies in homes and in the streets. Then, the fires.

Stores and homes burn, engulfed in flames.

He burns down the houses they live in and the stores they work in, he kills people that owe them money. And like that, he was gone. Underground. No one has ever seen him again. He becomes a myth, a spook story that criminals tell their kids at night.[74]

Because the images that would arrest the attention of a spectator in the cinema lack detail in the scene text, Verbal's proportionately more prominent narration accordingly receives greater attention in the screenplay.

The stunning final revelation is that much of what we have seen in the film is just a tale that Verbal has been improvising serendipitously from scraps of texts pinned on a notice board behind his questioners. Scenes played out before our eyes must now be retrospectively reinterpreted as his inventions. This is a little less shocking in the screenplay, because the textual sign system has concentrated attention on Verbal as a narrator. It still surprises, however, because while the unreliable narrator is a familiar convention in prose fiction, it is almost forbidden in cinema.

There is a crucial difference between *The Usual Suspects* and a spate of superficially similar films that followed in its wake, including *Fight Club* (David Fincher, 1999), *The Sixth Sense* (M. Night Shyamalan, 1999), and *A Beautiful Mind* (Ron Howard, 2001). In each of these later examples, the spectator finally recognises that many of the events previously shown are to be interpreted as the projection of events in the mind of a central character possessed by an extreme subjectivity (an idea deliciously parodied in the story attributed to Donald Kaufman in *Adaptation*). The protagonist is mentally ill, or dead, and does not realise that the world in which he appears to move is, to a large extent, his own mental construction. The reassuring solidity of the cinematic world, which film audiences have come to accept as real in a 'suspension of disbelief', dissolves. In other words, these films are variations on a kind of cinematic expressionism with a long history, stretching back at least as far as *The Cabinet of Dr Caligari* (Robert Wiene, 1919), in which the meaning of the entire film was altered by the controversial addition of a frame story that casts all of the events as the delusion of a madman.

In *The Usual Suspects*, however, the principal narrator, Verbal, is not deluded. He invents the plot that the spectator sees to gain a tactical advantage in the here-and-now; he is attempting to secure his escape. Although by the end the ontological status of many of the events remains uncertain, some, if not all, are to be understood as the fabrications of what had until this point appeared a relatively minor character. There is a significant difference between this and a lie told by a character on the stage, since the latter does not alter the perceptual space of the theatrical set. In the theatre, words will always be scrutinised for their reliability, and all speech acts will change the relationships between the characters on stage, but they will not physically alter the stage itself. In *The Usual Suspects*, however, the audience is finally forced to reinterpret whole sequences as visual representations of a story Verbal is making up: the action in such sequences is a representation of Verbal's speech. The challenge then lies in determining what degree of reliability to give to any of the scenes in the film.

The exchange between the lawyers is clearly an incident that is not invented by Verbal, since it is in response to the legal procedures that he begins to fabricate the story. Equally but conversely, the episode of Söze and the Hungarians is explicitly presented as a story told in voice-over by Verbal, who stresses that he is merely reporting a tale that may or may not be true. There is a certain complicity here between Verbal as an embedded narrator and the problematic 'image-maker' who is the impersonal narrator, or implied author, of *The Usual Suspects*. Just as the former stresses that nobody knows what Söze looks like, so the latter reports that when Söze enters the house, '[w]e are never allowed to see his face' (p. 90). This definitive statement has a different effect when followed in the film, because film tends to imply that such decisions are a choice of the director rather than an instruction in the screenplay. Nevertheless, as the unreliability of this particular episode about Söze has clearly been signalled to both reader and spectator, there is no great difficulty at this point.

The problem emerges at the end of seeing the film or reading the text. Now alert to the unreliability of everything Verbal says, there is a compulsion to go back and examine retrospectively the verifiability of every scene in the film. In many cases this is far from straightforward. Previously, Verbal has recounted under police interrogation the history of another mass killing that we know to have taken place from several pieces of independent corroboration, and which has left the authorities dumbfounded. Knowing that although the police investigation is 'real' much of Verbal's account is a fabrication, a question now surrounds the transitions from one to the other, as in the following:

KUJAN

Now what happened after the lineup?

Verbal sneers at Kujan, unable to change the subject.

EXT – POLICE STATION – NEW YORK – NIGHT *SIX WEEKS PRIOR*

Keaton stops at the top of the front steps of the police station and lights a cigarette. Edie comes out behind him, fuming mad. (p. 46)

Although the syntax indicates that the scene outside the police station represents Verbal's response to Kujan's question, the absence of any textual indicator of subjectivity (such as a dissolve or a voice-over) introduces an ambiguity. Customarily, film permits the conflation of these two possibilities: a transitional device indicating subjective memory may segue imperceptibly into an objective record of events, with the narrator's recollection taking on the status of accepted fact. If there is reason to doubt the reliability of the witness, the spectator will usually be made aware of this, as happens even in such a problematic case as *Rashomon* (Akira Kurosawa, 1950).

But it is extremely unusual for the spectator to be compelled to reinterpret a scene as a lie. The notorious precedent is *Stage Fright* (Alfred Hitchcock, 1950), in which a character's narration introduces a flashback that is only revealed at the end of the film to have been an untruth: the character himself had committed a murder, and the scene presented on the screen is the story he has told to cover his tracks. The film fails because the scene is not integrated into any larger structure that would call the cinematic narration as a whole into question; one scene, and one scene only, is a deception, and as the audience can have had no way of knowing this, the effect is of a cheap contrivance.

The Usual Suspects is different, because it calls into question the reliability of its narrational strategies in general. It is not simply the historical bias in favour of cinematic realism that creates an illusion of truth, it is also a result of the unfolding of cinematic time in the present tense. Each element of the story that the discourse reveals to us takes place in the continuous present, even when it is presented within the frame of a flashback. The same is also the case in the screenplay text. If *The Usual Suspects* were written as prose fiction, the narrator would cast the confrontation between Kujan and Verbal into the past tense ('Verbal sneered at Kujan'). The scene with Keaton and Edie would not only be narrated in the past tense but would also be revealed, by the presence or absence of inverted commas, to be either an event recounted by the narrator or embedded narration spoken by Verbal. This would alert the reader to the need for caution in assessing what degree of credence to give the narration.

Instead, the screenplay reader is faced with an ambiguity that is temporarily irresolvable other than by the conventional presumption in favour of the truth of the image. This is supported by the statement that the events happened 'six weeks prior', an assertion that is not attributed to Verbal. The director will have to decide whether and how to indicate this time frame to the spectator, but (slightly unconventionally) McQuarrie has given no indication within the script of how this is supposed to be done. Accordingly, the words are likely to strike the reader as a small piece of omniscient narration, although in retrospect it appears that this is probably another of Verbal's fabrications.

Faced with these doubts, attention shifts from the unreliability of Verbal's narration to that of the screenplay itself. The problem arises because some of the images and events are not to be interpreted either as mere fabrications by Verbal (since there is independent corroboration in the police reports), or as unmediated representations of events that have really happened in the story world. Instead, they are a visual *interpretation* of his words, and (if we are to make diegetic sense of the film) not an interpretation supplied by the director, nor by his auditors (the police, but also the spectators in the cinema), but by Verbal himself. This becomes apparent in the final twists, after Verbal has left the police station. A fax machine receives a copy of an image of Keyser Söze drawn by a survivor, following which Verbal is picked up by a man in a car:

INT. DISPATCHER'S OFFICE
Jasper Briggs pulls the sheet out of the fax machine and turns it over, revealing the composite sketch of Keyser Söze.

Though crude and distorted, one cannot help but notice how much it looks like Verbal Kint.

EXT. STREET
The car stops. The driver gets out.

It is Kobayashi, or the man we have come to know as such. (p. 133)

The conjunction of the two images plays havoc with the differences between the semiotic systems of screenplay and film. That the sketch of Keyser Söze resembles Verbal immediately begins the process of retrospective analysis, as we will start to consider whether the actions attributed to the former could in fact have been carried out by the latter. The image of Kobayashi, however, creates mayhem. Throughout the script, we have known of Kobayashi, Keyser Söze's lawyer, only from Verbal's account. A shot near the end shows us that Verbal has simply borrowed the name from that of the manufacturer of a coffee cup. The arrival of 'Kobayashi' in the getaway car at the end, however, complicates matters. Verbal has taken the signifier 'Kobayashi' and attached it to an associate, who must 'really' be called something else, in a textbook illustration of the arbitrary relationship between signifier and signified in Saussurean linguistics. The problem is that signifieds are mental concepts, raising the bewildering question at the end of *The Usual Suspects*: whose mental concept is the signified of 'Kobayashi'? On reading the screenplay, one will have formed a certain visual impression of Kobayashi. Or not: *The Usual Suspects* is very perfunctory in describing the physical appearance of its characters. For reasons noted Chapter 7, screenplay texts in general rarely offer the concrete visualisation of characters routinely found in realist fiction. In any case, the reader legitimately assumes a certain interplay with the text in the creation of the character. In this concluding moment, however, the screenplay seems suddenly to have usurped that autonomy and told us what we have been visualising all along.

The film is no less disorientating, but for the opposite reason. Now the answer to the question 'what does the mental concept "Kobayashi" look like?' is 'he looks exactly like the English actor Pete Postlethwaite, heavily suntanned'. Suddenly, someone other than Kobayashi, but with an identical facial appearance, emerges at the very end of the film. Again, the obvious explanation is that this is because 'Kobayashi' is *Verbal's* mental concept. The bafflingly unanswered questions that remain after either reading or seeing *The Usual Suspects* are therefore the result of the unresolved interplay of three different ontological fields: that of realism (the police and the lawyers, searching for clues within the diegetic world of the film); that of the reader or spectator, who when told a story naturally supplies the mental concepts for herself; and that of the narrator (whoever that is) of the screenplay or film, who has usurped this autonomy of the reader by asking us to accept that certain scenes are presented directly from the inside of Verbal's head. That this does not fully add up is partly due to the idea that Verbal has actually been improvising a story from signifiers pinned to the notice board that do not fully cohere within a consistently and coherently imagined world.

The Usual Suspects exploits with exceptional subtlety the resources of dialogue within the screenplay. The quasi-realistic scenes concerning the investigation initially follow a dramatic structure well known in detective fiction, whereby the authorities act as readers constructing a discourse which attempts to decode a story 'written' by the criminals. Like many contemporary films, such as those analysed by Temenuga Trifonova and discussed at the end of Chapter 1 of this book, this leads to the disturbing possibility that there is also, or instead, a non-realistic pre-text for the story, which is nothing other than the screenplay itself. McQuarrie's brilliant innovation is to introduce to this fascinating but relatively familiar idea the conceit that the film is an act of oral improvisation. Instead of referring back to a story, Verbal is to be regarded as actually creating the discourse that we see on the screen. This introduces a new level of interaction between two aspects of the screenplay, in which the voice-over of the dialogue text is seen to be responsible for the creation of the scene text (and of the dialogue of the other characters within it). In so doing, however, McQuarrie's script creates a new kind of palimpsest, in which a story that would make complete sense always appears to be almost within view, but is at the same time being rubbed out by the voice-over. Instead of the convention that a voice-over provides expressive revelation, Verbal's provides tactical concealment. In creating these interlocking dramas between the dialogue text and the scene text, the story and the discourse, *The Usual Suspects* takes the screenplay into new and challenging fields.

Epilogue: *Sunset Boulevard*

'... before you hear it all distorted and blown out of proportion, before those Hollywood columnists get their hands on it, maybe you'd like to hear the facts'.[1] The facts in the case of *Sunset Boulevard* (Billy Wilder, 1950) concern the melodramatic encounter of the failing screenwriter Joe Gillis and a faded star of the silent years, Norma Desmond, who imagines that Gillis can transform her own script of *Salome* into a vehicle for her triumphant return. Unable to accept that he does not love her, and that her plans for a comeback are delusional, Norma shoots Gillis as he attempts to leave.

From the beginning, the script is obsessed with writing, with text, even with orthography: 'START the picture with the actual street sign: SUNSET BOULEVARD, stencilled on a curbstone' (p. 9). The credit titles are to be superimposed in the same style, as they accompany the police who have been called to a crumbling mansion where a body lies in a swimming pool. The dead man is a writer; other writers, men from the papers, surround the pool. The screenplay, by Charles Brackett, Billy Wilder, and Dave Marshman, Jr., starts to play games with the text. Gillis's voice-over in the right-hand column in the script tantalisingly syncopates the personal pronouns and changing time-frame of his narration with the images described in the column on the left: the B-movie writer in the pool is a 'he', but six months earlier it is an 'I', Gillis, who sits beside the typewriter in the Alto Nido apartment. Gillis must be the man in the pool, but how? The writer has drawn us in: he will tell us 'the whole truth' (p. 9) – except that, in the event, he won't – but only in his own time; and if he is speaking from beyond the grave, what time is that?

Norma's beloved silent movies are full of faces; sound films, as she says, are full of 'talk, talk, talk', and writing is just 'words, words' (p. 27).

167

The screenplay of *Sunset Boulevard* is bursting with words, with texts and stories. Later we will see that the walls of the producer Sheldrake's office at Paramount, and of Norma Desmond's house, are festooned with pictures of Hollywood stars, but in Gillis's apartment there is no iconography of the movies; nothing except the tossed-aside pages of rejected scripts. As a text, the screenplay of *Sunset Boulevard* shows a concern with the fate that befalls other texts like this. They get physically mangled: the forty-page outline of 'Bases Loaded' is condensed into two by Betty Schaefer, Sheldrake's assistant and Gillis's future lover, who later pulls apart another Gillis story, 'Dark Windows', to get at the six-page flashback that interests her; and Gillis literally as well as metaphorically pulls to pieces Norma's encyclopaedic retelling of the story of Salome.

Dismemberment does not kill these texts, however. No matter how definitively they appear to have been killed off, they always return from the dead. 'Bases Loaded' is disinterred from the Paramount Readers' Department and mockingly resurrected by Sheldrake as a musical about 'a girls' softball team' ('It Happened in the Bull Pen – the Story of a Woman' [p.17]). Betty writes up the fragment of 'Dark Windows' into 'twenty pages of notes', and persuades Sheldrake that 'it could be made into something'; '[a] lampshade?', suggests Gillis (pp. 77–8). Instead, it will be made into a new screenplay, a collaboration by Betty and Gillis that also occasions their affair and leads to his fatal showdown with Norma. As so often in stories about Hollywood (Mamet's *Speed-the-Plow*, Kaufman's *Adaptation*), the battle of the sexes is played out as a proxy battle of the texts.

Sunset Boulevard is also full of other tales that provide magnificent touches of the grotesque, from story events represented within the discourse (the moonlit burial of a chimpanzee in a white coffin), to those verbally narrated by one of the characters (Max's story of the Maharajah who strangled himself with one of Norma's stockings). And, throughout, it plays off conventional notions of high and low culture in ways that raise the question of the literary status of its own pre-text as a screenplay. The constant rewrites of hackneyed stories ('plot 27-A' [p. 16]) are but one manifestation of a Hollywood text machine that includes sensationalist newspapers, gossip columns, and fan magazines. Gillis's disdain for such material is displayed in his references to highbrow literary fiction (*Great Expectations*, Joyce, Dostoevsky, Norman Mailer's recently published first novel *The Naked and the Dead*), while his anxiety about having his car repossessed is the same fear that troubles F. Scott Fitzgerald's failed screenwriter, Pat Hobby. The irony here, as in all such stories about Hollywood, is that while the lowbrow script may be a manifestation of the worst kind of mass commercial production, 'high' culture seems even worse, a dead hand determined to squeeze the life out of whatever is vital and new and threatening to its status.

The particular manifestation of this drama in *Sunset Boulevard* lies in the opposition of the sound movies for which Gillis writes to the silent films that Norma forces him to watch as she clasps her hand around his arm. Erich von Stroheim, the great silent director who plays Norma's ex-husband and loyal retainer Max von Mayerling, 'never liked the role', and recognised that Wilder was twisting a knife in the body of a Hollywood that was twenty years dead.[2] Norma's movies are unrepresentable within the screenplay; when a snatch of one of them is to be shown, it is perfunctorily described as 'not a funny scene', 'old-fashioned', but 'show[ing] her incredible beauty and screen presence' (p. 43).

In one sense, this lacuna in the screenplay text is simply an acknowledgement of its own limitations, like the gaps in the scenarios for Warners musicals that call for the later addition of songs and choreography. Yet it also implies a certain wilful illiteracy in Norma's silent films, painfully evident when, in response to Gillis's observation that her 'Salome' script needs 'a little more dialogue', she responds: 'I can say anything I want with my eyes' (p. 33). Although the film of *Sunset Boulevard* is, perhaps, more ambivalent, the screenplay is defiantly not an act of homage to the silent movie; it is a celebration of the talk and words that not only Norma, but a dominant tradition in film theory, wish to suffocate out of existence.

Gillis won't stop talking; he is fascinated by the circumstances of his own narration and with his performance as a storyteller. As in *Double Indemnity*, *Sunset Boulevard*'s voice-over presents itself as a confessional text: Gillis is going to tell us 'the whole truth', and nothing but the truth. Like any good narrator, however, he is going to hold things back, teasingly delaying the full revelation of the 'little plot of my own' that he is concocting, letting slip that '[l]ater, I found out that Max was the only other person in that grim Sunset castle, and I found out a few other things about him...' (pp. 31–2). Gillis is an embedded narrator within the text constructed by Wilder, Brackett, and Marshman, but at times he almost seems to be responsible for the organisation of the screenplay itself, which in keeping with Wilder's custom is divided into five 'sequences', like the acts of a play. At the end of sequence A, Gillis delivers the curtain line: 'queerer things were yet to come' (p. 37).

We will never know the whole truth about 'Bases Loaded', or 'Dark Windows', or Norma's 'Salome', because they appear only as reported fragments scattered throughout *Sunset Boulevard*. This is the one story that purports to be complete, but the fact we most want to hear is the one it doesn't tell us: the one about how it comes to be narrated by a man floating face-down dead in a swimming pool. Following the discovery of the corpse in the opening sequence, Wilder and Brackett had originally written an additional scene set in a morgue that 'explained' the voice-over, by having Gillis discuss the afterlife with other cadavers of the recently departed. This was cut after a preview audience, which must have known more about movies than the Pomona crowd that did for *The Magnificent Ambersons*, hated it. Wilder, who knew a lot about movies, admitted that without the scene the resulting film was 'illogical; but that doesn't matter; it's not boring. And as long as it's riveting, they will swallow it'.[3]

The deleted footage rested in peace until it was disinterred for the extras package of a 2003 DVD reissue, alongside the corresponding pages from the shooting script, which are not present in the published draft. Those pages are required, because the surviving footage does not have sound. It is truly uncanny: a morgue scene from a sound film about the death of silent movies re-emerges from a vault as a soundless fragment, and only the screenplay, the artefact that movies seek to erase, can speak for it. Tagged for identification like the other corpses, the dead screenwriter speaks – though we cannot hear him – of how he came to meet what was, until that moment, his end. Eisenstein must have seen some such image in his head, but he was writing decades before the creation of *Sunset Boulevard* when he remarked that '[a] numbered script will bring as much animation to cinema as the numbers on the heels of the drowned men in the morgue'.[4] And he didn't think it would be re-animated. Perhaps André Bazin, writing about the ontology of cinema in the first sentence in the first essay in the first volume of *What Is Cinema?*, was closer to the mark: '[i]f the plastic arts were put under psychoanalysis, the practice of embalming the dead might turn out to be a fundamental factor in their creation'.[5]

Screenwriting, as Gillis knows and as its history attests, is 'ghost writing' (p. 46), and the text of *Sunset Boulevard* is the autobiography of a corpse. In its creative exploitation of its own instability, its knowledge of an afterlife in which it circulates unpredictably, and its demonstration of the potential of a pointlessly maligned form, it is the definitive, or definitively provisional, parable of the death and resurrection of the screenplay.

Appendix: Extract from *Hellfire* by David Hughes and Ronan O'Leary

For those unfamiliar with some of the conventions of screenplay form, the following extract presents a facsimile of the first nine pages of *Hellfire*, by David Hughes and Ronan O'Leary. One of the most important reasons why critical analysis of the screenplay lags behind that of other forms is that copyright ordinarily resides with the studio rather than the writer. Even if this were not the case, the individual quality of a particular screenplay is often a matter of structure, and this is not easily illustrated other than by the quotation of passages that will frequently exceed in length the terms provided for in 'fair use'. I am therefore very grateful to David Hughes for granting permission to present a substantial extract from this screenplay.

A further reason for reproducing this extract is that *Hellfire* is unfilmed and unpublished, and will be unknown to the reader. A contention of the present book is that although screenplays owe their existence to film, they present no particular difficulties for the non-professional. The reader may wish to test this assertion by examining the extract either now, or after reading the following discussion, which elaborates upon the account given of the formal properties of 'master-scene' screenplays at the beginning of Chapter 7.

'FADE IN' is a widely used, but by no means mandatory, opening. It is less a direction for a particular kind of shot than a conventional beginning in this particular form, the screenwriter's equivalent of 'once upon a time'. Until quite recently it was commonplace for a writer to conclude each scene with the direction 'CUT TO:' followed by the next slug line. This is much less widespread today. 'CUT TO' is another pure convention: in practice, it is the director who will ordinarily decide which transitional device to deploy between scenes. Nevertheless, writers will often insert a transitional direction if they consider it helpful to the narrative flow of the script: here, the 'SMASH CUT' at the bottom of p. 3 offers a visual correlative to the violent sounds of the storm and cannons, while the 'DISSOLVE' on p. 4 captures the serenity of the dawn aftermath.

The material in bold type (EXT. FIELDS – DAY) is the 'slug line', usually composed of three elements that indicate interior or exterior location, the name of the location itself, and whether the scene takes place during the day or night, although a more specific time may sometimes be indicated, as in the 'dawn' scene on p. 4. Screenplays are sometimes segmented by shot numbers (as is the case with Evan Hunter's drafts of *The Birds*), but this is relatively infrequent in the writer's (as opposed to the director's) version, as the writer is poorly placed to know how the director will wish to break a scene down into a sequence of shots. In a numbered script, the shot number will appear in the left-hand margin.

Hellfire is, instead, written in the more common 'master-scene' format, in which the unit of segmentation is not the shot but the scene. Slug lines therefore indicate scene divisions, although there is room for debate about where such divisions should fall. Very unusually, the first three scenes of *Hellfire* all have the same slug line. This is because the end of each of the first two scenes is followed by an 'insert', in which the script directs the reader's attention to a specific image. Accordingly, inserts are usually close-ups: either of an object within the scene, or of an object in an unspecified time and/or place, or of objects distinct from the scene in time or space. Here, the juxtaposition of inserts of violent battle within scenes of the bloody aftermath clearly establishes that these are analepses ('flashbacks', as opposed to the proleptic flash forwards): the insert is from the same place, but not the same time, as the material in the rest of the scene. The writer has accordingly decided that the use of the insert occasions a change of scene; a different writer might have presented the material as one scene while keeping the inserts, while in a different form of script the inserts (and other shots) would simply be numbered. Much more clearly, the change of location to the Philadelphia meeting house demands a new slug line; although Franklin's speech here is a continuation of the speech heard in voice-over (V.O.) in the preceding scenes, any change in visible location instigates a new scene.

'V.O.' indicates that that the speaker is temporally and/or spatially detached from the scene. If the speaker is understood to be present, but simply not visible at this moment, the speaking voice is off-screen (O.S.). Where a speech continues, but is interrupted within the text by slug lines or scene descriptions (as here), most writers would insert (CONT.), for 'continued', following the speaker's name at each resumption of the speech. Hughes has here omitted this direction, perhaps because it is clear that the speech is indeed continuous, and he reserves the 'continued' direction for speeches interrupted by a page break, as at the top of p. 7. We are only given Franklin's name once we see him in the meeting house because prior to this point the film audience would have no indication of who is speaking, and this movement from ignorance to knowledge is matched in the screenplay by the transition from 'MAN'S VOICE' to 'FRANKLIN' in the speech heading. A screenplay will often be purposely reticent concerning the figures we see; on p. 6, for example, the identity of the 'two SHADOWY FIGURES' who observe Franklin's approach is not revealed, creating an air of suspense and foreboding. Occasionally a screenwriting manual will insist that such characters be identified on first appearance, on the grounds that the screenplay is a document intended for the use of the production team who must, of course, know which actors are required for each scene.[1] This, however, erases the distinction between a 'selling script', which aims to secure the interest of the studio reader, and the 'shooting script', a much later document prepared for the production crew. The suspense would be eliminated for the reader had Hughes followed this stipulation.

Nevertheless, selling scripts ordinarily preserve the essentially industrial functions of the screenplay. Margins, offsetting, use of capital letters, and functional prose all developed to meet the needs of various workers operating in a system that required a tightly specified division of labour. The slug line, for instance, is structured as it is for the aid of production and location managers, while the use of capital letters within description similarly indicates material for the attention of specific members of the production team, and speaker names and dialogue are offset for ease of reading for actors. While distinctions need to be drawn between selling and shooting scripts, the selling script must demonstrate that it is filmable, and accordingly is written in a way that anticipates production and which became standardised across the major Hollywood studios in the 1930s. This has altered slightly since the 1950s, especially in the matter of shot specification (which is now widely discouraged), and in recent years some film writers have recommended more idiosyncratic styles of presentation to attract the attention of readers or to capture better the peculiar qualities of an individual script. Nevertheless, most screenplays still follow a standardised format, and differ from poetry or novels (but not stage plays) in incorporating within their form the anticipation of their realisation within another medium.

Two questions arise in the present context. First, does the distinctive form of the screenplay text make it inherently more difficult to read than other kinds of text? No extensive empirical research appears to have been conducted that could provide a definitive answer. *Hellfire* was selected from the range of screenplays available for use in this appendix because it displays in its opening pages a very large number of the conventions that might be felt to present a problem. Action moves rapidly between locations; the same speaker's voice is presented first in voice-over and then within a scene; the extensive use of voice-over makes it uncertain whether all of the speech is to be understood as being delivered in the meeting house, or whether instead some of it is part of Franklin's dream on the boat; Franklin moves from man to boy and back again, symptomatic of the non-linear presentation of story events in these particular pages; there are frequent inserts, the significance of some of which (especially that of the young woman) is unclear at this point, and so on. Nevertheless, I would argue that the conventions of the screenplay form enable the alert reader to follow the text without difficulty, and facilitates the rapid movement and counterpointing of image and dialogue in ways that would be no easier to achieve within prose fiction.

The second question that arises is whether these conventions make the screenplay less literary than other forms. To some extent the answer has to be yes, because it is by definition characterised by a particular form of ekphrasis: that is, it seeks to approximate a visual and auditory medium within a textual form. It does this not because of the literary challenge presented by ekphrasis, as does (say) Walter Pater, but simply because of its industrial function. The use of capital letters within prose description, for example, has nothing to do with style and everything to do with film production. Aside from the dialogue, then, the screenplay arguably makes fewer demands on the writer to combine words in ways that achieve particular effects of style.

Another way of looking at this question, however, would be to say that the difference between the two media occasions different experiences and different emphases. As noted in the discussion of *The Usual Suspects* in Chapter 8, many screenplays unavoidably invite greater attention to the spoken word, and less to the image. One can imagine that a production of *Hellfire* would seek to exploit the visual and auditory potential of the images of battle and the storm at sea, while arguably the primary appeal of the 'costume drama' lies in the sensation of being transported back to another time that is fully realised on the screen. The screenplay can only indicate this visual world and invite the reader to imagine the rest. On the other hand, the written text draws particular attention to the dialogue. In the case of *Hellfire* the reader is drawn immediately to Franklin's wit, and aside from the pleasure it affords, the questions it invites are essentially literary ones: how much of the dialogue is transcribed from writings by or about Franklin? In what ways has the writer modified the speech to cater to the needs of dramatisation? These questions touch on broader questions of adaptation that are, again, as much literary and scholarly as they are cinematic.

Finally, it should be noted that screenplays, like some short stories (but unlike, perhaps, most novels), often do not benefit from close analysis of individual passages without reference to the broader narrative structure. As noted in Chapter 2, an individual image or event in a screenplay rarely has an immanent meaning; instead, its significance emerges within the structure of the story as a whole. In this respect it presents in narrative form something approximating aspects of Eisensteinian montage or the Kuleshov effect in Soviet cinema, whereby the meaning of a shot is determined not by the shot itself but by its relation to others. *Hellfire* invites speculation as to the meaning of particular images – the unfortunate woman fleeing into the street, the silent watchers of Franklin's arrival – that will only be answered later. This differs from Hitchcockian suspense, in which the meaning of the image (a bomb hidden under a table, for instance) is readily apparent, and the audience becomes rapt in anticipation of an event of which it has knowledge but the characters do not.

What the reader of this *Hellfire* extract (which ends for convenience at the conclusion of a scene) cannot know, without reading the script in its entirety, is that the genre of the piece is about to change. Until this point, it has appeared to be simply a historical drama; soon, it will turn into a murder mystery, with Franklin taking on the role of detective investigating murders at the notorious Hellfire club, the proclivities of which are well summarised by Fothergill on p. 9. The literary interest in adaptation persists, but the screenplay now becomes a more commercial entertainment, with historical fidelity taking a back seat and Franklin's verbal dexterity vying for attention with sex, violence, and comic intrigue in settings that recall Stanley Kubrick's *Eyes Wide Shut* (1999).

If cinema is conventionally (if problematically) associated primarily with image, and dialogue with words, then what connects image and text most closely in Western film-making is the shared commitment to story. Equally, however, if (as the manuals always say) what binds the screenplay to film is that it tells a story in cinematic terms, what binds it to literature is that it tells that story exclusively in words. Whether it is itself 'literature' begs the questions considered throughout this book.

FADE IN: *

EXT. FIELDS - DAY   *

The camera passes over FIELDS littered with the detritus of   *
battle: lost WEAPONS, fallen SOLDIERS in red and blue   *
uniforms, BLAST DAMAGE from cannons, etc.   *

FADE UP the sounds of battle, echoing and distant.   *

           MAN'S VOICE (V.O.)   *
       Gentlemen, with Amherst's defeat   *
       of the French in Newfoundland,   *
       the seven year war is at an end.   *

INSERT : A brief, jarring CLOSE-UP of SOLDIERS in battle.   *

EXT. FIELDS - DAY   *

Then the camera continues its passage over the FIELDS.   *

           MAN'S VOICE (V.O.)   *
       Voltaire said that this war,   *
       fought over "a few acres of   *
       snow", has cost more than all of   *
       Canada is worth. I do not share   *
       his view.   *

INSERT : Another brief CLOSE-UP of SOLDIERS in battle.   *

EXT. FIELDS - DAY   *

Over the fields, the sky is darkling: STORM CLOUDS gather.   *

           MAN'S VOICE (V.O.)   *
       The Proprietors have used the war   *
       as an excuse for tyrannical and   *
       inhuman taxes...   *
          (beat)   *
       ...extorting privileges from the   *
       people with the knife of savages   *
       at their throat.   *

Various VOICES are heard, signalling dissent.   *

INT. MEETING HOUSE, PHILADELPHIA - DAY   *

BENJAMIN FRANKLIN, a tall, stout and bewigged man with the   *
constitution and energy of a man half his age (57), is   *
addressing a gathering of rambunctious COLONIAL OFFICIALS.   *

When he speaks (a continuation of the VOICEOVER), his voice   *
has the effect of quieting the rabble: FRANKLIN clearly has   *
the respect of his audience.   *

2.

<pre>
                    FRANKLIN   *
      Their actions, if left unchecked,   *
      could light the kindling for a   *
      conflagration which spread   *
      throughout the Colonies... and   *
      may yet spark a Revolution to   *
      engulf this fledgling nation, and   *
      its Colonial masters!   *
</pre>

FRANKLIN looks around at the expectant faces before him.   *

<pre>
                    FRANKLIN   *
      Tomorrow, I voyage to England,   *
      land of our forebears, on a noble   *
      and just quest: to petition the   *
      Privy Council and, if necessary,   *
      His Majesty, for a fair system of   *
      taxation, interdependent from the   *
      whims of the Penns.   *
</pre>

EXT. FIELDS - DAY   *

The camera continues over the FIELDS to a HILL, where a   *
DISTANT FIGURE can be seen, flying a KITE.   *

As the camera moves in on him, we see that it is a younger *
FRANKLIN, flying his kite in the midst of a thunderstorm. *

<pre>
                  FRANKLIN (V.O.)   *
      In the years since my first   *
      journey to England, as a young   *
      man, I have worn many coats: *
      printer, post-master,   *
      philosopher, politician. Yet my   *
      achievements have lately been   *
      measured against a length of wet   *
      string attached to a kite.   *
</pre>

We hear various members of his audience laugh.   *

A sudden FLASH OF SPARKS as a BOLT OF LIGHTNING strikes the *
KITE, electrifying the WET STRING, and the KEY suspended   *
from it. FRANKLIN, holding the STRING, recoils, burned.   *

The camera moves up the string to the KITE.   *

<pre>
                  FRANKLIN (V.O.)   *
      On that day, I was lucky to   *
      escape with a burn to my hand and   *
      a slight injury to my dignity...   *
                                                 *
</pre>

INSERT : A strikingly beautiful, raven-haired YOUNG WOMAN *
grips the rail of a staircase, as though her life depends *
on it.   *

3.

                    FRANKLIN   *
        I can scarce predict what fate   *
        awaits me in England...   *

She is wrapped in a BLOODIED SHEET which snags momentarily,   *
exposing her naked back. Her skin red with welts and the   *
marks of lashes.   *

                    FRANKLIN   *
        ...and yet I feel the same sense   *
        of anticipation...   *

EXT. SKY WITH GATHERING STORM CLOUDS - DAY   *

The camera moves on through the storm clouds, as THUNDER   *
RUMBLES, broken by periodic FLASHES OF THUNDER.   *

                    FRANKLIN (V.O.)   *
        Mark my words, gentlemen. A storm   *
        is coming...   *

INSERT : The YOUNG WOMAN stumbles barefoot into a COBBLED   *
STREET, where she is almost KNOCKED DOWN by a HORSE-AND-   *
COACH. The horse REARS UP as she COLLAPSES on the cobbles.   *

EXT. SKY WITH GATHERING STORM CLOUDS - DAY   *

Back to the clouds, as the camera moves down to take in a   *
CLIPPER SHIP, pitching and yawing in a storm-tossed sea. On   *
the stern, the words 'GEORGIUS REX' shine in the moonlight.   *

The thunder we heard before is now CANNON FIRE.   *

                    FRANKLIN (V.O.)   *
        If the King refuses to view the   *
        Colonies as anything more than a   *
        market, the consequences for his   *
        influence over us may be dire.   *

In the midst of the storm, the camera moves down to take in   *
a CLIPPER SHIP, pitching and yawing in a dark sea.   *

                    FRANKLIN (V.O.)   *
        I seek to pour oil on these   *
        troubled waters. I will not fail.   *
        I cannot fail.   *

The Georgius Rex is fired upon by another vessel, FLASHES   *
OF CANNON FIRE lighting up the sky, echoing the lightning.   *

A THUNDEROUS BOOM   *

                            SMASH CUT TO: *

4.

INT. CABIN ABOARD THE 'GEORGIUS REX' - NIGHT   *

FRANKLIN starts awake, jolted from sleep by the noise.   *

We follow his P.O.V. to --   *

A HANDSOME YOUNG MAN, aged about 30, stands at the door of *
the CABIN where FRANKLIN was sleeping. This is FRANKLIN's   *
son, WILLIAM, and we will soon learn that intelligence, wit *
and a sense of humour are just some of the things he has   *
failed to inherit from his father.   *

              WILLIAM   *
     Father?   *

              FRANKLIN   *
     I was dreaming... I...   *

He is interrupted by a LOUD CRACK OF THUNDER.   *

              FRANKLIN   *
     Is that... cannon fire?   *

              WILLIAM   *
     No, father! Thunder.   *

FRANKLIN, relieved, sinks back onto his COT.   *

A LOUD BOOM OF CANNON FIRE   *

              WILLIAM   *
     <u>That</u> is cannon fire.   *

FRANKLIN does a double-take, looking wearily at WILLIAM as   *
though this kind of remark is typical of his son.   *

              FRANKLIN   *
     Perhaps they are unaware that the   *
     war is over.   *

EXT. ATLANTIC OCEAN - NIGHT   *

The GEORGIUS REX takes evasive action from the FRENCH   *
WARSHIP, sailing into a FOG BANK, and melting from view.   *

At last, the sounds of THUNDER and CANNON FIRE fade.   *

                           DISSOLVE TO: *

EXT. FALMOUTH - HARBOUR - DAWN   *

The sight of the GEORGIUS REX seems ethereal in the weak   *
but welcome light of an early dawn.   *

Two gentlemen, one thin and fashionably dressed (JOHN
FOTHERGILL, physician), the other red-faced and fashionably
fat (WILLIAM STRAHAN, printer) wait at the dock.

They light up at the sight of BENJAMIN FRANKLIN climbing
stiffly ashore, aided by WILLIAM. Behind them, Two NEGRO
SERVANTS, PETER and KING, struggle manfully with BAGGAGE.

> FOTHERGILL / STRAHAN
> Benjamin! / Franklin!

Both gentlemen offer hearty handshakes and claps on the
back.

> FRANKLIN
> Mr. Strahan and... Dr.
> Fothergill, I presume? Allow me
> to introduce my son, William.

> FOTHERGILL / STRAHAN / WILLIAM
> Delighted! / An honour. /
> Welcome! [etc., ad lib.]

More formal handshakes are exchanged, but FRANKLIN is
clearly the centre of attention.

> STRAHAN
> Franklin, you look wonderful!

> FRANKLIN
> We have never met, sir. Therefore
> I can only deduce that I compare
> favourably with the miniature I
> enclosed with my most recent
> correspondence.

STRAHAN bellows with laughter.

> STRAHAN
> Indeed! And a sight more
> animated, to be sure... Tell me,
> how was the crossing?

> FRANKLIN
> (stiffly)
> Truthfully? We were fired upon by
> French privateers, the food was
> inedible, and I remain a martyr
> to the gout.

> FOTHERGILL
> (bedside manner)
> Tsk, tsk. No matter, my dear
> fellow: lodgings befitting a man
> of your status have been
> procured, a mere stone's throw
> from Parliament.

6.

FRANKLIN   *
Let us pray that stone-throwing   *
will not be necessary!   *

STRAHAN's uproarious laughter carries the four away to   *
FOTHERGILL'S CARRIAGE, the NEGRO SERVANTS lagging behind.   *

ANOTHER P.O.V.   *

From a high vantage point, FRANKLIN's arrival is observed   *
by two SHADOWY FIGURES.   *

EXT. WILTON HOUSE, WILTON, SALISBURY - DAY   *

FOTHERGILL'S CARRIAGE enters the magnificent grounds of   *
Wilton House, country seat of the Earl of Pembroke.   *

EXT. WILTON HOUSE, WILTON, SALISBURY - MOMENTS LATER   *

The new arrivals stroll through the gardens with Henry   *
Herbert, the 10th Earl of PEMBROKE, a handsome 30-year-old   *
whose confidence and commanding presence belie his youth.   *

PEMBROKE   *
This is indeed an honour, Dr.   *
Franklin. The air positively   *
crackles in your presence!   *
(winning smile)   *
Or perhaps you carry some residue   *
of your electrical experiments?   *

FRANKLIN enjoys the man's wit.   *

FRANKLIN   *
You have followed my dabblings   *
with the electrical fluid?   *

PEMBROKE   *
Come, come, Doctor. Your fame   *
precedes you.   *

FRANKLIN   *
And, I dare say, flatters me.   *

FRANKLIN glances at WILLIAM, who is distracted by the sight   *
of two LOVELY YOUNG LADIES, giggling in the distance.   *

PEMBROKE   *
You are too modest, sir!   *
Prometheus himself would be   *
impressed by what you call   *
'dabblings!'   *
(gravely)   *
But I warn you, Doctor.   *
(MORE)

          PEMBROKE (cont'd)
You will find the Privy Council   *
rather more difficult to tame   *
than the lightning.   *

          FRANKLIN   *
I believe you may be correct?   *

          WILLIAM   *
          (helpfully)   *
Perhaps this Prometheus could   *
help you put your case?   *

Everyone looks at WILLIAM. He quickly gets the familiar   *
feeling he has just said something incredible stupid.   *

          WILLIAM   *
          (clears his throat)   *
Uh, tell me, Lord Pembroke. Who   *
are those delightful young   *
ladies?   *

          PEMBROKE   *
          (turning to look)   *
Ah! My "delightful" sisters.   *
Margaret and Mary. Since the   *
passing of my father, it has been   *
my unenviable task to seek   *
husbands for them both. But,   *
alas, they have a streak of   *
independence which is...   *
singular. My friend Casanova   *
begged for an introduction...   *
          (practiced comic timing)   *
...but I feared they might   *
corrupt him!   *

FRANKLIN laughs.   *

          WILLIAM   *
          (intrigued)   *
Indeed?   *

PEMBROKE turns back to FRANKLIN, all business.   *

          PEMBROKE   *
Your mission is a worthy one,   *
Franklin. I support you. The   *
Prime Minister, however, may not.   *
His position grows increasingly   *
fragile.   *

          FRANKLIN   *
Is that so? I confess my   *
surprise... Has he not presided   *
over a comfortable victory?   *

As they talk, WILLIAM stops to admire some FLOWERS. The   *
others walk on, oblivious at having left him behind.   *

8.

PEMBROKE
True enough. But the terms of the
treaty have all but eroded his
popularity. The concessions he
has made to the French... why,
one would think *they* had been the
victors!

STRAHAN
It is true, Benjamin! Bute
offered the French the whole of
Canada, or a sugar plantation in
the Caribbean.

PEMBROKE
Fortunately, for England and for
Bute, they chose the plantation!

They all have a good laugh at the expense of the French.

FRANKLIN
I suppose we should be grateful
that the Frenchman's short
sightedness is matched only by
his sweet tooth.

(Away in the distance, MARGARET and MARY can be seen waving
and beckoning in WILLIAM's direction. He brightens, and
begins walking, casually yet purposefully, towards them.)

PEMBROKE
Perhaps a more favourable
strategem might be to meet with
Sir Francis Dashwood. The
Chancellor of the Exchequer.

FOTHERGILL seems offended by the mere mention of the man's
name.

FOTHERGILL
And the most dissolute rake in
all of England, sir! A gambler,
an idler, as corrupt and wicked a
man as ever walked the Strand.

FRANKLIN is amused by his friend's disapprobation.

FRANKLIN
Indeed? He sounds somewhat over-
qualified for the post he
occupies!

PEMBROKE enjoys the joke. But FOTHERGILL is serious.

PEMBROKE
Nevertheless, as keeper of the
nation's books, he'll doubtless --

9.

```
                    FOTHERGILL                        *
                  (interrupting)                      *
            A blasphemer! He profanes all            *
            that good men hold dear...               *

                     STRAHAN                          *
                  (to FOTHERGILL)                     *
            Come, come, my dear Doctor...             *

FOTHERGILL waves off STRAHAN.                         *

                    FOTHERGILL                        *
            I'll not be drawn into idle              *
            gossip...                                 *
                 (but of course he will)             *
            ...but it is said that his most          *
            recent blasphemy is the re-              *
            creation of a secret order of           *
            disorder --                               *

(Beyond them, WILLIAM is surprised when the two black *
servants, PETER and KING, cut across his path, hurrying *
towards MARGARET and MARY. Realizing his mistake -- it was *
the black servants being beckoned over -- he changes *
direction abruptly, pretending to admire a BUSH.)    *

                     STRAHAN                          *
            Fotty refers to nothing more than        *
            the infamous Dilettanti Society --       *

                    FOTHERGILL                        *
            Piffle! I was going to say that          *
            he has lately presided over the          *
            resurrection of the forbidden            *
            Hell-Fire Club! Devoted to               *
            worship of the Devil.                     *

                     FRANKLIN                         *
            Gentlemen, please! Whatever this         *
            Dashwood's proclivities, they            *
            surely pale beside the cruel and         *
            unusual behaviour of the Penns!          *
                 (to PEMBROKE)                        *
            If you could arrange an                   *
            introduction, I would be greatly         *
            indebted to you.                          *

                     PEMBROKE                         *
            Nonsense. I would be delighted.          *

FRANKLIN and PEMBROKE shake on it. FRANKLIN looks around. *

                     FRANKLIN                         *
            Now, where is that errant son of         *
            mine?                                     *

He turns to see WILLIAM stomping towards them, glowering. *
```

Notes

1 Authorship

1. See http://www.guardian.co.uk/film/video/2009/jan/22/oscars-katewinslet, accessed on 23 January 2009.
2. See http://www.oscar.com/nominees/?pn=nominees, accessed on 23 January 2009.
3. For a recent account of the historical development of screenwriting, see Marc Norman, *What Happens Next: A History of American Screenwriting* (London: Aurum, 2008).
4. Tom Stempel, *Framework: A History of Screenwriting in the American Film*, 3rd edn (New York: Syracuse University Press, 2000), p. 5.
5. Lizzie Francke, *Script Girls: Women Screenwriters in Hollywood* (London: BFI, 1994), p. 5.
6. Nora Ephron made this remark to Marsha McCreadie, *The Women Who Write the Movies: From Frances Marion to Nora Ephron* (New York: Birch Lane Press, 1994), p. 3; Francke (p. 2) records writer Eleanor Perry overhearing a similar remark in a hotel lobby.
7. Francke, p. 6.
8. McCreadie, p. 4.
9. Francke, p. 45.
10. McCreadie, p. 4.
11. See, for example, many of the essays collected in Christine Gledhill (ed.), *Home Is Where the Heart Is: Studies in Melodrama and the Woman's Film* (London: BFI, 1987).
12. Francke, p. 6.
13. Edward Azlant, 'The Theory, History, and Practice of Screenwriting, 1897–1920' (unpublished doctoral thesis, University of Wisconsin, 1980), pp. 144–5.
14. Richard Fine, *Hollywood and the Profession of Authorship* (Ann Arbor, Michigan: UMI Research Press, 1985), p. 13.
15. Fine, p. 14.
16. Stanley Fish, *Is There a Text in This Class? The Authority of Interpretive Communities* (Cambridge, Mass.: Harvard University Press, 1980).
17. For a full collection of essays on the subject of film authorship, see John Caughie, ed., *Theories of Authorship* (London: Routledge, 1981).
18. Richard Corliss (ed.), *The Hollywood Screenwriters* (New York: Avon, 1972), pp. 11, 19.
19. Andrew Sarris, 'Preface for a Dialectical Discussion', in Richard Corliss, *Talking Pictures: Screenwriters in the American Cinema* (New York: Overlook, 1985), p. xv.
20. Thomas R. Schatz, *The Genius of the System: Hollywood Filmmaking in the Studio Era*, rev. edn (New York: Owl, 1996), p. 5.
21. Sarris, p. xiv.

22. Richard Corliss, *Talking Pictures: Screenwriters in the American Cinema* (New York: Overlook, 1985), p. xx.
23. Corliss, *Talking Pictures*, p. xxv.
24. Corliss, *Talking Pictures*, pp. xviii–xix.
25. David Simpson, 'Romanticism, Criticism and Theory', in Stuart Curran, ed., *The Cambridge Companion to British Romanticism* (Cambridge: Cambridge University Press, 1993), p. 4.
26. Jonathan Bate (ed.), *The Romantics on Shakespeare* (Harmondsworth: Penguin, 1992), pp. 21, 2.
27. Simpson, p. 5.
28. Brian Vickers, *Shakespeare, Co-Author: A Historical Study of Five Collaborative Plays* (Oxford: Oxford University Press, 2002).
29. Jack Stillinger, *Multiple Authorship and the Myth of Solitary Genius* (Oxford: Oxford University Press, 1991), p. 183.
30. Stillinger, p. 187.
31. Stillinger, p. 193.
32. Michael Crick, *Jeffrey Archer: Stranger Than Fiction* (London: Fourth Estate, 2000).
33. Peter Carey, *True History of the Kelly Gang* (London: Faber, 2002), pp. 423–4.
34. 'Rough Crossings: The Cutting of Raymond Carver', *New Yorker*, 24 December 2007, pp. 92–4.
35. Stillinger, p. 16.
36. Zachary Leader, *Revision and Romantic Authorship* (Oxford: Oxford University Press, 1996).
37. Marjut Salokannel, 'Cinema in Search of Its Authors: On the Notion of Film Authorship in Legal Discourse', in Virginia Wright Wexman, ed., *Film and Authorship* (New Brunswick, NJ: Rutgers University Press, 2003), p. 168.
38. *Theatrical and Television Basic Agreement* (Los Angeles: Writers Guild of America, 2001), p. 1.
39. *Screen Credits Manual* (Los Angeles: Writers Guild of America, undated), p. 18. Page numbers of subsequent references are given in parentheses.
40. Tad Friend, 'Credit Grab', *New Yorker* (20 October 2003), pp. 165–6.
41. David Mamet, *Hannibal*, unpublished screenplay, 8 September 1999; Steven Zaillian, *Hannibal*, unpublished screenplay, revised first draft, 7 January 2000. Both scripts are held in the library of the Writers Guild of America in Los Angeles.
42. Tom Stempel, 'The Collaborative Dog: *Wag the Dog* (1997)', *Film and History* 35.1 (2005), pp. 60–4; see also Steven Price, *The Plays, Screenplays and Films of David Mamet: A Reader's Guide to Essential Criticism* (Basingstoke: Palgrave Macmillan, 2008), pp. 133–4.
43. Friend, p. 167.
44. Friend, p. 163.
45. For discussion of the distinctions between mass, folk, and popular culture, see Dominic Strinati, *An Introduction to Theories of Popular Culture* (London: Routledge, 1995), pp. 1–33.
46. John Ellis, 'What Does a Script Do?', *Yearbook of English Studies* 20 (1994), p. 64.
47. Michel Foucault, 'What Is an Author?', in Paul Rabinow (ed.), *The Foucault Reader* (Harmondsworth: Penguin, 1991), p. 101. Subsequent references are to this edition.

48. See Yannis Tzioumakis, 'Marketing David Mamet: Institutionally Assigned Film Authorship in Contemporary American Cinema', *Velvet Light Trap* 57 (2006), pp. 60–75.
49. François Truffaut, 'A Certain Tendency of the French Cinema', in Bill Nichols, ed., *Movies and Methods: An Anthology* (Berkeley: University of California Press, 1976), pp. 228, 233, italics in original.
50. Richard Corliss (ed), *The Hollywood Screenwriters*, p. 9.
51. Temenuga Trifonova, 'Time and Point of View in Contemporary Cinema', *Cineaction* 58 (2003), p. 22.
52. Trifonova, p. 14.

2 From Work to Text

1. Quoted in Julian Murphet and Lydia Rainford, eds, *Literature and Visual Technologies* (Basingstoke: Palgrave Macmillan, 2003), p. 1.
2. Ernest Betts, 'Introduction', *The Private Life of Henry VIII* (London: Methuen, 1934), p. ix.
3. John Gassner, 'The Screenplay as Literature', in Gassner and Dudley Nichols, eds, *Twenty Best Film Plays* (New York: Crown, 1943), p. x.
4. Douglas Garrett Winston, *The Screenplay as Literature* (Cranbury, NJ: Associated University Press, 1973), p. 199.
5. Yaakov Malkin, *Criticism in Creation and the Screenplay as a New Literary Form* (Jerusalem: Israel Film Archives, 1980), p. 1.
6. Gary Davis, 'Rejected Offspring: The Screenplay as a Literary Genre', *New Orleans Review* 11.2 (1984), p. 90.
7. Nina Baym et al., eds, *The Norton Anthology of American Literature*, 4th edn, vol. 2 (New York: Norton, 1994).
8. Claudia Sternberg, *Written for the Screen: The American Motion-Picture Screenplay as Text* (Tübingen: Stauffenburg Verlag, 1997).
9. Barbara Korte and Ralf Schneider, 'The Published Screenplay – A New Literary Genre?', *AAA – Arbeiten aus Anglistik und Amerikanistik* 25.1 (2000), pp. 89–105.
10. Kevin A. Boon, *Script Culture and the American Screenplay* (Detroit, MI: Wayne State University Press, 2008), pp. 25–37.
11. Steven Maras, *Screenwriting: History, Theory and Practice* (London: Wallflower, 2009), pp. 12, 6.
12. Gassner, p. x.
13. Gassner, p. xviii.
14. Gassner, pp. vii–viii.
15. John Howard Lawson, *Theory and Technique of Playwriting and Screenwriting* (New York: G. P. Putnam, 1949), p. 368.
16. Winston, pp. 13–14.
17. Winston, p. 93, italics in original.
18. Winston, pp. 201–2, italics in original.
19. Winston, pp. 22–3.
20. Richard Corliss, *Talking Pictures: Screenwriters in the American Cinema* (New York: Overlook, 1985), p. 1.
21. Corliss, p. 124.

22. Sternberg, p. 91.
23. Sternberg, p. 59.
24. Sternberg, p. 232.
25. Andrey Tarkovsky, *Sculpting in Time: Reflections on the Cinema*, rev. ed., trans. Kitty Hunter-Blair (London: Faber, 1989), p. 126.
26. Gassner, p. viii.
27. Sternberg, p. 64.
28. Malkin, p. 1.
29. Abraham Polonsky, 'Une expérience utopique', in John Schultheiss and Mark Schaubert (ed.), *Force of Evil: The Critical Edition* (Northridge, CA: Center for Telecommunication Studies, 1996), p. 187.
30. Sarah Kozloff, *Overhearing Film Dialogue* (Berkeley: University of California Press, 2000), p. 69.
31. Davis, pp. 92–3.
32. Kevin Alexander Boon, 'The Screenplay, Imagism, and Modern Aesthetics', *Literature/Film Quarterly* 36 (2008), p. 262.
33. Quoted in Boon, 'The Screenplay', p. 262.
34. Ethan Coen and Joel Coen, *Fargo* (London: Faber, 1996), p. 1; quoted in Boon, 'The Screenplay', p. 263.
35. Boon, 'The Screenplay', p. 263.
36. Boon, 'The Screenplay', p. 264.
37. Frank S. Nugent, *The Searchers* (Ipswich: ScreenPress, 2002), p. 5.
38. Allan Scott and Chris Bryant, *Don't Look Now* (London: Sight and Sound [British Film Institute], 1997), p. 7.
39. Coen, p. 1.
40. Roland Barthes, 'From Work to Text', in *Image – Music – Text*, trans. Stephen Heath (New York: Hill and Wang, 1977), p. 156. Subsequent page references are to this edition.
41. Roland Barthes, 'The Death of the Author', in *Image – Music – Text*, trans. Stephen Heath (New York: Hill and Wang, 1977), p. 146.
42. Philip Brophy, 'Read My Lips: Notes on the Writing and Speaking of Film Dialogue', *Continuum* 5.2 (1992), p. 260.
43. Ian W. MacDonald, 'Disentangling the Screen Idea', *Journal of Media Practice* 5.2 (2004), p. 90.

3 Ontology of the Screenplay

1. William Horne, 'See Shooting Script: Reflections on the Ontology of the Screenplay', *Literature/Film Quarterly* 20.1 (1992), p. 48.
2. Toby Mussman (ed.), *Jean-Luc Godard: A Critical Anthology* (New York: Dutton, 1968), p. 110; quoted in Douglas Garrett Winston, *The Screenplay as Literature* (Cranbury, NJ: Associated University Press, 1973), p. 17.
3. Quoted in Winston, p. 16.
4. Elizabeth Ezra, *Georges Méliès: The Birth of the Auteur* (Manchester: Manchester University Press, 2000), p. 72.
5. Quoted in Winston, p. 16.
6. Claudia Sternberg, *Written for the Screen: The American Motion-Picture Screenplay as Text* (Tübingen: Stauffenburg Verlag, 1997), p. 28.

7. For a detailed consideration of the blueprint metaphor from a different perspective, see Steven Maras, *Screenwriting: History, Theory and Practice* (London: Wallflower, 2009), pp. 117–29.
8. Dudley Nichols, 'The Writer and the Film', in John Gassner and Dudley Nichols, eds., *Twenty Best Film Plays* (New York: Crown, 1943), p. xxxv.
9. Janet Staiger, 'Blueprints for Feature Films: Hollywood's Continuity Scripts', in Tino Balio, ed., *The American Film Industry*, rev. edn (Madison: University of Wisconsin Press, 1985), pp. 173–92.
10. Kristin Thompson, *Storytelling in the New Hollywood: Understanding Classical Narrative Technique* (Cambridge, Mass.: Harvard University Press, 1999), p. 346.
11. Cherry Potter, *Screen Language: From Film Writing to Film-Making* (London: Methuen, 2001), p. xiii.
12. Syd Field, *Screenplay: The Foundations of Screenwriting*, rev. edn (New York: Dell, 1994), p. 4.
13. Sternberg, p. 50.
14. Sternberg, p. 57.
15. Sternberg, p. 50.
16. Quentin Tarantino, *Natural Born Killers* (London: Faber, 1995), p. 3.
17. For examples of blueprints and plans of interior sets, see the reproductions of the floor plan of the Amberson mansion in Robert L. Carringer (ed.), *The Magnificent Ambersons: A Reconstruction* (Berkeley: University of California Press, 1993), p. 74, and of the Bates house in *Psycho*, in Bill Krohn, *Hitchcock at Work* (London: Phaidon, 2000), p. 227.
18. Quoted in Winston, p. 166.
19. Krohn, p. 9.
20. Sternberg, p. 50.
21. Dore Schary [and Charles Palmer], *Case History of a Movie* (New York: Random House, 1950), p. 27.
22. Carl Foreman, 'Foreword: Confessions of a Frustrated Screenwriter', in Richard Corliss (ed), *The Hollywood Screenwriters* (New York: Avon, 1972), p. 32.
23. Peter Wollen, *Signs and Meaning in the* Cinema, 3ʳᵈ ed. (Bloomington: Indiana University Press, 1972), p. 113. On the screenplay and music, see also Maras, p. 127.
24. Winston, p. 20.
25. Nichols, p. xxxii.
26. W.K. Wimsatt, Jr. and Monroe C. Beardsley, 'The Intentional Fallacy', in W. K. Wimsatt, Jr., *The Verbal Icon: Studies in the Meaning of Poetry* (Lexington: University of Kentucky Press, 1954), p. 3.
27. Tad Friend, 'Credit Grab', *New Yorker* (20 October 2003), p. 163.
28. Sternberg, p. 27.
29. Sternberg, p. 57.
30. John Collier, *Milton's Paradise Lost: Screenplay for Cinema of the Mind* (New York: Knopf, 1973).
31. Ian W. MacDonald, 'Disentangling the Screen Idea', *Journal of Media Practice* 5.2 (2004), p. 90.
32. Andrey Tarkovsky, *Sculpting in Time: Reflections on the Cinema*, rev. ed., trans. Kitty Hunter-Blair (London: Faber, 1989), p. 126.
33. Sergei Eisenstein, 'The Form of the Script', in *Selected Works, vol. 1: Writings, 1922–34*, trans. and ed. Richard Taylor (London: BFI, 1988), p. 134.

34. Pier Paolo Pasolini, 'The Screenplay as a "Structure that Wants to Be Another Structure"', *American Journal of Semiotics* 4.1–2 (1986), p. 59; italics in the original.
35. John Ellis, 'What Does a Script Do?', *Yearbook of English Studies* 20 (1994), p. 61.
36. Quoted in David Cook, *A History of Narrative Film*, 4th ed. (New York: Norton, 2004), p. 367.
37. François Truffaut, *Hitchcock*, rev. ed. (London: Paladin, 1984), p. 131.
38. Sternberg, p. 52.
39. Sternberg, p. 107.
40. Tarkovsky, p. 134.
41. Andrei Tarkovsky, *Collected Screenplays*, trans. William Powell and Natasha Synessios (London: Faber, 1999).
42. Jacques Derrida, 'The Ghost Dance: An Interview with Jacques Derrida', trans. Jean-Luc Svobada, *Public* 2 (1989), p.61; quoted in Andrew Bennett and Nicholas Royle, *Introduction to Literature, Criticism and Theory*, 3rd edn (London: Longman, 2004), p. 138.
43. Kevin Boon, *Script Culture and the American Screenplay* (Detroit, MI: Wayne State University Press, 2008), p. 35. Perhaps the most helpful discussion of invagination in the present context is found in Jacques Derrida, 'The Law of Genre', *Critical Inquiry* 7.1 (1980), pp. 55–81.
44. Robert Bresson, *Notes on the Cinematographer*, trans. Jonathan Griffin (London: Quartet, 1996), p. 13.
45. Dudley Andrew, *Concepts in Film Theory* (Oxford: Oxford University Press, 1984), p. 96.
46. Thomas Leitch, 'Hitchcock and His Writers: Authorship and Authority in Adaptation', in Jack Boozer, ed., *Authorship in Film Adaptation* (Austin: University of Texas Press, 2008), p. 79.
47. Deborah Cartmell, 'Introduction', in Deborah Cartmell and Imelda Whelehan (eds), *Adaptations: From Text to Screen, Screen to Text* (London: Routledge, 1999), pp. 23–4.
48. Cartmell, p. 24.
49. Thomas Leitch, 'Twelve Fallacies in Contemporary Adaptation Theory', *Criticism* 45.2 (2003), p. 161.
50. Brian McFarlane, *Novel to Film: An Introduction to the Theory of Adaptation* (Oxford: Oxford University Press, 1996), p. vii.
51. McFarlane, p. 13.
52. McFarlane, p. 13.
53. McFarlane, p. 26.
54. Pauline Kael, *5001 Nights at the Movies* (New York: Holt, Rinehart and Winston, 1982), p. 355; quoted in Leitch, 'Twelve', p. 152.
55. Boon, pp. 154–5.
56. Leitch, 'Twelve', p. 152.
57. Gene Gauntier, 'Blazing the Trail', unpublished manuscript, quoted in Tom Stempel, *Framework: A History of Screenwriting in the American Film*, 3rd. edn (New York: Syracuse University Press, 2000), p. 9.
58. Jonathan Culler, *On Deconstruction: Theory and Criticism after Structuralism* (London: Routledge, 1983), p. 123.
59. Patrick McGilligan, *Alfred Hitchcock: A Life in Darkness and Light* (New York: HarperCollins, 2003), p. 719; quoted in Leitch, 'Hitchcock', p. 73.

60. Charlie Kaufman and Donald Kaufman, *Adaptation: The Shooting Script* (London: Nick Hern, 2002), p. 2. Subsequent page references are to this edition.

4 Stages in Screenplay Development

1. Steven Maras, *Screenwriting: History, Theory and Practice* (London: Wallflower, 2009), pp. 22, 27–43.
2. Charles Fleming, *High Concept: Don Simpson and the Hollywood Culture of Excess* (London: Bloomsbury, 1998), p. 14.
3. Fleming, p. 29.
4. Edward Dmytryk, *On Screen Writing* (London: Focal Press, 1985).
5. Dore Schary [and Charles Palmer], *Case History of a Movie* (New York: Random House, 1950), pp. 7–8.
6. Art Linson, *What Just Happened?: Bitter Hollywood Tales from the Front Line* (London: Bloomsbury, 2002), p. 28.
7. Carl Foreman, 'Anatomy of a Classic: *High Noon*', 20 February 1976, American Film Institute; unpublished seminar transcript 1, BFI.
8. Schary, p. 27.
9. Scott Frank, speaking at the WGA Pre-Conference Craft Day, 2002 Film and TV Writers Forum, 'Words into Pictures', June 6–9 2002, Hilton Hotel Universal City, California; audio recording held at Writers Guild of America library, Los Angeles.
10. Austin E. Quigley, *The Pinter Problem* (Princeton, N. J.: Princeton University Press, 1975), pp. 13–16.
11. David Mamet, *A Whore's Profession* (London: Faber, 1994), p. 360.
12. David Mamet, *Jafsie and John Henry* (London: Faber, 1999), pp. 97–8.
13. Maras, p. 86.
14. David Bordwell, Janet Staiger, and Kristin Thompson, *The Classical Hollywood Cinema: Film Style and Mode of Production to 1960* (London: Routledge, 1985).
15. Maras, pp. 79–96.
16. James F. Boyle, 'Foreword', in Judith H. Haag and Hillis R. Cole, Jr., ed, *The Complete Guide to Standard Script Formats, Part 1: The Screenplay* (Los Angeles: CMC, 1980), pp. ix–x.
17. Schary, pp. 30–34.
18. Kevin Jackson, *The Language of Cinema* (Manchester: Carcanet, 1998), p. 230.
19. For more detail, see Haag and Cole, pp. 111–14.
20. Robert L. Carringer, *The Magnificent Ambersons: A Reconstruction* (Berkeley, CA: University of California Press, 1993), pp. 2, 33, italics in original.
21. Boyle, p. x.

5 *The Birds*

1. Thomas Leitch, 'Hitchcock and His Writers: Authorship and Authority in Adaptation', in Jack Boozer, ed., *Authorship in Film Adaptation* (Austin: University of Texas Press, 2008), p. 84, n. 45.
2. Leitch, pp. 67–8.
3. Leitch, p. 75.
4. Leitch, p. 78.

5. Tony Lee Moral, *Hitchcock and the Making of Marnie* (Manchester: Manchester University Press, 2002), pp. 21–53.
6. Dan Auiler, *Vertigo: The Making of a Hitchcock Classic* (London: Titan, 1998), pp. 27–62.
7. Unless otherwise noted, the discussion of all primary materials relating to *The Birds* is derived from the author's study of the files on *The Birds* held at the Margaret Herrick Library, Academy of Motion Picture Arts and Sciences, Los Angeles.
8. Kyle B. Counts, 'The Making of Alfred Hitchcock's *The Birds*: The Complete Story behind the Precursor of Modern Horror Films', *Cinefantastique* 10.ii (Fall 1980), p. 15.
9. Counts, p. 16.
10. Evan Hunter, *Me and Hitch* (London: Faber, 1997), p. 10.
11. Hunter, p. 11.
12. Hunter, p. 12.
13. Hunter, p. 23.
14. Hunter, p. 14.
15. Hunter, p. 17.
16. Bill Krohn, *Hitchcock at Work* (London: Phaidon, 2000), p. 251.
17. Hunter, p. 47.
18. Krohn, p. 250.
19. Krohn, p. 243.
20. Krohn, p. 256.
21. Patrick McGilligan, *Alfred Hitchcock: A Life in Darkness and Light* (New York: HarperCollins, 2003), p. 624.
22. Krohn, p. 9.
23. Hunter, p. 31.
24. Counts, p. 18.
25. Hunter, p. 31.
26. Counts, p. 20.
27. Counts, p. 18.
28. Robert E. Kapsis, *Hitchcock: The Making of a Reputation* (Chicago: University of Chicago Press, 1992), p. 74.
29. Counts, p. 20.
30. Counts, p. 32.
31. Hunter, p. 55.
32. Krohn, p. 258.
33. Krohn, p. 259.
34. Krohn, p. 262.
35. Counts, p. 34.

6 Editing and Publication

1. For further examples and discussion of 'the position of screenwriting in the sociological system of literature', see Barbara Korte and Ralf Schneider, 'The Published Screenplay – A New *Literary* Genre?', *AAA – Arbeiten aus Anglistik und Amerikanistik* 25.1 (2000), pp. 91–3.
2. *Sunrise*, DVD (Eureka 2005); *Sunset Boulevard*, *DVD* (Paramount, 2003).

3. *Pierrot le Fou: A Film by Jean-Luc Godard*, trans. Peter Whitehead (London: Lorrimer, 1969); *The Cabinet of Dr Caligari*, trans. R.V. Adkinson (London: Lorrimer, 1984).
4. *Pandora's Box (Lulu)* (London: Lorrimer, 1971, rev. 1984).
5. *Eisenstein: Two Films [October and Alexander Nevsky]*, ed. Jay Leyda, trans. Diana Matias (London: Lorrimer, 1984), p. 13.
6. *The Rules of the Game*, trans. John McGrath and Maureen Teitelbaum (London: Lorrimer, 1970), p. 4.
7. *Stagecoach* (London: Lorrimer, 1971), p. 4.
8. *Singin' in the Rain* (London: Lorrimer, 1986), p. xiv.
9. Ingmar Bergman, *Wild Strawberries: A Film*, trans. Lars Malmström and David Kushner (London: Lorrimer, 1970).
10. The studies that have most closely informed the following discussion are Jerome J. McGann, *The Textual Condition* (Princeton, N. J.: Princeton University Press, 1991), and Jack Stillinger, *Multiple Authorship and the Myth of Solitary Genius* (Oxford: Oxford University Press, 1991).
11. Stillinger, p. 195.
12. McGann, pp. 58, 75.
13. McGann, pp. 85–6.
14. McGann, p. 14.
15. Esther Luttrell, *Tools of the Screen Writing Trade*, rev. ed. (Mt. Dora, Fla.: Broadcast Club of America, 1998), p. 10, italics in the original.
16. McGann, pp. 29–30.
17. Tino Balio, 'Foreword' to *42nd Street*, ed. Rocco Fumento (Madison, Wisc: University of Wisconsin Press, 1980), pp. 7–8.
18. Rocco Fumento, 'Introduction: From Bastards and Bitches to Heroes and Heroines', *42nd Street*, ed. Rocco Fumento (Madison, Wisc: University of Wisconsin Press, 1980), pp. 36–7.
19. *42nd Street*, pp. 196, 21.
20. *42nd Street*, p. 20.
21. *42nd Street*, p. 193.
22. *Meet Me in St. Louis*. MGM, 1944. Screen Play by Sarah Y. Mason and Victor Heerman. Victor Heerman collection, MHL, 5–f.7.
23. *42nd Street* folder, Warner Brothers collection, USC.
24. Billy Wilder and Raymond Chandler, *Double Indemnity*, intro. by Jeffrey Meyers (Berkeley: University of California Press, 2000), p. 11.
25. Richard J. Anobile, ed., *The Maltese Falcon* (London: Picador, 1974), p. 5.
26. John Schultheiss and Mark Schaubert, eds, *Force of Evil: The Critical Edition* (California State University, Northridge: Center for Telecommunication Studies, 1996), p. 17.
27. Robert L. Carringer, *The Magnificent Ambersons: A Reconstruction* (Berkeley: University of California Press, 1993), p. 3. Subsequent page references are to this edition.

7 The Scene Text

1. Claudia Sternberg, *Written for the Screen: The American Motion-Picture Screenplay as Text* (Tübingen: Stauffenburg Verlag, 1997), p. 71. Subsequent references in parentheses.

2. *Citizen Kane*, shooting script, by Herman J. Manciewicz and Orson Welles, in *The Citizen Kane Book* (London: Methuen 1985), p. 86.
3. Pier Paolo Pasolini, 'The Screenplay as a "Structure that Wants to Be Another Structure"', *American Journal of Semiotics* 4.i–ii (1986), p. 53. Subsequent page references are given in parentheses; italics in the original.
4. Sergei Eisenstein, 'The Form of the Script', in *Selected Works, vol. 1: Writings, 1922–34*, trans. and ed. Richard Taylor (London: BFI, 1988), pp. 134–5.
5. James F. Boyle, 'Foreword', Judith H. Haag and Hillis R. Cole, Jr., *The Complete Guide to Standard Script Formats, Part 1: The Screenplay* (Los Angeles: CMC, 1980), p. v.
6. Gérard Genette, *Narrative Discourse: An Essay in Method* (Ithaca: Cornell University Press, 1980).
7. Alain Robbe-Grillet, *Last Year at Marienbad: A Ciné-Novel*, trans. Richard Howard (London: Calder, 1961), pp. 7–8.
8. Ernest Hemingway, 'The Killers', *Men without Women* (London: Granta, 1977 [1928]), p. 49.
9. William Peter Blatty, *The Exorcist* (London: Faber, 1998), p. 3.
10. Christian Metz, *Film Language*, trans. Michael Taylor (Oxford: Oxford University Press, 1974), p. 21.
11. Edward Branigan, *Narrative Comprehension and Film* (London: Routledge, 1992), p. 38.
12. David Bordwell, *Narration in the Fiction Film* (London: Methuen, 1985), p. 15.
13. Bordwell, p. 62.
14. Sternberg, p. 109.
15. Paul Schrader, *Taxi Driver* (London: Faber, 1990), p. 1.
16. Patrick McGilligan, *Alfred Hitchcock: A Life in Darkness and Light* (New York: HarperCollins, 2003), pp. 445–7; Thomas Leitch, 'Hitchcock and His Writers: Authorship and Authority in Adaptation', in Jack Boozer, ed., *Authorship in Film Adaptation* (Austin: University of Texas Press, 2008), pp. 69–70.
17. Bill Krohn, *Hitchcock at Work* (London: Phaidon, 2000), pp. 115–6.
18. Krohn, p. 119.
19. Christopher McQuarrie, *The Usual Suspects* (London: Faber, 1996), p. 7.
20. Charles Dickens, *Bleak House*, ed. Norman Page (Harmondsworth: Penguin, 1985), pp. 768–9.
21. For a very full discussion of character and structure in film, see Richard Dyer, *Stars*, 2nd edn (London: BFI, 1998), pp. 87–131.
22. David Mamet, *True and False: Heresy and Common Sense for the Actor* (New York: Random House, 1997), p. 9.
23. David Mamet, *A Whore's Profession* (London: Faber, 1994), p. 346.
24. Rick Altman, 'A Semantic/Syntactic Approach to Film Genre', in Barry Keith Grant (ed.), *Film Genre Reader II* (Austin: University of Texas Press, 1995), pp. 26–40.
25. Munsterberg, quoted in Edward Azlant, 'The Theory, History, and Practice of Screenwriting, 1897–1920' (unpublished doctoral thesis, University of Wisconsin, 1980), pp. 22–3.
26. Quoted in Azlant, p. 46.
27. Roland Barthes, 'Introduction to the Structural Analysis of Narrative', in *Image – Music – Text*, trans. Stephen Heath (New York: Hill and Wang, 1977), pp. 79–124.

28. Azlant, p. 139, quoting Lewis Jacobs.
29. Dore Schary [and Charles Palmer], *Case History of a Movie* (New York: Random House, 1950), p. 8.
30. Schary, pp. 8–9.
31. Michael Hauge, *Writing Screenplays That Sell* (London: Elm Tree, 1989), p. 11.
32. David Mamet, *Plays: Three* (London: Methuen, 1996), p. 177.
33. Will Wright, *Six Guns and Society: A Structural Study of the Western* (Berkeley: University of California Press, 1975), pp. 25–6.

8 The Dialogue Text

1. Mary Devereaux, 'Of "Talk and Brown Furniture": The Aesthetics of Film Dialogue', *Post Script* 6.1 (1986), p. 35.
2. Devereaux, p. 38.
3. Mary Devereaux, 'In Defense of Talking Film', *Persistence of Vision* 5 (1987), p. 17.
4. Devereaux, 'Of "Talk"', p. 43.
5. Siegfried Kracauer, *Theory of Film* (Oxford: Oxford University Press, 1960), p. 106.
6. Devereaux, 'Of "Talk"', p. 39.
7. Noël Carroll, 'The Specificity Thesis', in Gerald Mast, Marshall Cohen, and Leo Braudy (eds), *Film Theory and Criticism*, 4th ed. (Oxford: Oxford University Press, 1992), pp. 278–85.
8. Kevin Boon, *Script Culture and the American Screenplay* (Detroit, MI: Wayne State University Press, 2008), pp. 89–113.
9. Robert McKee, *Story: Substance, Structure, Style, and the Principles of Screenwriting* (London: Methuen, 1997), p. 393.
10. Syd Field, *Screenplay: The Foundations of Screenwriting* (New York: Dell, 1979), pp. 173–4.
11. Lew Hunter, *Screenwriting* (London: Robert Hale, 1994), pp. 79–81, 124–8; Michael Hauge, *Writing Screenplays that Sell* (London: Elm Tree, 1988), pp. 133–44.
12. McKee, p. 393.
13. Sarah Kozloff, *Overhearing Film Dialogue* (Berkeley: University of California Press, 2000), p. 28, italics in the original.
14. Devereaux, 'Of "Talk"', p. 46.
15. Claudia Sternberg, *Written for the Screen: The American Motion-Picture Screenplay as Text* (Tübingen: Stauffenburg Verlag, 1997), pp. 94–102.
16. Kracauer, p. 106.
17. Kozloff, p. 47.
18. Jean Chothia, *Forging a Language: A Study of the Plays of Eugene O'Neill* (Cambridge: Cambridge University Press, 1979), pp. 7–8; quoted in Kozloff, p. 16.
19. Kozloff, pp. 15–16.
20. Sternberg, p. 93.
21. Devereaux, 'Of "Talk"', pp. 46–7.
22. Kozloff, pp. 33, 90, italics in the original.
23. Richard Corliss, *Talking Pictures: Screenwriters in the American Cinema* (New York: Overlook, 1974), p. xx.

24. David Thomson, *The Whole Equation: A History of Hollywood* (London: Abacus, 2006), p. 198.
25. Philip Brophy, 'Read My Lips: Notes on the Writing and Speaking of Film Dialogue', *Continuum* 5.2 (1992), p. 260.
26. Kozloff, p. 64.
27. Kozloff, pp. 33–4.
28. Keir Elam, *The Semiotics of Theatre and Drama* (London: Methuen, 1980), pp. 27, 140.
29. Manfred Pfister, *The Theory and Analysis of Drama*, trans. John Halliday (Cambridge: Cambridge University Press, 1988), p. 258.
30. Pages from the screenplay are reproduced in the DVD release of the film (British Film Institute, 2002).
31. William Aubrey Burlington, *Through the Fourth Wall* (London: Brentano, 1922), pp. 110–14.
32. Laurence Olivier, 'The Making of *Henry V*', in *Henry V* (London: Lorrimer, 1984), n.p.
33. Olivier, n.p.
34. Kenneth Branagh, *Henry V, by William Shakespeare: A Screen Adaptation by Kenneth Branagh* (London: Chatto and Windus, 1989), pp. 9–11.
35. Branagh, p. 16.
36. Branagh, pp. 11–12.
37. Russell Jackson, 'From Play-Script to Screenplay', in Russell Jackson, ed., *The Cambridge Companion to Shakespeare on Film*, 2nd edn (Cambridge: Cambridge University Press, 2007), p. 19.
38. Branagh, p. 12.
39. Peter Brook, *The Shifting Point: Forty Years of Theatrical Experience, 1946–1987* (London, 1988); quoted in Jackson, p. 22.
40. J. L. Austin, *How to Do Things with Words* (Oxford: Oxford University Press, 1962), pp. 6, 139, 145.
41. Andrew K. Kennedy, *Dramatic Dialogue: The Duologue of Personal Encounter* (Cambridge: Cambridge University Press, 1983), p. 9.
42. Austin E. Quigley, *The Pinter Problem* (Princeton, N.J.: Princeton UP, 1975), p. 54.
43. David Mamet, *Glengarry Glen Ross* (London: Methuen, 1984), p. 18, italics in the original.
44. Mamet, pp. 19–23.
45. Roman Jakobson, 'Linguistics and Poetics', in Thomas A. Seboek (ed.), *Style in Language* (Cambridge, Mass.: M.I.T. Press, 1960), p. 356.
46. Austin, pp. 18–19.
47. Kennedy, p. 23.
48. Pfister, pp. 117–8.
49. Kozloff, p. 19.
50. Kozloff, pp. 16–17.
51. Quentin Tarantino, *Pulp Fiction* (London: Faber, 1994).
52. Billy Wilder and Raymond Chandler, *Double Indemnity* (Berkeley: University of California Press, 2000), pp. 17–18.
53. See http://www.afi.com/tvevents/100years/quotes.aspx#list.
54. Brophy, p. 259.
55. Tad Friend, 'Credit Grab', *New Yorker*, 20 October 2003, p. 166.

56. Brophy, p. 253.
57. Brophy, p. 253.
58. Brophy, p. 258.
59. Brophy, p. 259.
60. Brophy, pp. 264–5.
61. Harold Pinter, 'Writing for the Theatre', in *Plays: One* (London: Methuen, 1976), p. 11.
62. David Mamet, *A Whore's Profession* (London: Faber, 1994), p. 163.
63. Sidney Lumet, *Making Movies* (New York: Knopf, 1995), p. 37.
64. David Mamet, *Homicide* (New York: Grove, 1992), p. 103.
65. Graham Greene, *The Third Man* (London: Faber, 1988), p. 100.
66. Sarah Kozloff, *Invisible Storytellers: Voice-Over Narration in American Fiction Film* (Berkeley: University of California Press, 1988), pp. 33–4.
67. Kozloff, *Invisible*, pp. 17, 106.
68. Kozloff, *Invisible*, p. 5, emphasis added.
69. Samuel Beckett, *The Complete Dramatic Works* (London: Faber, 1990), pp. 399, 435.
70. Beckett, pp. 323–4.
71. Kozloff, *Invisible*, p. 52.
72. *Double Indemnity*, pp. 10–11. In reproducing extracts from this screenplay I have attempted to preserve the lineation of the facsimile.
73. Christopher McQuarrie, *The Usual Suspects* (London: Faber, 1996), pp. 31–3. Subsequent page references are to this edition.
74. *The Usual Suspects*, p. 91. Instead of using the '(cont.)' convention to indicate the resumption of speech in the dialogue text after an interruption by elements of the scene text, McQuarrie's published screenplay presents the scene text in italics.

Epilogue

1. *Sunset Boulevard* (Berkeley: University of California Press, 1999), p. 9. Page references are to this edition.
2. Jeffrey Meyers, introduction to *Sunset Boulevard* (Berkeley: University of California Press, 1999), p. ix.
3. Quoted in Meyers, p. xii.
4. Sergei Eisenstein, 'The Form of the Script', in *Selected Works, vol. 1: Writings, 1922–34*, trans. and ed. Richard Taylor (London: BFI, 1988), p. 134.
5. André Bazin, 'The Ontology of the Photographic Image', in *What is Cinema?*, vol. 1, trans. Hugh Gray (Berkeley: University of California Press, 2005), p. 9.

Appendix

1. Esther Luttrell, *Tools of the Screen Writing Trade*, rev. ed. (Mt. Dora, Fla.: Broadcast Club of America, 1998), p. 79.

Select Bibliography

Unpublished materials

42nd Street files, Warner Brothers collection, University of Southern California.
The Birds files, Alfred Hitchcock Collection, Margaret Herrick Library, Academy of Motion Picture Arts and Sciences, Los Angeles.
Meet Me in St. Louis, by Sarah Y. Mason and Victor Heerman, Victor Heerman collection, Margaret Herrick Library, Academy of Motion Picture Arts and Sciences, Los Angeles.
Strangers on a Train, final draft, 18 October 1950, unpublished, British Film Institute library, London, S18186.
Foreman, Carl, 'Anatomy of a Classic: *High Noon*', 20 February 1976, American Film Institute; unpublished seminar transcript 1, BFI.

Published screenplays

I have followed below the convention followed by most librarians, whereby screenplays are catalogued by title and not by author. This carries a presumption of corporate authorship that sits uneasily with many of the screenplays listed below; but I have opted for consistency at the risk of absurdity.

42nd Street, by Rian James and James Seymour, ed. Rocco Fumento (Madison, Wisc: University of Wisconsin Press, 1980).
Adaptation: The Shooting Script, by Charlie Kaufman and Donald Kaufman (London: Nick Hern, 2002).
Cabinet of Dr Caligari, The, by Robert Wiene, Carl Mayer and Hans Janowitz, trans. R. V. Adkinson (London: Lorrimer, 1984).
Citizen Kane, shooting script, by Herman J. Manciewicz and Orson Welles, in *The Citizen Kane Book* (London: Methuen 1985), pp. 85–171.
Don't Look Now, by Allan Scott and Chris Bryant (London: Sight and Sound [British Film Institute], 1997).
Double Indemnity, by Billy Wilder and Raymond Chandler, intro. by Jeffrey Meyers (Berkeley: University of California Press, 2000).
Eisenstein: Two Films [October and Alexander Nevsky], ed. Jay Leyda, trans. Diana Matias (London: Lorrimer, 1984).
Exorcist, The, by William Peter Blatty (London: Faber, 1998).
Fargo, by Ethan Coen and Joel Coen (London: Faber, 1996).
Film, by Samuel Beckett, in *The Complete Dramatic Works* (London: Faber, 1990), pp. 322–34.
Force of Evil, by Abraham Polonsky, in John Schultheiss and Mark Schaubert, eds, *Force of Evil: The Critical Edition* (California State University, Northridge: Center for Telecommunication Studies, 1996).
Henry V, by Laurence Olivier (London: Lorrimer, 1984).

Henry V, by William Shakespeare: A Screen Adaptation by Kenneth Branagh (London: Chatto and Windus, 1989).

High Noon, by Carl Foreman, in George P. Garrett, O. B. Hardison, Jr., and Jane R. Gelfman (eds), *Film Scripts Two* (New York: Appleton-Century Crofts, 1971).

Homicide, by David Mamet (New York: Grove, 1992).

Last Year at Marienbad: A Ciné-Novel, by Alain Robbe-Grillet, trans. Richard Howard (London: Calder, 1961).

Magnificent Ambersons, The, by Orson Welles, in Robert L. Carringer, ed., *The Magnificent Ambersons: A Reconstruction* (Berkeley: University of California Press, 1993).

Maltese Falcon, The, by Huston, ed. Richard J. Anobile (London: Picador, 1974).

Natural Born Killers, by Quentin Tarantino (London: Faber, 1995).

Pierrot le Fou: A Film by Jean-Luc Godard, trans. Peter Whitehead (London: Lorrimer, 1969).

Pulp Fiction, by Quentin Tarantino (London: Faber, 1994).

Rules of the Game, The, by Jean Renoir, trans. John McGrath and Maureen Teitelbaum (London: Lorrimer, 1970).

Searchers, The, by Frank S. Nugent (Ipswich: ScreenPress, 2002).

Stagecoach, by Dudley Nichols (London: Lorrimer, 1971).

Sunset Boulevard, by Charles Brackett, Billy Wilder, and Dave Marshman, Jr. (Berkeley: University of California Press, 1999).

Taxi Driver, by Paul Schrader (London: Faber, 1990).

Third Man, The, by Graham Greene (London: Faber, 1988).

Usual Suspects, The, by Christopher MacQuarrie (London: Faber, 1996).

Wild Strawberries: A Film, by Ingmar Bergman, trans. Lars Malmström and David Kushner (London: Lorrimer, 1970).

Other

Andrew, Dudley, *Concepts in Film Theory* (Oxford: Oxford University Press, 1984).

Austin, J. L., *How To Do Things With Words* (Oxford: Oxford University Press, 1962).

Azlant, Edward, 'The Theory, History, and Practice of Screenwriting, 1897–1920' (unpublished doctoral thesis, University of Wisconsin, 1980).

Barthes, Roland, 'From Work to Text', in *Image – Music – Text*, trans. Stephen Heath (New York: Hill and Wang, 1977), pp. 155–64.

Barthes Roland, 'The Death of the Author', in *Image – Music – Text*, trans. Stephen Heath (New York: Hill and Wang, 1977), pp. 142–8.

Bate, Jonathan (ed.), *The Romantics on Shakespeare* (Harmondsworth: Penguin, 1992).

Bazin, André, *What is Cinema?*, vol. 1, trans. Hugh Gray (Berkeley: University of California Press, 2005).

Beckett, Samuel, *The Complete Dramatic Works* (London: Faber, 1990).

Bennett, Andrew, and Nicholas Royle, *Introduction to Literature, Criticism and Theory*, 3rd edn (London: Longman, 2004).

Betts, Ernest, 'Introduction', *The Private Life of Henry VIII* (London: Methuen, 1934), pp. ix–xvii.

Boon, Kevin A[lexander], *Script Culture and the American Screenplay* (Detroit, MI: Wayne State University Press, 2008).

Boon, Kevin Alexander, 'The Screenplay, Imagism, and Modern Aesthetics', *Literature/Film Quarterly* 36 (2008), pp. 259–71.

Boozer, Jack, (ed.), *Authorship in Film Adaptation* (Austin: University of Texas Press, 2008).

Bordwell, David, *Narration in the Fiction Film* (London: Methuen, 1985).

Bordwell, David, Janet Staiger, and Kristin Thompson, *The Classical Hollywood Cinema: Film Style and Mode of Production to 1960* (London: Routledge, 1985).

Boyle, James F., 'Foreword', in Judith H. Haag and Hillis R. Cole, Jr., *The Complete Guide to Standard Script Formats, part 1: The Screenplay* (Los Angeles: CMC, 1980), pp. i–xi.

Branigan, Edward, *Narrative Comprehension and Film* (London: Routledge, 1992).

Bresson, Robert, *Notes on the Cinematographer*, trans. Jonathan Griffin (London: Quartet, 1996).

Brophy, Philip, 'Read My Lips: Notes on the Writing and Speaking of Film Dialogue', *Continuum* 5.2 (1992), pp. 247–66.

Burlington, William Aubrey, *Through the Fourth Wall* (London: Brentano, 1922).

Carey, Peter, *True History of the Kelly Gang* (London: Faber, 2002).

Carroll, Noël, 'The Specificity Thesis', in Gerald Mast, Marshall Cohen, and Leo Braudy (eds), *Film Theory and Criticism*, 4th edn (Oxford: Oxford University Press, 1992), pp. 278–85.

Cartmell, Deborah, and Imelda Whelehan (eds), *Adaptations: From Text to Screen, Screen to Text* (London: Routledge, 1999).

Cook, David, *A History of Narrative Film*, 4th edn (New York: Norton, 2004).

Corliss, Richard (ed.), *The Hollywood Screenwriters* (New York: Avon, 1972).

Corliss, Richard, *Talking Pictures: Screenwriters in the American Cinema* [1974] (New York: Overlook, 1985).

Counts, Kyle B., 'The Making of Alfred Hitchcock's *The Birds*: The Complete Story behind the Precursor of Modern Horror Films', *Cinefantastique* 10.ii (Fall 1980), pp. 14–35.

Culler, Jonathan, *On Deconstruction: Theory and Criticism after Structuralism* (London: Routledge, 1983).

Davis, Gary, 'Rejected Offspring: The Screenplay as a Literary Genre', *New Orleans Review* 11.2 (1984), pp. 90–4.

Derrida, Jacques, 'The Law of Genre', *Critical Inquiry* 7.1 (1980), pp. 55–81.

Devereaux, Mary, 'In Defense of Talking Film', *Persistence of Vision* 5 (1987), pp. 17–27.

Devereaux, Mary, 'Of "Talk and Brown Furniture": The Aesthetics of Film Dialogue', *Post Script* 6.1 (1986), pp. 35–52.

Dmytryk, Edward, *On Screen Writing* (London: Focal Press, 1985).

Eisenstein, Sergei, 'The Form of the Script', in *Selected Works, vol. 1: Writings, 1922–34*, trans. and ed. Richard Taylor (London: BFI, 1988), pp. 134–5.

Elam, Keir, *The Semiotics of Theatre and Drama* (London: Methuen, 1980).

Ellis, John, 'What Does a Script Do?', *Yearbook of English Studies* 20 (1994), pp. 60–4.

Ezra, Elizabeth, *Georges Méliès: The Birth of the Auteur* (Manchester: Manchester University Press, 2000).

Field, Syd, *Screenplay: The Foundations of Screenwriting*, rev. edn (New York: Dell, 1994).

Fine, Richard, *Hollywood and the Profession of Authorship* (Ann Arbor, Michigan: UMI Research Press, 1985).

Fleming, Charles, *High Concept: Don Simpson and the Hollywood Culture of Excess* (London: Bloomsbury, 1998).

Foreman, Carl, 'Foreword: Confessions of a Frustrated Screenwriter', in Richard Corliss, ed., *The Hollywood Screenwriters* (New York: Avon, 1972), pp. 19–35.

Foucault, Michel, 'What Is an Author?', in Paul Rabinow, ed., *The Foucault Reader* (Harmondsworth: Penguin, 1991), pp. 101–20.

Francke, Lizzie, *Script Girls: Women Screenwriters in Hollywood* (London: BFI, 1994).

Friend, Tad, 'Credit Grab', *New Yorker* (20 October 2003), pp. 160–9.

Gassner, John, 'The Screenplay as Literature', in John Gassner and Dudley Nichols (eds), *Twenty Best Film Plays* (New York: Crown, 1943), pp. vii–xxx.

Haag, Judith H., and Hillis R. Cole, Jr., ed., *The Complete Guide to Standard Script Formats, Part 1: The Screenplay* (Los Angeles: CMC, 1980).

Hauge, Michael, *Writing Screenplays That Sell* (London: Elm Tree, 1989).

Hemingway, Ernest, 'The Killers', in *Men without Women* (London: Granta, 1977 [1928]), pp. 49–58.

Horne, William, 'See Shooting Script: Reflections on the Ontology of the Screenplay', *Literature/Film Quarterly* 20.1 (1992), pp. 48–54.

Hunter, Evan, *Me and Hitch* (London: Faber, 1997).

Jackson, Kevin, *The Language of Cinema* (Manchester: Carcanet, 1998).

Jackson, Russell, 'From Play-Script to Screenplay', in Russell Jackson, ed., *The Cambridge Companion to Shakespeare on Film*, 2nd edn (Cambridge: Cambridge University Press, 2007), pp. 15–34.

Jakobson, Roman, 'Linguistics and Poetics', in Thomas A. Seboek, ed., *Style in Language* (Cambridge, Mass.: M.I.T. Press, 1960), pp. 350–77.

Kapsis, Robert E., *Hitchcock: The Making of a Reputation* (Chicago: University of Chicago Press, 1992).

Kennedy, Andrew K., *Dramatic Dialogue: The Duologue of Personal Encounter* (Cambridge: Cambridge University Press, 1983).

Korte, Barbara and Ralf Schneider, 'The Published Screenplay – A New *Literary* Genre?', *AAA – Arbeiten aus Anglistik und Amerikanistik* 25.1 (2000), pp. 89–105.

Kozloff, Sarah, *Invisible Storytellers: Voice-Over Narration in American Fiction Film* (Berkeley: University of California Press, 1988).

Kozloff, Sarah, *Overhearing Film Dialogue* (Berkeley: University of California Press, 2000).

Kracauer, Siegfried, *Theory of Film* (Oxford: Oxford University Press, 1960).

Krohn, Bill, *Hitchcock at Work* (London: Phaidon, 2000).

Lawson, John Howard, *Theory and Technique of Playwriting and Screenwriting* (New York: G. P. Putnam, 1949).

Leitch, Thomas, 'Twelve Fallacies in Contemporary Adaptation Theory', *Criticism* 45.2 (2003), pp. 149–71.

Leitch, Thomas, 'Hitchcock and His Writers: Authorship and Authority in Adaptation', in Jack Boozer, ed., *Authorship in Film Adaptation* (Austin: University of Texas Press, 2008), pp. 63–84.

Linson, Art, *What Just Happened? Bitter Hollywood Tales from the Front Line* (London: Bloomsbury, 2002).

Luttrell, Esther, *Tools of the Screen Writing Trade*, rev. ed. (Mt. Dora, Fla.: Broadcast Club of America, 1998).

MacDonald, Ian W., 'Disentangling the Screen Idea', *Journal of Media Practice* 5.2 (2004), pp. 89–99.

McFarlane, Brian, *Novel to Film: An Introduction to the Theory of Adaptation* (Oxford: Oxford University Press, 1996).

Malkin, Yaakov, *Criticism in Creation and the Screenplay as a New Literary Form* (Jerusalem: Israel Film Archives, 1980).

Mamet, David, *Glengarry Glen Ross* (London: Methuen, 1984).

Mamet, David, *A Whore's Profession* (London: Faber, 1994).

Mamet, David, *True and False: Heresy and Common Sense for the Actor* (New York: Random House, 1997).

Mamet, David, *Jafsie and John Henry* (London: Faber, 1999).

Maras, Steven, *Screenwriting: History, Theory and Practice* (London: Wallflower, 2009).

McCreadie, Marsha, *The Women Who Write the Movies: from Frances Marion to Nora Ephron* (New York: Birch Lane Press, 1994).

McGann, Jerome J., *The Textual Condition* (Princeton, N. J.: Princeton University Press, 1991).

McGilligan, Patrick, *Alfred Hitchcock: A Life in Darkness and Light* (New York: HarperCollins, 2003).

McKee, Robert, *Story: Substance, Structure, Style, and the Principles of Screenwriting* (London: Methuen, 1997).

Metz, Christian, *Film Language*, trans. Michael Taylor (Oxford: Oxford University Press, 1974).

Murphet, Julian, and Lydia Rainford (eds), *Literature and Visual Technologies* (Basingstoke: Palgrave Macmillan, 2003).

Nichols, Dudley, 'The Writer and the Film', in John Gassner and Dudley Nichols, *Twenty Best Film Plays* (New York: Crown, 1943), pp. xxxi–xl.

Norman, Marc, *What Happens Next: A History of American Screenwriting* (London: Aurum, 2008).

Pasolini, Pier Paolo, 'The Screenplay as a "Structure that Wants to Be Another Structure"', *American Journal of Semiotics* 4.1–2 (1986), pp. 53–72.

Pfister, Manfred, *The Theory and Analysis of Drama*, trans. John Halliday (Cambridge: Cambridge University Press, 1988).

Pinter, Harold, 'Writing for the Theatre', in *Plays: One* (London: Methuen, 1976), pp. 9–16.

Polonsky, Abraham, 'Une expérience utopique', in John Schultheiss and Mark Schaubert (eds), *Force of Evil: The Critical Edition* (Northridge, CA: Center for Telecommunication Studies, 1996), pp. 186–88.

Potter, Cherry, *Screen Language: From Film Writing to Film-Making* (London: Methuen, 2001).

Quigley, Austin E., *The Pinter Problem* (Princeton, N.J.: Princeton UP, 1975).

Rainford, Lydia, 'How to Read the Image? Beckett's Televisual Memory', in Julian Murphet and Lydia Rainford (eds), *Literature and Visual Technologies* (Basingstoke: Palgrave, 2003), pp. 177–96.

Salokannel, Marjut, 'Cinema in Search of Its Authors: On the Notion of Film Authorship in Legal Discourse', in Virginia Wright Wexman, ed., *Film and Authorship* (New Brunswick, N.J.: Rutgers University Press, 2003), pp. 152–78.

Sarris, Andrew, 'Preface for a Dialectical Discussion', in Richard Corliss, *Talking Pictures: Screenwriters in the American Cinema* (New York: Overlook, 1985), pp. xi–xvi.

Schary, Dore, [and Charles Palmer], *Case History of a Movie* (New York: Random House, 1950).

Schatz, Thomas R., *The Genius of the System: Hollywood Filmmaking in the Studio Era* (New York: Owl, 1996).

Screen Credits Manual (Los Angeles: Writers Guild of America, n.d.).

Simpson, David, 'Romanticism, Criticism and Theory', in Stuart Curran, ed., *The Cambridge Companion to British Romanticism* (Cambridge: Cambridge University Press, 1993).

Staiger, Janet, 'Blueprints for Feature Films: Hollywood's Continuity Scripts', in Tino Balio, ed., *The American Film Industry*, rev. edn (Madison: University of Wisconsin Press, 1985), pp. 173–92.

Stempel, Tom, *Framework: A History of Screenwriting in the American Film*, rev. ed. (New York: Syracuse University Press, 2000).

Stempel, Tom, 'The Collaborative Dog: *Wag the Dog* (1997)', *Film and History* 35.1 (2005), pp. 60–4.

Sternberg, Claudia, *Written for the Screen: The American Motion-Picture Screenplay as Text* (Tübingen: Stauffenburg Verlag, 1997).

Stillinger, Jack, *Multiple Authorship and the Myth of Solitary Genius* (Oxford: Oxford University Press, 1991).

Tarkovsky, Andrey, *Sculpting in Time: Reflections on the Cinema*, rev. ed., trans. Kitty Hunter-Blair (London: Faber, 1989).

Theatrical and Television Basic Agreement (Los Angeles: Writers Guild of America, 2001).

Thompson, Kristin, *Storytelling in the New Hollywood: Understanding Classical Narrative Technique* (Cambridge, Mass.: Harvard University Press, 1999).

Thomson, David, *The Whole Equation: A History of Hollywood* (London: Abacus, 2006).

Trifonova, Temenuga, 'Time and Point of View in Contemporary Cinema', *Cineaction* 58 (2003), pp. 11–31.

Truffaut, François, 'A Certain Tendency of the French Cinema', in Bill Nichols, ed., *Movies and Methods: An Anthology* (Berkeley: University of California Press, 1976), pp. 224–37.

Truffaut, François, *Hitchcock*, rev. ed. (London: Paladin, 1984).

Wexman, Virginia Wright (ed.), *Film and Authorship* (New Brunswick, N.J.: Rutgers University Press, 2003).

Winston, Douglas Garrett, *The Screenplay as Literature* (Cranbury, N.J.: Associated University Press, 1973).

Wollen, Peter, *Signs and Meaning in the* Cinema, 3rd edn (Bloomington: Indiana University Press, 1972).

Wright, Will, *Six Guns and Society: A Structural Study of the Western* (Berkeley: University of California Press, 1975).

Index

In view of the problems surrounding film (and screenplay) authorship, films and screenplays are indexed by title and date; other written texts are indexed by title and author.